After ten years working as a lawyer, Emma Beddington is now a freelance writer, who has contributed to: *ELLE*, *The Times*, the *Sunday Times*, the *Guardian*, *O Magazine* and *Red*. She is also the author of the acclaimed blog Belgian Waffle (www.belgianwaffling.com). She lives in Brussels with her husband and two sons.

'A must-read for anyone who's ever lived, or thought about living, abroad, Francophile or otherwise'   *Sunday Herald*

'Tender, funny, sad, and brutally honest, I devoured this book like I would have eaten Parisian patisserie. I loved every page (as did my husband!)'   JoJo Moyes, author of *Me Before You*

'I loved Emma Beddington's funny, poignant memoir, which made me laugh – and cry'   Nina Stibbe, author of *Love Nina*

'*We'll Always Have Paris* is a joy. So much resonated as I read it in a café wearing my Breton T-shirt'   Cathy Rentzenbrink

'I totally loved this gorgeous, funny, honest, adorable book: *formidable*'   Jenny Colgan

'Searingly funny, searingly honest, searingly good cake'   Sarah Franklin, Costa Prize judge and director of *Short Stories Aloud*

'I loved *We'll Always Have Paris*. Love, grief and cake. Often sad and hellishly funny'   Lissa Evans, author of *A Crooked Heart*

'Charged with love, longing and lots of cake, Emma Beddington's warm and witty memoir of her romance with the City of Light is a treat for anyone whose Parisian dreams encompass café crème at Les Deux Magots, macarons at Ladurée . . . and instinctively recognizing the gender of a *lave-vaisselle*'
Kathryn Flett, author of *Separate Lives*

'Extremely funny, emotionally acute and often very moving. Writing about yourself and your life without giving in to navel gazing or self-interest is a rare trick and one Emma Beddington pulls off with aplomb; instead she turns her sideways gaze on the world and its absurdities with a wink and a wry smile. *We'll Always Have Paris* has all this, but in addition a big dose of genuine warmth and wisdom'   Jessica Ruston,
author of *The Lies You Told Me*

'Emma Beddington's adorably breathless tale bravely explores her fraught adolescent fancies, adult fears and finally her happy homecoming to being wholly herself'   *Saga*

'From frites to Breton stripes, chic women to romantic men, Emma Beddington's memoir *We'll Always Have Paris* explores our enduring fascinating with France and what happens when childhood dreams of a French idyll collide with reality' *Tatler*

'[A] warm, candid account of a life abroad' *Sunday Express*

'A droll and unexpectedly raw memoir to read with a stiff drink – preferably a glass of Chablis' *Glamour*

'Fascinating on the cultural differences between Britain and France' *The Times*

EMMA BEDDINGTON

We'll Always Have
PARIS

Trying and Failing to Be French

PAN BOOKS

First published 2016 by Macmillan

First published in paperback 2017 by Pan Books
an imprint of Pan Macmillan
20 New Wharf Road, London N1 9RR
Associated companies throughout the world
www.panmacmillan.com

Copyright © Emma Beddington 2016

The right of Emma Beddington to be identified as the
author of this work has been asserted by her in accordance
with the Copyright, Designs and Patents Act 1988.

The publishers gratefully acknowledge the following for permission to reproduce copyright material:

© Christine Rochefort, *Les Petits Enfants du Siècle* © Editions Bernard Grasset, 1961.

By W. G. Sebald, translated by Michael Hulse, from THE RINGS OF SATURN,
copyright © 1995 by Vito von Eichborn GmbH & Co Verlag KG. Translation © 1998 by
The Harvill Press. Reprinted by permission of New Directions Publishing Corp.

'*Méfiez-vous de Paris*', words and music by Joseph Kosma and Jean Renoir.
Published by Peermusic (UK) Limited.

All rights reserved. No part of this publication may be reproduced,
stored in a retrieval system, or transmitted, in any form, or by any means
(electronic, mechanical, photocopying, recording or otherwise)
without the prior written permission of the publisher.

Pan Macmillan does not have any control over, or any responsibility for,
any author or third-party websites referred to in or on this book.

1 3 5 7 9 8 6 4 2

A CIP catalogue record for this book is available from the British Library.

Printed and bound by CPI Group (UK) Ltd, Croydon, CR0 4YY

This book is sold subject to the condition that it shall not, by way of
trade or otherwise, be lent, hired out, or otherwise circulated without
the publisher's prior consent in any form of binding or cover other than
that in which it is published and without a similar condition including
this condition being imposed on the subsequent purchaser.

Visit **www.panmacmillan.com** to read more about all our books
and to buy them. You will also find features, author interviews and
news of any author events, and you can sign up for e-newsletters
so that you're always first to hear about our new releases.

To my mother

toujours gai

Méfiez-vous de Paris
De ses rues, d'son ciel gris

Beware of Paris
Of its streets, its grey sky

'Méfiez-vous de Paris' by Jean Renoir
(originally performed by Léo Marjane in
Elena et les Hommes)

PART ONE

Paris, plus vague de l'Océan, miroitait donc aux yeux d'Emma dans une atmosphère vermeille.

So Paris, vaster than the ocean, glittered in Emma's eyes with a rosy glow.

Gustave Flaubert, *Madame Bovary*

Elle

At the age of sixteen, I decide what I want to be when I grow up: French.

Being sixteen has little to recommend it, other than not being fifteen any more. On Saturday lunchtimes, puffed up with our own daring, my best friend Alex and I and a group of sundry social C-listers from school can at least now go to the only pub in York that serves shifty teenagers, no questions asked. There we linger over a half of lager, watching The Bee Gees on the video jukebox, observed impassively by the elderly gentlemen who make up the remainder of the Brewer's Arms' clientele. This forms a significant new strand of our social life, hitherto limited to listening to Radio 1 in one or other of our bedrooms, loitering in McDonalds or Rough Trade records, trying on clothes in River Island and eating all the free samples of cake from under the plastic cloche in Bettys tearoom. Boredom hangs around us like a low mist on the River Ouse. My attempts to launch York Youth CND have foundered on a combination of ideological differences and inertia and the members of Wind Band, in which I play the clarinet badly, are even further down the school pecking order than I am. I am too chicken to go to

Leeds, which we view as the acme of civilization, and even if I went, I would not know what to do when I got there.

Mainly, I mope in my bedroom reading and listening to The Smiths, much as I did at fifteen. When my moping infuriates my mother to the point where she tries to suggest unpalatably worthy occupations for me ('if you're so bored, you could volunteer at the nursing home down the road?' she suggests several times and I roll my eyes in disgust), I trudge down to school to sit in the library and read there instead. And it is here that I encounter French *Elle* for the first time.

No one has a satisfactory explanation of how a boys' Quaker boarding school that has only recently admitted girls has ended up with a subscription to French *Elle*. Clerical error? Librarian insurrection? It's not an overtly Quaker place in some ways, though: the music teacher thumps out Hymns Ancient and Modern at the grand piano instead of silent worship on Friday mornings ('Jerusalem', 'Dear Lord and Father', 'Immortal, Invisible') and most of the pupils are farmers' kids from the Vale of Wetherby, not real Quakers. Whatever the reason, French *Elle*'s incongruous candy-coloured cover with a photograph of a pretty girl draws my eye one afternoon in the mock Tudor-beamed, wood-panelled library and I take a copy off the rack, and start to read. Having flicked through the first copy with growing interest, I go back, find several more, and sit down to give them my full attention.

Much of French *Elle* is impenetrable to me. I do not know who the people in the articles are: authors, politicians or actresses. Almost everyone the magazine interviews does something called '*barre au sol*', which bemuses me (a bar on the ground? How is this exercise? It sounds like going over trotting poles on the fat Shetland pony at the riding school in Escrick) and everyone is *épanouie* (blooming, says the dictionary) or becoming an *égérie* of something (a muse?), which I don't really understand. The magazine also tends to talk about '*le couple*' as if it were a needy houseplant requiring constant attention. I concentrate initially on the make-up and fashion pages, which are full of desirable items you cannot find in Browns department store (I know because I write them down, and go and check). But my interest is piqued and I find I want to know more. *Elle* has stories about lipstick, sex and film stars, but also about literature and philosophy and politics. The film stars interviewed about their latest romantic comedies will discuss serious, abstract topics without any awkwardness. Sometimes they discuss facial serums, Victor Hugo and their relationship with their fathers in the same sentence and no one thinks this is unusual. Sex is ever-present, but not in the way it is ever-present in the hormonal fug of the lower sixth common room. In French *Elle* it is discussed seriously, and in depth. Indeed it is apparent quite quickly that pleasure of all kinds is a serious business in *Elle*: food, sex, culture or bath oils. The founding fathers of Quakerism would not have approved.

I fall in love with the world portrayed in French *Elle* over my seventeenth year, from the *bûche de Noël* taste tests in winter to the '*régime maillot*' diets in summer and all points in between, rushing to the library each Thursday to read the new edition. In the world French *Elle* presents, you are allowed to be interested, without any apparent contradiction, in books, films and politics, men, éclairs and pretty bras and this is what I want; this is what, without really realizing it, I have been aspiring to. No one in French *Elle* is embarrassed or apologetic, while I am one or the other all the time, and often both at once. Finally, there seems to be a destination at the other side of this mortifying trudge through a North Yorkshire adolescence: France.

I am not necessarily predisposed to fall in love with France. We have a French memory card game with pictures of typically French scenes and items, so initially France for me is the frustrating search for the second picture of Nougat de Montelimar and trying to snatch the wheels of Brie before my mother on wet afternoons. We go there on holiday sometimes, long queasy hot car journeys, me vomiting in lay-bys, my father getting tetchy. On one trip my mother becomes so enraged with me and my half-brother that she orders us horse steak just so she can tell us about it years later and watch our reaction. Another time, on a tense extended family holiday, I get locked in the loo of a draughty gîte in Brittany for a whole afternoon and have to be humiliatingly released by the local handyman. During another teenage summer, my father rents, very cheaply, a decaying chateau with a stuffed bear: the attic is full of relics of the German occupying officers, fly larvae wriggle under the wallpaper and the stagnant pond in the garden is full of dying frogs. Later, we go to Lot-et-Garonne and I try to sunbathe topless lying in the garden listening to awful Europop, ending up horribly burnt, while my sister gets bitten by an adder and has to go to hospital. The consolation for all our many minor disasters and disappointments in France is always the same: cake. Before I fall in love with French *Elle* I fall hard for French cake, *pains aux raisins* and pretty raspberry tartlets and wobbly, trembling *flans* topped with plump apricot halves.

I have also suffered under the yoke of French lessons from a friend of my mother's, a semiotics lecturer. The lessons, I am later given to understand, were less intended for my benefit than hers (she needed the extra income). This makes sense, since they were no fun at all for me. The semioticist would wait in the playground to collect me from school one afternoon a week, a thin, rather forbidding figure whose presence did not scream of roaring good times. She would escort me to a nearby café and attempt to drill into me the basics: my name, my age, did I have any pets, colours, cheerless songs in which some chickens would go to a field and then return or puppets would turn around three times and leave. I dreaded everything about these strained and awkward afternoons – it was plain even to me that her heart was not in it – except the cake I was allowed to choose to accompany our conversation. A serial quitter of extra-curricular activities that inconvenienced my minutely planned schedule of reading the Famous Five and pretending to be a horse, I petitioned hard to be allowed to give up; eventually my mother acquiesced.

'She sat at Derrida's feet!' she protested when I remonstrated with her many years later, as if this in some way reinforced the semioticist's credentials for teaching me to count to twenty.

Now, in secondary school, I am good at French, but the lessons are indescribably dreary and uninspiring. Our teacher, Madame Cockroft – the French faculty is mainly composed of French women with Yorkshire names, exiled in our misty shire for love – is a great fan of repetitive written and oral exercises and we spend hours each week conjugating irregular verbs, agreeing our adjectives and asking each other about our ailments. I have chosen French A-level more because I am good at it than because I enjoy it, and the dreary drills and exercises continue. There is a token element of 'culture', but this has been largely limited to learning the location of the power stations of Haute-Normandie, studying Norman cheese production and watching a couple of grainy videos about the port of Le Havre. Our other French teacher, Monsieur Collins, who seems to be permanently teetering on the brink of a nervous breakdown, sometimes reads us poetry, de Vigny and Verlaine, but we just find this embarrassing, a pink-cheeked Irish man getting misty-eyed about sepia-tinted men in frock coats. '*Seul le silence est grand*,' he declaims, tremulously. '*Tout le reste est faiblesse.*' This is at least appropriate for a Quaker school, but it doesn't exactly speak to us.

Occasionally, however, the French A-level group is herded to City Screen, York's sole art-house cinema, to watch films starring Gérard Depardieu. All French films in the late 1980s and 1990s seem to feature Gérard Depardieu in some capacity, as if without him they would not be fully French. His face becomes inseparably associated with French culture to us as we watch him fall in love with his secretary to a soundtrack of Schubert Impromptus (*Trop Belle Pour Toi*), recite verse with a prosthetic nose (*Cyrano de Bergerac*) and reminisce about playing a viol in a curly wig (*Tous Les Matins du Monde*). 'He is not handsome,' says Madame Lofthouse (another of our Yorkshire–French teachers) thoughtfully, during our conversation sessions after these films, '*mais* he has something.'

On our own, my best friend Alex and I go and see *Les Valseuses*, in which a much younger Gérard – who indisputably 'has something' at this point – wears extravagant flares and has arousing, alarming sex with strange women who apparently find him and his co-star Patrick Dewaere irresistible. We like *Les Nuits Fauves* best, because the director and principal actor Cyril Collard is beautiful, bisexual and tragic and because there is lots of sex and drama. The rumoured ménage à trois in *Jules et Jim* (no Gérard in this one) is a bitter disappointment in contrast (what on earth is even going on? We are mystified), but I do add a postcard of a still from the film – Jeanne Moreau running across the bridge in her chic, oversized man's sweater, baggy trousers and charcoal moustache – to the mosaic of moody black and white Robert Doisneau and Cartier-Bresson shots above my desk. At home with my mum and stepfather we watch *Au Bout de Souffle* and I ignore the plot entirely to fantasize about walking through Paris with a pixie cut and Capri pants and kissing the cop-killing rogue Jean-Paul Belmondo's lubricious, Jagger-esque lips. Because not only do I want to *be* French, my sexual orientation is now firmly French. I lust after Belmondo, and Alain Delon, after Daniel Auteuil, Vincent Lindon and *Valseuses* era Depardieu (though I draw the line at Jean Rochefort).

Soon, France is my worst crush ever, worse than the man from House and Sons Electricians on Monkgate, worse than Gary Speed of Leeds United, worse than Dafydd, the double bass player who lives down our street. I listen to Nina Simone's version of 'Ne Me Quitte Pas' in my bedroom, rolling my 'r's extravagantly, and look round York's second-hand shops for a leather jacket like Romane Bohringer's. Sadly, my outlets for Frenchness are very limited. There is staticky, dull France Inter on longwave on my radio. Our neighbour Geoff is translating *Madame Bovary* and he lets me read the manuscript (or rather, lets me keep the manuscript on my bedside table and say to myself in the mirror 'yeah, I'm reading a new translation of *Madame Bovary*', because I find all the bits about the countryside tedious and search in vain for the sex scenes). My mum buys me *Le Grand Meaulnes* (deeply improbable but stirring) and Simone de Beauvoir's *Memoirs of a Dutiful Daughter* (I like the bits about getting flashed at in a Catholic bookshop and drinking gin fizz, but skim over whole chapters of dry Sorbonne disagreements about Hume). But my latent Frenchness does not receive any fuller expression until my French exchange trip, Easter 1992.

*

It is actually not strictly speaking a 'French' exchange, because my exchange partner, although French, lives in Casablanca. This rather eccentric arrangement comes about through my stepfather's mother spotting a small ad in the classifieds section of the *Catholic Herald* and after some exchanges of letters and an awkward phone call, an arrangement is put in place for me to go and stay with Aurélie, the daughter of two French expats and an accomplished ballet dancer and model, no less, and for Aurélie to return to us in the summer.

I set off with a suitcase full of nineteenth-century novels and Monsoon summer dresses and spend the next three weeks in a state of deep, dream-like culture shock. Casablanca is the strangest place I have ever been. It is not so much the centre, which is broadly recognizable as a North African city from reading Paul Bowles or watching television (a souk of heaped olives and cakes and insistent pressing bustle, the roar and odour of poorly fitted exhaust pipes, groups of men sitting around in purposeful idleness). The strangeness comes in the suburbs, the flat plains of desert where Aurélie's leathery, enigmatic family live. Driving back to their house from the airport we pass through huge swathes of nothing but grey-brown scrub, the emptiness broken only by the occasional donkey or goat. Then, rising from nothing, come a series of huge, stupid, white elephants of villas. They are outlandish, architectural follies, the kind of mansions you discover when a dictator is deposed and the rebel forces parade around, showing off the gold-plated toothbrush holders and His and Hers lavatories. One is shaped like an ocean liner and another like a Deep South colonial bayou. They are all in poor repair, buffeted by desert winds and exfoliated by sand, and it's impossible to imagine who, if anyone, lives there.

Aurélie's own suburb is called 'La Californie' and it is just about conceivable why, since it is made up of low-rise, white-painted bungalows, the high protective garden walls overhung with bougainvillea. Inside, the house is surprisingly small: three bedrooms, a tiny bathroom and a kitchen no one but the maid seems to enter. Seven cats and four dogs of wildly differing shapes and varieties sprawl all over the house, lounging on the modish L-shaped sofa module, following the maid into the kitchen to beg for scraps, drawing the intermittent ire of the gardener. The humans are more uniform: both Aurélie and her brother Ludo are almost comically attractive. Aurélie is tall and almond-eyed, her hair cut into a highlighted shaggy mane, her cheekbones conferring the instant illusion of sophistication. Ludo is boy band handsome with a floppy dark wave of hair falling over his face, emitting strong teenage boy waves of contempt. Aurélie's mother wears thigh-high fringed suede boots and her eyes are heavily kohl ringed. Her father is tiny, neat and bronzed, almost always silent, one of those Giscard d'Estaing style French men who wear navy blue suits and striped shirts with brown brogues, and who carry man bags, which they do not consider for a second might impugn their masculinity.

Aurélie and I, thrown together by the *Catholic Herald*, share not only a room, but, to my prudish horror, a *bed*. We put one of those bolster pillows down the middle so as not to roll onto one another in the night, but it is still odd to sleep so close to someone you have known for a matter of hours. It gets stranger still when I wake to realize the maid is bedding down on a mat in the corner of the room. Over the next few weeks I wake occasionally to a low murmur and turn over, befuddled with sleep, to see her performing *salat* in the dim pre-dawn. More often, I am woken by one of the cats, claws out, impassively massaging my leg.

No one seems to have any idea what to do with me. Aurélie and I do not bond; we are strangers, two people sharing nothing more than a bed. Aurélie has her boyfriend, the jockish, monosyllabic Robert, her modelling, her dance classes and her Slimfast-based regime. She has no time for me and my floral dresses and my Victorian novels, dithery and tongue-tied and painfully embarrassed. I only go to school with her once (it's terrifying, a giant purpose-built Lycée in downtown Casa full of lithe, brown French kids) and the rest of the time I am thrown on the kindness of Aurélie's mother and of the neighbours. Dozy with culture shock and sleep deprivation, I wake late, to be greeted by a pile of pancakes, specially prepared for me, soft and full of holes like giant crumpets, butter and honey seeping through to the plate; then I hang around, awkwardly, reading or playing with the animals until someone finds me something to do. Once I get to watch Aurélie's ballet class, and another time she takes me to watch her record a lo-fi soft drink commercial. It's Ramadan, and filming stops at nightfall so the crew can go and eat dates and drink bowls of *harira*, the traditional Ramadan soup, in a tent behind the studio.

But things are far better when Aurélie can't be persuaded to amuse me. I am handed over to a fierce, semi-fascist elderly lady who lives down the road, who holds forth to me on various subjects close to her heart, then takes me on the train to Rabat. We tour the city, which is completely fascinating to me: the beautiful fortifications, the ornate Mohammed V mausoleum and the Tour Hassan, but also the modernity of it, the accommodations of old and new. Later, Aurélie's mother takes me to Marrakech for the weekend. The drive is an enchantment, a fairy story with camels and herds of floppy-eared goats sitting in the middle of the road and the snow-topped Atlas mountains sparkling improbably in the distance. We stay in a riad in the Medina, where the lush tiled courtyard gardens hidden behind plain alleyway doors with peeling paint bewilder me with their beauty. The souk is a familiar image from a thousand films and photographs, but I am not prepared for the lambs gathered shitting in terror in its narrow lanes in anticipation of Eid, or for the rivulets of blood, made sticky and slow-moving by the yellow dust, the smells of spice and dirt and decay. We walk across the Djema el-Fna at dusk, all twinkling lights and smoke and hissing and I feel overwhelmed and cracked open, like the 1970s hippies. It's all a very long way from North Yorkshire.

And then there is Karim.

I have never had a boyfriend, not a proper one. I have 'gone out' with a couple of Wind Band nerds, more because they were available than because I liked them and it has always been dreadful, excruciatingly awkward, a festival of sweaty hand-holding, silence and clashing orthodontics. Each time, there is a moment of triumph at the idea that I have demonstrated my normality, but each time it is swiftly replaced by a desperate desire to get as far away from these boys as possible. My fantasy crushes are far more satisfying: distant figures like the electrician, Dafydd the double bass player and Gary Speed. No one attainable has ever seemed desirable to me, and vice versa.

But now there is Karim, a friend of the family (his sister dances with Aurélie) who comes round to Aurélie's house one night for some reason, and who, for some reason, asks me out. I say yes, of course I do. He is older than me, in his early twenties, confident and funny with that fair Moroccan colouring, green eyes and dark golden curls. Why on earth wouldn't I say yes?

Karim picks me up in the warm blue Casablanca night and we go to the cinema. It's ten o'clock. I don't even think there are screenings that late in York: how would you get home? We drive through the barren suburbs and along the dual carriageway lined with scrubby palm trees, towards the city where the white cubes are closer together and strip-lit night shops alternate with dark alleys. As he drives, we talk, or we try to, a halting mix of English and French. I understand, but speaking is harder, I fumble my answers and point, my chest tight and fizzy with anticipation.

The cinema is showing some daft recent action film, dubbed into French, with Arabic subtitles. It feels ineffably sophisticated to be doing something so ordinary in such a strange place and I observe the audience covertly, young and old, snacking on paper cones of pumpkin seeds and drinking cans of Coke. After the film ends, the sky is darker blue still and as we drive, a vast inky mass appears to my right: the sea. It is the first time I have spotted it since my arrival and I insist on getting out of the car and walking down the debris-strewn beach, the twinkling lights of the refineries and chemical plants in the distance. I do not care. A warm salty wind blows into my face and nothing has ever felt so exotic, so romantic in my entire life. We kiss, and before Karim drops me back at the bougainvillea-covered bungalow, we conclude with a breathy hormonal grapple in the dark, to the soundtrack of his Prefab Sprout cassettes. This is almost certainly the high point of my life to date.

Our fling continues for the remainder of my stay. Almost every night, Karim is there to take me out on adventures. There is something incredibly freeing about being somewhere where no one knows who I am and what I am supposed to be like. In York, I am an introverted, vegetarian semi-goth. In Casablanca, I can be someone entirely different, and I am. With Karim and his sisters, I go to nightclubs and dance and we drive around the city in the pink dawn to buy hamburgers. I sit on the floor at packed house parties as French stoners talk over me about The Doors, and ride horses through the desert. I have a delicious feeling of uncertainty: I never quite know where I am or what will happen next, but rather than worrying I abandon caution and trust entirely. Nothing bad happens. Usually, we end up back at Karim's house drinking mint tea with his parents and playing Pictionary. I sleep in his bedroom sometimes. We don't have sex – for all my abandoned caution, I just can't surrender to that extent – but it's all a great deal more satisfying than my excruciatingly awkward encounters with the Wind Band nerds. I lose myself, lose the inhibition and the doubt and the distaste for my own body in the warm darkness.

It is there that they come to find me in the small hours of my very last morning, Karim's sister banging on the door, phone in hand, reminding me my flight leaves in a few hours. After a mad rush to pack – boxes of Moroccan patis-series stuffed in my backpack wrapped in those Monsoon dresses, the unread *Effi Briest* and *War and Peace* – Aurélie's parents see me off, waving a last-minute goodbye as I run to my departure gate. My heart lurches as the plane taxis, then climbs (last view of palms, white low-rise city, sand, refineries, churning grey sea). Something has shifted in me: I feel older, taller, Frencher.

My bubble is swiftly burst on my return to York. Karim never replies to my gushing letters and when I tell people at school that I rode Arab stallions in the desert, it causes an outbreak of juvenile sniggering. Aurélie's return trip to England does not seem to affect her anything like as deeply, either. We take her to a damp National Trust cottage in the Lake District, where we introduce her to our traditional holiday pursuits: long, sodden walks, the occasional visit to a tearoom and a great deal of solitary reading, occasionally punctuated by a hysterical (to us) game of Racing Demon. Each morning, Aurélie rows gloomily across the lake in the mist to maintain her '*poitrine*'. She seems distinctly less excited than the rest of the family by the momentous discovery of a dead mole by the back door, or by the large tick lodged in my sister's shoulder. She does, however, learn that '*cagoule*' has another meaning in English, so the trip is not entirely wasted from an educational perspective. On our return to York, we take her to the newly opened multiplex cinema, and to my friends' houses for viewings of *Single White Female* and Spar popcorn. My male friends stare at her in open lust, a fact Aurélie accepts with a total and complacent absence of surprise. It is true that she is magnificent. The problem is that she is also very boring. We part without regret at the end of her stay and soon our correspondence dies an inevitable death.

For me, however, the die is cast. Casablanca, Aurélie and Karim have shown me the transformative power of abroad: being in another place and speaking another language has allowed me to be someone else entirely. If my identity can be up for grabs in this unexpected and welcome fashion, then I can pursue my plan with every expectation of success: I will become French.

1, 2, 3 Soleil

When my placement comes through for my *assistante*-ship, my stepfather Joe looks it up in our huge *Times* atlas and shows me, then I laugh, hollowly. Madame Cockroft would be happy: I am going to sodding Normandy. Will my knowledge of the nuclear power stations and cheeses, the industrial hinterland of the port of Le Havre and the meadowlands of the Pays de Caux finally be put to good use?

I am going to be a classroom assistant in a secondary school on my year off and the school to which I have been assigned is in Canteleu, on the outskirts of Rouen in Normandy. Joe, who likes a task, researches Canteleu, cycling down to the library, returning with several reference volumes plus the collected works of Guy de Maupassant and Flaubert, both of whom have Normandy connections. Flaubert's house is actually on the outskirts of Canteleu it transpires, and has an illustrious literary past, having welcomed Zola, Turgenev and George Sand among others. Canteleu was a pretty, bucolic Normandy hamlet back then, a short carriage trip from Rouen. Emile Zola, attending Flaubert's funeral, describes it as '*un coin touffu de la grasse Normandie qui verdoie dans une nappe de soleil*', a densely planted corner of fertile Normandy, blossoming under a carpet of sun. Modern Canteleu is a whole other story, as I will soon discover.

I arrive in Rouen by train on a Sunday afternoon in January after a two-day induction course during which I learn nothing, except that red wine is fantastically, improbably cheap in Paris and that no one here cares if I am old enough to drink it. It's sort of terrifying the way we are all just left to our own devices to find our way to our schools, but I manage to acquire a ticket and find a train (no one else is heading in my direction, since most of the other *assistantes* are based down south). Sitting by the window, I watch as the Paris *banlieues* give way to orchards and farmland, and I track the wide meandering willow-lined course of the Seine. As we near Rouen, the fields give way again to several miles of flat industrial wasteland, illuminated in the gathering darkness. When I alight, uneasily, at the station the English teacher, Madame Martine, is waiting for me, as arranged. She is a wispy woman in her fifties in a brown roll-neck, with an air of resignation and little to say, but she does take me to the station café where, still English despite myself, I order tea and boggle in silent horror at what arrives: a tiny metal pot of lukewarm water, a Lipton Yellow teabag on the side, no milk. Some of the children, she says, can be difficult, she uses the word '*insolent*', but it will be fine. Probably. I think back to my brief conversation with my predecessor, who told me he was held up in the car park of the nearby supermarket by one of his students, who stole a bottle of vodka from him. I had assumed he was joking, but now I am less sure.

After I have finished my awful beverage, she drives me to

my new home. We start to climb the hill to Canteleu – the wide, winding road fringed by meadows and wheatfields and poplars that Zola described barely recognizable – when Madame Martine's decrepit Renault is suddenly overtaken by ten vans full of CRS (the French riot police), sirens blaring, *pin pon pin pon pin pon*. She shakes her head sorrowfully.

'More trouble.'

With the sirens still audible and flashing lights reflecting off the apartment blocks, Madame Martine is unwilling to leave her car unattended (*'Voyous,'* she mutters, 'vandals, *brigands'*). She drops me and my luggage at the front gate, gives me the key to my apartment (which is apparently within the school grounds) and drives away, promising we will catch up on Monday. The *collège* is a modern low-rise, a squat heap of grey and white metal in the middle of a *cité* of pebble-dashed tower blocks.

My room is on the first floor of the administrative block. It is small, with a single bed and a small table and two hard metal chairs. The walls are made of metal too and are in fact the outside walls of the building: I am living in a metal box, an *'établissement Pailleron'* (so-named after the Paris school that famously burnt to the ground in twenty minutes in the 1970s, which is reassuring). A second, interestingly con-figured small room combines fridge, hotplate, lavatory and shower in two square metres of space that would give the UK Health and Safety Inspectorate enduring nightmares. As I settle in, putting posters on the walls and unpacking, a ballet of handbrake turns and sirens unfolds outside my window. When I venture to the phone box to tell my parents all is well, a small crowd of teenagers gathers outside, calling out 'Hello!', 'Fuck you!', 'Pussy!' but not with any menace. They seem bored, mainly, and hungry for distraction.

The area around the school is a sink estate; a large immigrant population living in poorly maintained social housing in an area of 30 per cent unemployment with few accessible shops or public services. There is, quite simply, nothing to do, so it is no surprise that my students trail me to the launderette and the phone box, or that they spend each night stealing and joy-riding cars and smoking weed, engaging in half-hearted clashes with the CRS riot police at weekends.

Teaching, it turns out, is not teaching at all, it's baby-sitting. This is not the kind of environment where you can think big thoughts about the horizon-broadening, mind-expanding role of education. Why bother with school, the older children regularly ask us (homework undone, third written warning sent home and ignored), when there are no jobs, when your name marks you out as *beur*, Arab, in a society where that means an instant black mark against you? They are funny and bright, mainly, but they have no sense they have a future and who am I to suggest otherwise, coming from my white, prosperous city centre life?

School is not even a place of safety for these kids. The yard is lawless and frightening, humming with tension. There are drug deals and fights and on one occasion one of the older children holds another kid's arm against a burning hot radiator until he suffers second-degree burns. The police are on site most weeks for one reason or another and the staffroom has bars on the windows. Ashen-faced, resigned-looking men and women huddle around the coffee machine, smoking and talking about their most recent bout of industrial action. The English teacher goes on long-term sick leave shortly after I arrive, never to be seen again. The younger children, the ones I teach, fall into two groups. There are the swaggerers, who deal with the open and veiled threats they face with bluster and violence, and then there are those who try to become invisible. I watch sometimes as the smaller, more diffident kids cross the yard, hampered by their vast school bags and I will the big boys, the casually violent invincible *caïds*, not to notice them. I don't really teach anyone anything and after a few weeks I refine my lessons to two: either I hand out copies of *Smash Hits* and we chat about song lyrics (in French) or we play bingo.

This France is so very far from Laetitia Casta modelling Dolce & Gabbana swimwear in French *Elle*, or from Gérard Depardieu playing the viol in a powdered wig, I barely recognize it and reading Maupassant short stories is no preparation for this Normandy. It feels bleak and hopeless: the tower blocks create vicious wind tunnels and it rains diligently for weeks, a solid, turbo-charged drizzle that feels as if it will never stop. There isn't even really anywhere I can buy decent patisserie in Canteleu; rather I live on radishes and Haagen Dazs ice cream from the supermarket (which is worryingly, in view of my predecessor's experiences, called 'Atac').

In these days before Mathieu Kassovitz's vividly bleak

slap in the face portrait of *cité* life, *La Haine*, explodes our preconceptions, I know almost nothing about the *banlieue*. Most of what I know is gleaned from Bertrand Blier's surreal, dream-like film *1, 2, 3 Soleil*, where the grimy, half-derelict Marseilles *cité* becomes strangely sublime, baking in the sun to a soundtrack of cicadas. There is deprivation and violence and sex, but also solidarity and magic and unexpected acts of kindness, like the old man who 'tames' a child-burglar by leaving him small amounts of money and food. In Blier's *banlieue*, anything can happen: people come back from the dead; adults become children again. It's quite a vision for Canteleu to live up to.

The remainder of my knowledge of the *banlieue* comes from Christine Rochefort's *Les Petits Enfants du Siècle*, a 1960s 'issues' novel we studied for A-level French. The action in *Les Petits Enfants du Siècle* takes place as the *cités* around Paris are under construction – their expansion is both backdrop and plot point. Josyane, the teenage narrator, is a child of social housing, the oldest of a feckless, ever-expanding family living on welfare in a tower block and she falls for Guido, a builder working on the construction of the surrounding towers (Guido is at least thirty and Josyane is twelve, it is not exactly a healthy relationship). When Guido leaves, she embarks upon a despairing journey to find him, via sex with most of the *cité* (what was Monsieur Collins thinking?).

In one scene Josyane heads off to try and find Guido in the newly constructed suburb of Sarcelles, where his crew is rumoured to have been spotted, and is brought to a stand-still by the vision of the ideal, as yet unsullied structures: kilometres of white towers, lawns, shops and youth centres.

'It was beautiful. Green, white, orderly. You could sense the organization. They had done everything to make us feel at home, they had asked themselves: what do we need to put in for them to feel good? And they had put it.'

She gets lost amidst this architecture of optimism, wan-dering confused up and down identical streets named for poets: Rue Verlaine, Mallarmé, Paul-Claudel, Victor Hugo.

This part, at least, I recognize: Canteleu has similar, similarly named streets down which you can get lost. In the early weeks I walk in the rain along Allée Bovary and Boule-vard Monet and Rue Pissarro, exploring, trying to find my way to and from school or to the bank, bewildered by the ranks of identical tower blocks. It is not as if there is much to see, and after a few such outings, I tend not to venture out alone except to Atac, which I can see from my room. My main refuge, other than my metal-sided bedroom, is the *surveillants'* room. The *surveillants* are mainly students, working to fund their studies. They deal with fights in corri-dors and social dramas, supervise detentions and frisk the kids on the way into school. There is usually a good vein of gallows humour bouncing around us as we troop off to the canteen at half past eleven: who has thrown what piece of furniture at whom, what new and exotic insults have been dredged up in long-running feuds.

Surveillants come and go but there is a hard core of four: Marie-Laure, Sophie, Laurent and Olivier and over the *navarin d'agneau* (I have abandoned six years of vegetarianism overnight, when faced with the prospect of six months of baguette and/or boiled potato and have managed to eat everything except the tongue, a forest of unadorned grey organs jauntily arranged in the giant steel serving trays) and the terrible coffee, obviously, inevitably I suppose, I evaluate the two men. Laurent is dreamy, fair and chaotic and Olivier is the opposite. He's quite short, dark-haired and he vibrates with a barely suppressed energy. In the mornings as I lean out of my window to smoke a Gauloise Blonde Légère (my latest pretension), I watch him searching the kids at the front gate, instantly recognizable in a red, puffy down jacket. I am not particularly interested in him, but when he asks if I would like to come on a trip into Rouen one Wednesday afternoon (school finishes at twelve on Wednesdays), I say yes. The prospect of an afternoon in Canteleu is dismal (it has rained solidly for two weeks at this point) and if I take the bus into town, there are bound to be students on it, staring at my clothes and sniggering (I find the girls far more terrifying than the boys). I have also sized him up and decided that while I do not think he is a violent psychopath, if he does turn out to be one, he is quite small and slight, so I have a fighting chance.

So off we go. I don't think it's a date, but if it were a date, it's a pretty terrible one. We go to some outpost of regional administration to pick up a form, then we go to a large hardware store so he can buy some wood, then we have a coffee in the Rue du Gros-Horloge, Rouen's most tourist-infested medieval street and all the while Olivier is speaking to me in the most execrable, unbearable English. He seems like a nice man as far as I can elicit, but frankly, it's like talking to a halfwit. After fifteen minutes or so, with me supplying the words that elude him, I just can't stand it any more, and I say something to him in French.

'Oh!' he says, surprised. Then in French: 'But you're really good!' And he laughs, because he is not the kind of man to get offended about that kind of thing. He's right: I am really good and I'm quite proud of it. I don't know how, whether it's years of singing or Madame Cockroft or Gérard Depardieu. Maybe it's even the semioticist, but French has become something I can just do, the sounds trip off my tongue and the 'r's roll neatly.

Olivier orders us more coffee in his beautiful and, yes, sexy French and everything is so much better. Everything is great, actually, and we talk all afternoon, then we go for a Mexican meal and drink too much tequila. A few weeks later after several more successful dates, we kiss.

Before we even have sex, I stay over in his grimy little house, which is in a rather depressing, far-flung village and looks like something you might see on a local news report about a grisly, sexually motivated sequestration and murder. We share his mattress, which is on the floor in a first-floor room with no furniture, a single bare bulb and faded, peeling wallpaper that features the rock band Kiss. It seems legitimate to wonder whether I may be murdered, but instead, we fall asleep perfectly entwined like something from a fairy tale: arms and legs entangled, my head on his shoulder. It shouldn't be comfortable for more than five minutes but I wake in the morning and neither of us has moved an inch.

Dating Olivier makes absolute sense of my weird Normandy adventure; in fact it becomes my weird Normandy adventure. Almost instantly I move out of my metal box and into his grotty little house with the Kiss wallpaper and damp lino and he takes me to school each morning and brings me back in the afternoon. Sometimes, thrillingly, he brings me in on the back of his motorbike. At weekends we see his friends or go to the cinema, or lie in bed and eat oranges.

He's clever and open to anything and he makes me laugh properly by saying dark, horrible, funny things, but above all of it, above everything, he is French. Oh, but he is so, so French. He is French in the obvious ways: he listens to George Brassens and Serge Gainsbourg and uses the subjunctive effortlessly and has volumes of Montaigne's essays on his bookshelf. He wakes me with a sincere and beautifully expressed endearment, finds physical affection simple and buys me gifts. He likes a rambling, circular philosophical discussion. But what really fascinate me are the weird little idiosyncrasies of his Frenchness. The way he spreads sweetened condensed milk from a tube on a supermarket loaf cake at breakfast time, then dunks it in a soup bowl of black coffee. The awful, tartan old man slippers he wears religiously at home. In bars, he sometimes orders *menthe à l'eau*, that violently green mouthwash, and I marvel at how anyone could enjoy it. Frenchness is stamped all the way through him like a stick of rock. 'He looks so French!' says my mother, amused, when she comes to visit me in Rouen. 'He's very *French*,' says my father, his eyes narrowed in naked suspicion, when I finally pluck up the courage to introduce them some months later.

On Sundays, we go to his grandmother's dark little house for a proper three-course lunch, perhaps asparagus or scallops, then roast chicken, followed by a home-made apple tart or something from the patisserie in a big white cardboard box finished with a slippery knot of ribbon. Lunch is preceded by dainty glasses of muscat and salty crackers and discussions of what we are going to eat, and finished off with Nescafé from the good cups and chocolate squares out of the tin she keeps in the forbiddingly huge *armoire normande* (a giant, brown piece of furniture that could easily double as a family tomb), possibly accompanied by some kind of meditation on the awfulness of ageing and the imminence of death or, on better days, reminiscences about Olivier's childhood.

Later – considerably later, this is obviously a bigger psychological step – Olivier introduces me to his parents.

My picture of French family life is half drawn from those elegant films of bourgeois adultery and anomie that take place in grand Parisian apartments, and half from *Jean de Florette*. A French mother, thus, is a whippet-thin Kristin Scott Thomas smoking and saying cutting things or a bounteously sexy Emmanuelle Béart figure preparing tomatoes at a stone sink as the cicadas sing outside for a selection of rugged, shirt-sleeved sons of toil. Beyond that, everyone should be preoccupied with food to the extent British people are preoccupied with the weather, and talk openly about sex.

Olivier's parents are nothing like this and they fit in none of my cinematic boxes. His dad is quiet and gentle and bearded and his mum is little and loud and lively. They live in a brown, modern house in Rouen with Olivier's younger brother and a soppy Alsatian and they like riding bicycles through the forest and playing Scrabble. Olivier's mother once offers to loan me her copy of the 1960s erotic novel *Emmanuelle*, but obviously thinks better of it five minutes later; apart from that, no one tries to talk about sex, ever. Most shocking of all, they aren't particularly interested in food.

Perhaps that is unfair. Some of their food is good and they certainly *enjoy* eating, but buoyed by the convenience revolution of the 1970s Olivier's mother decided that she would not be spending her life cooking and she has stuck to this principle: tinned Buitoni ravioli is Olivier's version of Proust's madeleine. Vegetables are thrown into the *'cocotte minute'*, an intimidating monster of a pressure cooker, from whence they emerge soft, greying and defeated (except the artichokes, which are new to me and delicious and which we eat on the chilly terrace when Olivier's mother decrees it is warm enough, which is when the temperature hits 12°C). Puddings come from the supermarket in plastic boxes and for special occasions food is sourced from the *'traiteur'*. This special occasion food is pastel-coloured and moussey and often imprisoned in a trembling dome of aspic, though on one memorable occasion, Olivier's mother orders a vast pie from whose crust twelve charred bird heads emerge, with fantastic whimsy (Olivier's uncle picks off and crunches each individual head with relish, beak, bones and all).

These special occasions are something to behold. I attend a few of them because Olivier has what seems like several hundred cousins and they kindly invite me along to their christenings and weddings and anniversaries. I both like the feeling of being included and slightly dread the actual events at which large groups of family – often thirty or forty or fifty people – gather in village halls in far-flung corners of Normandy. First there is a flurry of cheek kissing, during which no one is quite sure which branch of the family does how many – two? three? four? – and which side to start (*bise* anxiety is a constant factor in my life). At this point, some bristly male relative can be guaranteed to trap me in a *bise* cycle as implacably relentless as a crocodile's death roll, from which I will be too embarrassed to extricate myself. Next we sit down for a meal of many, many courses, after an arbitrary number of which Calvados will be served as a palate cleanser. I am often seated near some elderly relative who speaks with as much clarity as Father Fintan Fay, the monkey priest in *Father Ted* ('It's OK,' Olivier says cheerfully on the way home, 'no one else understands him either'), which makes my Calvados-blurred perception of these events even blurrier. When people find out I am English, they tell me about their awful school trips and laugh about lamb and mint sauce and '*les* beans'. Everyone gets steaming drunk (usually not the children, though Olivier's mother does often claim they used to put Calvados in babies' bottles on her parents' farm) and the day and then the night slip away in loud, confusing merriment. Usually, the whole thing starts up again the next day. It is the wedding scene in *Madame Bovary* brought to life: best dresses, overwhelming piles of food, an endurance marathon of festivity ('. . . they ate until night. When they were too tired of sitting, they went for a stroll . . . the children had fallen asleep under the seats').

When we aren't with his family, Olivier is game for anything. We go on road trips to Brittany, museum visits and zoo outings. Sometimes we go to the forest that surrounds Canteleu to see the not-so-wild boar in the amateurish nature reserve: Olivier knows exactly where to scratch the piglets behind the ears so that they fall into a deep trance, fully unconscious for a whole minute.

I am never homesick, not once in my eight months. Life with Olivier is fun and intense and gratifying, like an extended holiday romance. It is *dépaysant*, all this cultural and sociological exploration and I am *dépaysée* in grey-green rainy Normandy. *Dépaysé* means something a little like homesick but it's hard to translate precisely because it is quite different from homesickness, there's no implication of longing and no sense that it is a bad thing. You have been taken away from what you know and that can mean anything, good or bad. For me, it means I am hungry for it all. What I really want is for all this to no longer be *dépaysant* but to become familiar, and to achieve this I become the most indiscriminate consumer of French life. I gobble up television sitcoms and talk shows, dubbed German cop series with Olivier's grandmother and dubbed *Love Boat*

(*La Croisière s'Amuse*) with his stoner cousin. We go to the cinema to watch trashy comedies with the improbably tanned and perfect Thierry Lhermitte, as wooden as an Action Man, costume dramas with Fabrice Luchini over-emoting in a frock coat and American blockbusters (also dubbed) alike. I eat couscous and *choucroute*, *rillettes*, Danette puddings from Carrefour (I still love a trip to the hypermarché with its ludicrously well-furnished yoghurt aisle) and puff pastry swans from our local bakery. I discover Sephora for lipstick, Princesse Tam Tam for underwear and Printemps for everything else. I can feel my vocabulary extend and my fluency grow and I definitely still want to be French, more than ever. This trip has just confirmed that, even if no one I meet looks like Daniel Auteuil or Isabelle Adjani.

But the school year draws to an end and it is time for me to go back home, and from there to university. I have assumed for many months that Olivier and I will bow to the inevitable and break up at this point but when the time comes, the obvious time when we stand in Charles de Gaulle airport and my flight is called and I need to turn and head up one of the escalators, we don't seem to be breaking up at all.

« 3 »

Betty Blue

My degree is in modern history, but for three years I do everything I can to make it all about France. I pick and choose courses to plug the gaps in my knowledge from the storming of the Bastille to the Liberation of Paris and I fill my head with Marat and Danton and Robespierre, with Manet and Apollinaire and Huysmans. I skim over the dry stuff – the land reforms, the Pépins and the Clovises and the arid rationality of the *Lumières* – and concentrate on the mad, bad and dangerous to know parts, especially the Revolution, the Communards and the *fin de siècle* poets and painters. I like anything with blood or sex or intrigue, neglecting the economic origins of the Franco-Prussian war in favour of Courbet and Baudelaire's friendship, Zola wading into the Dreyfus affair and Céline swooning at the occupying German army. I learn, selectively and with varying degrees of enthusiasm, and I start to build a more rounded picture of France in my head. One of the most important things I learn, however, is not part of my degree at all. I learn that it is almost impossible to have a functional relationship when you draw your role models from French cinema.

I have watched a lot of French cinematic fights by this

point and I have become something of an expert on them. There are *loads* of fights in 1990s French films and, I must say, many of them are excellent. French actors are really great at fighting. I don't mean they are good at fighting in a relentlessly logical, enlightened *cartésien* style they might have learned in the philosophy exams for the *baccalaureat*. The fights I watch in the cinema are illogical and mad and often just stupid, but they are fiery and articulate and everything that comes out of the protagonists' mouths sounds beautiful. French actors having fights sound like I imagine Rimbaud and Verlaine duelling would sound, even when they are throwing shoes at each other in their underwear. Victoria Abril, the Spanish actress who often appears in French comedies, is good; I like the way she lets rip with a volley of fury at Gérard Jugnot in the ludicrous war zone comedy *Casque Bleu* or at dozy Alain Chabat in the equally ludicrous 'oops, my wife is a lesbian!' farce *Gazon Maudit*. Josiane Balasko, playing her lover, does some good headbutting too. Isabelle Adjani is magnificent as the Medici queen, less for her fighting than her general attitude, battling and defying and carrying her lover's head in a burlap sack on her knee at the end of *La Reine Margot*. But Béatrice Dalle is my favourite.

In *37°2* (*Betty Blue* in English) – the preposterous 1980s cult classic of doomed love and stonewashed denim in a beachside shack on stilts – Dalle is the loosest of loose cannons, kicking off at the slightest provocation, throwing and breaking things and generally making an almighty nuisance of herself. There is not much of a plot to speak of (boy meets girl, girl goes mad, girl gouges out her own eye, boy smothers girl), but the sexual chemistry between Dalle and Jean-Jacques Beineix is heady and Dalle plays her part like a woman possessed, luminously beautiful, believably insane and unapologetic. At nineteen, I find this vision of love and relationships utterly persuasive: fuck logic, screw compromise, set everything on fire with a raging passion, have sex in front of the fire and then carry the embers on your lap in a burlap sack. Or something.

My love of cinematic drama means that when Olivier and I fight, which we do, almost constantly, I am obscurely satisfied by it. Our fights are awful, but according to my sources love is supposed to be unbearable and violent ('happiness is an abnormal state in love,' says Proust, who I read this year and who seems to elevate self-imposed misery to a fine art) so we must be doing it right. I take an unhealthy pleasure in standing in the corridors of my college, fighting with him in French on a payphone, which a small part of me thinks is rather glamorous and good for my image. I have taken great, ridiculous pains to cultivate my 'French' image at university – slightly distant and sophisticated is what I am aiming for – by going away often to Normandy, smoking Gauloises Blondes Ultra Légères that I import from France and walking the thirty minutes to the Maison Blanc patisserie to buy a millefeuille or a *tarte au cassis* in French. When I am in a good mood, I play Serge Gainsbourg records ('L'Anamour' or 'Le Poinçonneur des Lilas') on repeat, provoking the ire of the Dean, who lives downstairs. When I am not in a good mood, I play wistful, droopy ballads by men who look more like antiquarian book dealers than pop stars: Alain Souchon,

Francis Cabrel and William Sheller. I worry about their possible naffness, though, which is as hard to gauge in a foreign language as swearing. Am I listening to the equivalent of David Essex? Chris de Burgh? *Sting?* This fear haunts me often. I am odiously, ostentatiously French, and the dramatic French fight scenes fit perfectly with all this.

The only problem is, in reality I find the fighting very upsetting. We have lots of reasons to fight, Olivier and I, hissing at each other in my tiny college bedroom (he comes over at least two weekends a month), or racking up punishingly expensive silences on the payphone. He is deeply insecure about my new life in Oxford, and regards my friends and acquaintances with suspicion, verging on outright hostility, his eyes narrowing every time I mention a male name. He wants us to be together all the time, every possible minute: this is his conception of love. I have to concede that this is totally consistent with the French film version, but it is unreasonable and unfair and I am angry and frustrated. I need to have an independent life and make some friends without my boyfriend looming sulkily; I know that is a reasonable desire, but I can't convince him. He thinks he is being logical and *cartésien*, but often he sounds quite insane.

As for me, I am not good at fighting. For the first decade of my life my mother and I lived mainly alone (she and my father split when I was tiny) and we never fought, then my stepfather Joe, who is the kindest, gentlest, most conflict-averse man I have ever met, moved in. My sister is ten years younger than me; I simply have no experience of fighting and I don't really like it either; I want everyone to get on. I don't even like expressing mild dissent, or talking about what I want. Ideally, what I would like to happen is for Olivier just to intuit my feelings without me having to say anything, and act upon them. This is often my default: staring hard at him and trying to convey my thoughts nonverbally, in the manner of a mournful greyhound. Can't you just *guess*? I think, desperately. I have not had much success with this strategy so far.

The fact that we are fighting in French adds another layer of complexity. I know what I need to convey: it is, basically, 'back off'. I need to be able to explain to him, gently but quite firmly, that there are more ways of loving a person than he has the life experience to conceive of right now. That not everyone is as simply and absolutely happy in the company of one other person all the time as his parents and that for some people – including me – moments of separateness aren't a threat or a problem but a necessity. 'Look at my mum and Joe,' I want to say to him but of course, we've been together for less than a year and he hasn't really seen enough of them to understand what I mean and I don't have the linguistic ability to make him understand. He's staring at me all fiery and heartbroken and 'back off' seems too raw and too definitive. What can I say? I just don't have the subtleties of language at my disposal in French and I don't trust myself to find them.

So rather than get it wrong, I just clam up. Obviously I know the words or at least, I know some words, enough words, but they feel so powerful to me, I am terrified of misusing them. I am hung up on phrasing and tone and nuance, so instead of saying something that might come out wrong, or be misconstrued, I say nothing. I formulate and reformulate in my head – does this sound right? Is this what I really want to say? – and while I do, the silence builds until I haven't said anything for so long it feels too late. Unable to express my frustration, I turn it inwards on myself. Sometimes I rake my nails through the skin on my arms and legs until they bleed, sometimes I bang my head against a wall. Sometimes I just storm off and sleep in the bath or stomp through the streets of Oxford muttering to myself (obviously, this passes entirely unnoticed, most of the other people in Oxford city centre are also muttering to themselves). I'm seething: I can't reconcile these two incompatible lives and it makes me furious at myself.

I have, I suppose, a sort of breakdown. At the end of my first year, when exam stress combines with our continuing relationship meltdown, my hair starts to fall out – wisps, then tufts, then handfuls. By mid-vacation, back in France with Olivier, the bedroom floor is entirely coated in an unsettling carpet of my hair each day. We go off to the hills outside Rome for a disastrous holiday and the fighting gets worse, uglier, as bad as it has ever been – we scream at each other as we tour the Villa Hadriana, and drink too much cheap wine in thunderous silence in trattorias. I behave abominably – I even hit him once. Some irrational part of me feels like the hair loss is his fault, and I'm bereft and furious and scared. When we get back from holiday, I am still bald, exhausted and sick of fighting and I wonder if it's time to give up. I didn't really expect this relationship to survive and perhaps it has run its natural course? Olivier is so incredibly certain we should be together and it has been flattering and gratifying and romantic, but he can't be certain enough for both of us. We can't stay together through the sheer force of his will, strong as that is.

Somehow, though, we carry on. Olivier seems to mellow as I start my second year and he's tender and solicitous and patient as I trail from dermatologist to psychologist, helping me manage my horrible salt-free diet and my medication, encouraging me when I get low and coaxing me to take better care of myself. I am in worse shape than I have ever been at this point: bald, plump and moon-faced from high doses of steroids, obsessed with trying not to gain more weight, dozy with sedatives and behind on my work. I go to hardly any tutorials and I manage to learn absolutely nothing about the eighteenth century. I eat only Marks & Spencer diet ready meals and I drift around my shared house, barely interacting with my housemates. I can't drink with all the pills I am taking and I feel so tired all the time, I crash out at nine every night. Olivier is utterly solid through this time. He gets on slow ferries and packed coaches to visit me without complaint and when he arrives, he doesn't pick fights or get angry and suspicious. He cheers me up and cheers me on and makes me feel as if I am still as beautiful to him as ever, puffy and cross in my ginger wig. He is funny too, happy to put on my sister's platform shoes and an eyeliner moustache just to amuse me (he does this, one Christmas, just for the hell of it).

The time I spend with him in Normandy in the holidays, thankfully, is mainly very peaceful. Olivier is no longer frisking fifteen-year-olds for marijuana; he has a job in an engineering firm in a sleepy Normandy town called Elbeuf where the average age seems to be sixty-five, and has exchanged his Kiss wallpapered murder hovel for a much nicer flat with high ceilings and pretty wrought-iron balconies. We sometimes fight still – I sleep in his bath a few nights here too – but gradually we seem to learn how to be a little gentler with each other as space and time do their work.

Olivier leaves for work early and I doze, make breakfast and read the piles of Zola and Proust I have stacked by the bed. The very best thing about my degree is how many French novels I get to read and call 'work'. Zola is a gift for a historian because he placed himself at the heart of every current and preoccupation of his age and then wrote a book about it. Over the twenty novels of the Rougon-Macquart cycle, he tries to set out his then-modish theory of hereditary degeneracy (that hereditary character flaws, habitually revealed in physical characteristics, are inescapable and worsen over generations) and to critique the social mores and political impulses of the Second Empire, from labour relations to anti-clericalism, Impressionism to the Franco-Prussian war. I gobble up their thundering unsubtle prose, spending hours lost down the mines (*Germinal*), among the bonnets in a Parisian department store (*Au Bonheur des Dames*) or drunk, filthy and starving in the cupboard under the stairs (*L'Assommoir*).

Proust is trickier, but in those quiet Elbeuf mornings I can slow my heartbeat and my reactions sufficiently to get caught up in his waterfalls of words, the textures and the wallpapers, the brocades and silks, the elegant evocation of longing. I love the shapes of Proust in my mouth: often I read passages aloud in the echoing, high-ceilinged bedroom for the sheer physical pleasure of it. It helps me remember what I love about France, and why, and I start to get excited about work again: I want to read more, see more pictures; think harder.

When my head starts to throb or I get hungry, I go out and buy myself a cake (a *flan* usually, my favourite) and a copy of *Voici*, the salacious cheap gossip magazine whose front cover is often given over to apologies to the celebrities they have libelled, to find out what is happening in Johnny Halliday's marriage: I continue to maintain an equal opportunities approach to French culture, high, low, and anywhere in-between. I walk down to the river, where in the way of small provincial towns everywhere, old people on benches stare fixedly at me. Sometimes, I go to the cinema down the street for a matinee of whatever adultery-based comedy Christian Clavier has made most recently (the oleaginous Clavier has by the mid-1990s replaced Gérard Depardieu as the Actor For Whom a Quota of Film Appearances Seems to Be In Force). More often I stay at home and watch TV.

Some extraordinarily terrible things happen on French television, I discover: things that shake my faith in the superiority of French culture. Between the dubbed German cop shows and *Love Boat* repeats, the home-grown material stands out as infinitely worse. I watch a lot of sitcoms of brain-liquefying stupidity, including *Les Filles d'à Côté*, in which three shrieking harpies attempt to seduce their American neighbour. This would be grotesquely sexist were it not for the existence of a male equivalent, *Salut Les Musclés*, which is even worse (the Musclés, five single, be-mulletted musicians, share an apartment and high jinks ensue). The worst of all, though, is Patrick Sébastien. Gurning, sinister humourist Sébastien has a stranglehold on Saturday night television, keeping it stuck in the worst of the seventies through the sheer force of his personality. His shows feature accordion solos, bare-breasted circus acts, risqué songs stuffed with unfunny double entendres, Sébastien himself in awful prosthetics, and communal rugby chants. Who on earth is watching this stuff? It's as if there is a whole other France I can barely imagine out there and it has atrocious taste. The one thing I can rely on is the lunchtime news.

The lunchtime news on TF1 is presented by a genially avuncular man called Jean Pierre Pernaut, and it is more like a Gallic version of *That's Life* – all heartwarming animal rescues and oddly shaped tubers – than a serious news programme. The emphasis is on France's regions, their produce, particularities and *patrimoine* (heritage), and this is deliberate. Pernaut was once quoted in the weekly magazine *Télérama* saying, 'The one o'clock news is a French news programme intended principally for French people. If you want to know about Venezuela, watch Venezuelan TV. If you want to know about Sudan, watch African channels.' It is entirely normal for the principal headline on the one o'clock news to be the weather, followed by anything from cherry-stone spitting competitions or chocolate bunny makers to – the daily financial paper *Les Echos* suggested in exasperation – 'a Béarnese sheep bell maker'. It is 'a giant comforter' *Les Echos* continued while left-wing broadsheet *Libération* evokes 'a news broadcast in muddy clogs, revering pretty landscapes, forgotten crafts and *la maouche ardéchoise* (a vaguely obscene-looking sausage) the way granny used to make it'.

In my delicate state (I am still on antidepressants and high doses of steroids), the giant comforter is perfect and I sink gratefully into its marshmallow-like embrace. In my vacations, I follow the reassuring rhythms of the TF1 year assiduously, from the September reports on the worrying increase in the weight of school bags, through a winter of flu vaccines and opening ski resorts. At Easter I watch several days' worth of reports on trends in Easter chocolate (is fruit more popular this year? Animal motifs? Bright colours?) and the Paris couture shows are genuinely absorbing. The more parochial esoterica I absorb, the closer I feel to French-ness. I want to get all the cultural references effortlessly when we go out and Olivier's friends are chatting, and this is how I insinuate myself into the interstices of French low culture: *Voici*, the TF1 news and soap operas. I'm assiduously attentive too when Olivier tries to bolster my cinematic education with a selection of classic comedies. We watch Louis de Funès's magnificently silly *La Soupe aux Choux*, in which two elderly peasants are visited by a Martian, and *La Vie est Une Longue Fleuve Tranquille* with its deliciously horrible bourgeois Catholic family, all neat side partings, guitar-playing priests and repression.

In the evenings, we drive out along the Seine as the sun sets, the river flat and wide and Monet-hazy, banks dotted with willows, cow parsley waving in the breeze. We eat the cheapest set menu in half-timbered and chintzy fish restaurants and splash out on a bottle of Sancerre. Sometimes we drive out to the coast to a soundtrack of George Brassens and sit on the uncomfortable pebbly beach at Dieppe or search out cider farms and cows to admire in the lush greenery of Basse-Normandie. Sunday lunch with Olivier's grandmother remains a fixture. Although she has moved into sheltered accommodation, standards have not slipped remotely and the *armoire normande* full of biscuits and chocolate squares and lace doilies has accompanied her (it takes up half of the living space). We eat and then watch *Inspecteur Derrick*, the dubbed German detective series she loves, squashed up on her tiny sofa. We pitch a tent in Olivier's grandfather's field on a blustery Normandy cliff top and play dominoes with his other grandmother, who cries when she loses, then forces you to play again.

Gradually, our periods of tranquillity lengthen and we settle into something more comfortable: he trusts me now, finally I think, and I have seen how magnificently kind and loyal he is. We have weathered the worst of a long-distance relationship and both our insecurities have subsided. I feel a bit shattered by the past few years – I am bald now, for god's sake – but I have realized I do not want to conceive of my life without this man. We have become interwoven in each other's lives, with family weddings and holidays and the delicate business of where to have Christmas. Olivier's parents are completely accepting of me (he does not really give them any choice in the matter, but they are lovely nevertheless): Jacqueline provides me with special mayonnaise and aspic-free foods and I am invited to more and more of their gatherings of the clans. On my side, I think my illness has short-circuited some of my parents' reticence and given them a chance to see Olivier's essential kindness. My mother treats him as an ally and in the warmth of her regard – her love is a wonderful thing – he relaxes and blossoms, shows them he can be funny and relaxed as well as fiercely loving. As my finals approach and then pass, we can begin to think about what happens next.

The obvious thing, surely, is for me to move to France. What is keeping me in England? This is what I have been working towards for the past six years, isn't it? But actually, we hatch another plan. Olivier is going to do an MBA and I am going to train to be a lawyer: in London.

« 4 »

La Fille sur le Pont

We don't even consider moving to France until six years later, when my mother dies.

I find out she is dead on an indolent, clockwatching afternoon in the office in autumn 2003, the air suffused with the familiar scents of photocopier toner and vending machine coffee. I am sitting at my desk in a large law firm in the City, where I have recently qualified as a solicitor (European law, a discipline I hope will get me back to France eventually, though so far I have shown scant aptitude or enthusiasm for it). I am pregnant for the second time: our son Theo, who is one, is at nursery. In a couple of hours I need to go and collect him, so with a sigh I turn back to the spreadsheet I am laboriously composing when the phone rings.

It is my stepfather Joe, his voice strained and hesitant. I just have time to think, 'Joe never calls me', before he says: 'Em, there's been an accident in Italy. It's your mum.' Then there is a pause, quite a short one, and then he says, 'She's dead, Em.'

I don't really know what he says next. Something to do with a railway station in Rome. I hear him say he hasn't told my sister, that she isn't home yet and that he has to get ready to tell her, so I put the phone down and I stand up but then I don't really know what to do with myself. I don't doubt Joe at all; he has been admirably, devastatingly clear and I recognize the truth of his words as soon as he says them. But she was in our flat borrowing my dressing gown and cuddling Theo only a few days ago and what now? Shock leaves me befuddled and incompetent: I can't make a decision and my limbs are heavy and clumsy. Eventually someone calls Olivier and someone makes arrangements to collect Theo and somehow we are quite quickly back in our flat, and I am watching the architects in the office opposite go about their strip-lit business as Theo demands yoghurt and Olivier crouches in front of me, hands on my knees.

'We should go.'

'Go where?'

'To York. Come on. Just get yourself ready. I'll do the rest.'

So we go, heading out of the city northwards, Regent's Park then Swiss Cottage, Finchley Road and Brent Cross, as night draws in. Theo, strapped in his car seat in the back with a juice box and a breadstick, is delighted with this break from routine and amuses himself by pointing out his favourite vans and chatting to us, like a charming cocktail party guest. He is lovely at the moment, funny and ebullient. Having a baby so soon (I get pregnant at twenty-six, long before any of our English friends have even considered it) has been a sort of *folie à deux*, but we have leapt into the unknown hand in hand. Some of it has been a struggle: the exhaustion, the hyper-alert anxiety of the early months, Theo's severe eczema and the isolation of raising a baby in the grown-up heart of central London. But our son – our long-lashed, easily amused son who flirts with everyone, from the pensioners in John Lewis to the leather queens of Soho – is the distilled essence of delight. It's scarcely credible that the two of us have created this marvel and we enjoy him fiercely, proudly.

The last few months have been especially lovely. Theo's eczema has cleared up, and now he can speak I feel as if we are both emerging from the strange, scorched-earth weirdness of early motherhood and early babyhood. A real person is emerging with desires and opinions and a sweetly eccentric vocabulary, and every week brings a developmental leap. On my days off, Theo and I play in the fountains in Russell Square or run around the Great Court of the British Museum, we visit the sheep in Coram Fields and hang out in John Lewis toy department when it rains. Olivier makes Theo laugh by catching pigeons for him in Charlotte Street gardens (they can stalk them for hours). My school friend Kate sneaks out from Sotheby's for cups of tea and Maria downstairs allows Theo to chase her gigantic fluffy cat, Bambi, around, creating suffocating clouds of hair in her overheated flat. Early on Saturday mornings we walk down to Bar Italia for cappuccinos and pastries and watch the wild, funny, dirty city come to life. I love where we live, in the warren of streets between Oxford Street and Regent's Park (the Household Cavalry trot smartly up our street most Sunday mornings in a thunderous clattering of hooves); it's full of life and history and unexpected discoveries. I am thrilled to be pregnant again too: I feel lucky, buoyed by hormones and anticipation.

We arrive in York around midnight, park up and knock on my mother's red front door. My sister opens it and her features look indistinct with shock. She is only seventeen, for god's sake. This kind of thing shouldn't happen to seventeen-year-olds.

'I'm so glad you're here,' she says and we hold on to each other in confusion and relief and misery and my stepfather comes to join us, his big nicotine-stained hands around the two of us, and I'm so glad I'm here, too, in this little house I know so well: I can't imagine how I could be anywhere else. That night, after we all finally go to bed (it is strange, this, it doesn't feel right somehow but staying up all night won't help and I am so, so tired), I go to the loo, the baby pressing on my bladder. I find my way there instinctively, without turning on the lights. It's comforting to realize I know every inch of this place; that I can find my way around in the dark.

Over the next few days, we find out a little more. My mother – my beautiful, funny, ferociously loving mother – was walking through Rome's Termini Station that morning. She was on holiday with two old friends, Jack (her adored ex-husband, the man she married before she met my father) and his partner Brian. They had just stepped onto one of the flat mechanical walkways that carried passengers to the platforms and were moving along it, separated by a few yards, when the section that my mother was standing on collapsed inwards, crushing her in the mechanism. My mother was killed instantly, Jack and Brian told us, despite heroic attempts from passers-by to save her. Later we will find out that that the walkway was being repaired and had mistakenly been left open and accessible (the 'no entry' cones had been placed at the wrong walkway by maintenance staff), rendering it fatally dangerous. It was a happy morning, Jack and Brian assure us, and a good trip. My mother had been planning, Brian adds, to buy clothes for my new baby.

Whatever I have previously imagined grief to be like, from reading and television and my imagination, I am wrong. It is not operatically dreadful, a soaring, wailing, instant heartbreak accompanied by the rending of garments and the gouging of skin. Things carry on. We are still ourselves: we drink tea and talk and eat biscuits. I sleep, constantly: fatigue keeps coshing me round the back of the neck and I have to stagger off and lie down. Olivier spends a lot of time in the backyard smoking, keeping my stepfather, made garrulous by shock, company. The rest of the time he is on the phone to the consulate and the airlines and the coroner, using his vast energies to get my mother's body home (this takes on an inordinate importance; I need her to be back). It is a thick fog of logistics, tiredness and unease, with a considerable, inevitable, amount of life as usual, thanks to Theo. We go to feed the ducks, we visit the Railway Museum and play with the toy trains in the Early Learning Centre, between awful administrative tasks and visits from devastated friends and family.

There is a lot to be done. We have to choose a coffin (from an awful laminated catalogue; sitting on the slippery Co-op

Funeral couch I get the giggles and choose badly) and organize a funeral (venue, food and flowers). Piles of post begin to arrive from people whom I have never met or even heard of, detailing the ways in which my mother touched their lives. Others turn up on our doorstep: a huge contingent of family, brothers and sisters, a former neighbour with the slightly eccentric gift of a microwave, colleagues and acquaintances. A criminal prosecution is underway in Rome and we have to find representation, and my stepfather becomes very ill and ends up in hospital suffering the after-effects of shock.

Throughout it all, I feel detached. I function relatively well practically, but emotionally, I am almost entirely absent, enveloped in a thick cognitive fog, the insulating bulk of my pregnancy acting as a shock absorber. My mother is absent from my thoughts – her real, vital self, the person who was going to Rome to drink wine and admire ecclesiastical vestments and buy baby clothes for her new grandchild.

At her funeral I try, really try, to conjure her up. The sight of my mother's small coffin, carried by my father and Olivier, makes my sister and I clutch one another again and sob, but the feeling passes. My sister has done a magnificent job with the music and the readings, and the eulogies are beautiful and funny and right, but, for me, none of the melodic or lyrical grenades hit their target: 'Soave Sia Il Vento', the lovely quartet from *Cosi Fan Tutte*, Don Marquis's 'Song of Mehitabel' from *Archy and Mehitabel* ('wotthehell, archy, wotthehell', her favourite rallying cry), not even Harry, one of her university friends, a brilliant sweet-voiced tenor singing an unaccompanied Scottish folk song in the white-washed silence of the Methodist chapel. It's partly because there are too many people, there are hundreds of them, then the taxi driver refuses to turn down his soundtrack of ultra-sexy R 'n' B on the way to the cemetery, which just makes us laugh, and as we stand there in the rain and some men put my mother in a hole this is it, really it, but the feeling is elusive. I want this moment to mean something, but I just feel angry and embarrassed at how public it all is; there are still too many people, too many distractions. I can't find my mum in all this. I want to, but I can't: I have to think of her in private.

My mum was very little, barely 5'2", but she fought and laughed and danced and loved like a giant.

Born in a poor ex-steel town in the west of Scotland, one of seven children, she was the first in her family to go to university, leaving with a first in English, a wild eye for beauty and a lovely, gay husband, Jack. Her parents both died when she was in her early twenties and their deaths and the early experience of caring for them shaped her perception of life and family. She lived bigger, brighter and louder than I would ever dare to: moving to Ghent without a word of Dutch, moving in with my then-disreputable father and his menagerie in the Scottish Borders and stalking a pianist who had broken her heart round the concert halls of London.

She knew things you would never expect: how to get a table under the art nouveau *coupole* in the lovely Bofinger brasserie in Paris, the best churches for a quiet sit-down in most European capitals and any number of excellent cafés, and she had an anecdote for each. 'I had my bag blown up by the Bow Street police here,' she would say, tucking my arm into hers as we walked through the back streets of Covent Garden or, studying the flyers at the Wigmore Hall, 'When I was stalking that pianist, I sat in the front row during a recital here and glared at him the whole way through.' Her wardrobe was full of evidence of an intensely lived life: a daring crocheted Biba mini dress, lace-up plat-form boots, a psychedelic floral babydoll nightie. Jack fell in love, initially, with her red shoes, glimpsed across the univer-sity library.

In her professional life as a research fellow and subse-quently as a professor of social policy, she was instrumental in effecting seismic shifts in the way that child and other unpaid carers were treated. She knew, personally, what it meant to care for someone when there is no option and no support and she spent long hours listening to, recording and bearing witness to the lives of people caring for the profoundly disabled.

But she was also wickedly funny: she was a woman who stole chips from strangers and danced on tables and coloured in the holes in her tights with a ballpoint pen. She loved the opera and her tiny garden, other people's terriers, schmaltzy country music, nice bedlinen and Guerlain potions.

We were close, perhaps too close, bound together by love and dependency and a decade of physical proximity when it was just the two of us. My childhood memories are mainly of her: long train journeys to Glasgow, sitting with a pen and a packet of Smarties in the corner of her meetings, riding on the back of her bike and weekend mornings in Bettys tearoom in York with a round of granary toast and a hot chocolate, her reading the paper and me the *Beano*. Our closeness worried her sometimes: she thought she hadn't given me enough structure or discipline and perhaps she hadn't. She was a grade-A worrier, her appearance of insouciance hard won, her lightness of touch maintained by a real effort of will. Her love held me steady as much as it kept me afloat – I knew instinctively what would disappoint her. This kind of love is a massive – if unconscious – effort for the person doing the loving and many of us, the lucky ones, float complacently in the benign amniotic safety of maternal love, swatting away its unwelcome excesses, giving no thanks. I did.

When I was miserable in Oxford, she took me out for meals and sent me money for massages. Parcels arrived for me constantly: books, poems, carefully copied out in her familiar handwriting, Chanel lipsticks, and once, as I prepared for my finals, a huge bunch of spring flowers – my favourites, scented blue hyacinths, parrot tulips and dark tendrils of ivy – with a card that read 'nearly time to come out, Persephone'.

When, later, I struggled after Theo was born, isolated and anxious, she would make the two-hour train journey to visit us in London almost weekly, rocking Theo's tense colicky little body over her shoulder and dancing with his peach-fuzzy cheek against hers, one hand cradling his wobbly head as she sang 'Cheek to Cheek'. She tried to teach me what Olivier understood instinctively: how to enjoy the baby, to relax and savour the delicious animal warmth and otherness of him. I didn't quite get it then. Soon I will, when the new baby comes.

Now she is gone and it makes no sense. She was just here, my borrowed dressing gown too big for her little frame, drinking a cup of coffee and planning her Rome itinerary. I know exactly how it felt to hug her goodbye but I experience a complete imaginative failure at the idea of her dead. I *know* she is, but I can't feel it, so I just get on with things. Presumably it will sink in eventually.

After the funeral we return to London. My sister moves in with us – she can't stand to be in York – and we spend a grisly Christmas, whose only redeeming feature is that no one tries to pretend it's remotely OK, together in our flat with her and her father and the saddest, most stunted Christmas tree any of us has ever seen. Then, in the dark, short, dead days between Christmas and New Year, we head off to the abandoned Millennium Dome, where an optimistically named 'Christmas Wonderland' has been installed. We are hoping to amuse Theo but the scene before us is pretty dismal: a few scrappy fairground rides dotted here and there in the semi-darkness. It's chilly under the damp wet canvas and there's that muddy marquee smell, mingling with stewed hot-dog onions and the acrid burnt-sugar tang of candyfloss. I find a hard chair to sit on and watch as my sister takes Theo on a shudderingly slow miniature train. She is smiling, but the smile doesn't reach her eyes, which are blank with unhappiness. Theo, in contrast, is beaming unreservedly, his cheeks round and ruddy. He is wearing a bright yellow oilcloth coat like a tiny sea captain and his fat fists thump the plastic steering wheel in delight.

Olivier isn't watching, he's looking at me, with an odd, sort of appraising expression.

'*Quoi?*' We still speak French to each other all the time. His English has improved enormously, but it doesn't feel right – we fell in love in French and I'd rather he deal with my linguistic infelicities than I deal with his. It seems key to our relationship somehow.

'So what do you think about moving to Paris, seriously?'

He's raised this before but I haven't really been paying attention, have had other things on my mind, but now, next to the sweating hot dogs, it all comes out, properly.

His job (in a French investment bank), he believes, will not exist for very much longer; they are restructuring and things don't look good for him. There is, however, the possibility of doing the same job, or even a slightly better one, at head office, in La Défense in Paris. He thinks it's the best option, but we have to decide fast.

'Like, when?'

'Like, well, now, really. As soon as possible.'

I understand that it makes financial sense. But I can also see some fairly obvious downsides: I am about to give birth, my mother died two months ago and we have built a life here in London, family, friends (admittedly most of mine are local pensioners and shop assistants, but still) and jobs. My French yearnings have been in abeyance for a while: having a baby has catapulted me back into a set of instinctive responses learned in my own babyhood, the songs I sing to him and the words I use come automatically, summoned from some unconscious part of my brain. My mother's death too has left me a little homesick for the familiarity of York, where people know me and knew her and where the shape of her life is still vivid and distinct. I'm constantly fighting a desire to crawl back home and revert to childhood. What really prevents me from doing so is the knowledge that it won't actually feel right, because the person who made it home is gone. That's why my sister is here with us: she doesn't want to be in York, because it's in York that the wrongness of everything becomes so glaringly obvious.

I look across at Olivier. He is holding a pile of stuff – my bag, my sister's coat, Theo's comfort blanket, a half-drunk hot chocolate – and he looks as wired as I feel leaden. His eyes are darting round the gloom, vigilant as a meerkat, primed for the next challenge. He has met a lot of challenges in the last few months, doggedly, politely agitating to get my mother's body repatriated, smoking calmly in the back-yard with my stepfather when he was at his most febrile and loquacious, and signing up to run a marathon with my sister to keep her company. 'He's wonderful,' people said to me over and over again at the funeral, relieved to have something unreservedly positive to say, and they were right, he is. I have discovered how deep his commitment to us, his family, goes: he will simply do whatever he needs to for things to be OK. It's awe-inspiring, and slightly Sicilian. If he tells me he thinks this is the right thing to do, then I can be perfectly sure that he believes it is right for all of us.

Perhaps he's right? I don't know. On one obvious level it

sounds like a terrible idea: you don't run off to another country with a newborn and a two-year-old after – indeed during – the most cataclysmic time of your life. That sounds stupid and warning bells go off in my head, but then again, I don't really trust my own emotions. I don't actually *have* any emotions except a flat, permanent tiredness and a bolus of dread in the depths of my stomach. I don't know how to think about my mum and I don't really try. One frosty morning as I am crossing Bloomsbury Square Gardens on my way to work I find myself thinking about her grave and how cold it must be: she must be *freezing*, I think, why can't I do anything about it? We have to get her out of there. It's unbearable for a couple of minutes and I have to sit down and breathe through my mouth, trying to expel the terror with each breath. But then the feeling passes and life goes on; I go to work, look at spreadsheets, collect Theo, make dinner. It's sort of horrifying the way life goes on, but of course she knew all about that and had lived it: one of those parcels she sent me to Oxford contained Auden's 'Musée de Beaux-Arts' ('About suffering they were never wrong, The Old Masters') and an accompanying postcard of Breughel's *Fall of Icarus*.

So life will go on and why not in Paris? Paris! My dulled spirit feels a tiny fillip of excitement at the thought of it. Magical, beautiful Paris where everything is finer and brighter and more exalted. Paris is Juliette Binoche sitting on top of a statue of Henri IV drunk and mad and half-blind, and shooting her father's service revolver (*Les Amants du Pont-Neuf*). It's saturnine Jacques Dutronc being *le dauphin de la place Dauphine*, describing the city at dawn in his elegant, clever prose. It's Daniel Auteuil (oh, Daniel Auteuil, the most exquisite of raddled-looking French actors, my fantasy husband) playing a nihilistic knife thrower, smoking and saying to Vanessa Paradis, '*Vous avez l'air d'une fille qui va faire une connerie*' (you look like a girl who's about to do something stupid) before she jumps off the Passerelle Debilly into the Seine in the daft but stylish melodrama *The Girl on the Bridge*. Paris is obviously the place for strong emotions (although it may be best to avoid the bridges). We will go to Paris.

'OK,' I say. 'Let's do it.'

« 5 »

En Sourdine

As I get larger and even slower, Olivier starts to look for flats in Paris, bringing home sets of estate agents' particulars from his trips. It should be exciting, but somehow it isn't for me; it all seems very distant and unreal, whereas Theo's needs are immediate and pressing and easy to satisfy and they stop me from thinking too much. We are also selling our flat, so I spend a considerable amount of time putting away toys and hiding things in cupboards, which is dull but vaguely gratifying. The aim is that we will move almost as soon as the baby is born, in the springtime.

I feel utterly detached from the idea of moving to Paris, an idea that should thrill me to my core. I love Paris. Of course I do; everyone loves Paris. All my adolescent fantasies centred around living in Paris, drinking coffee in bars and smoking Gauloises, with a nice dog at my feet. Maybe I would wear men's shirts like Jane Birkin. Perhaps I would be a writer. Doubtless, I assumed, I would have lovers, though they took no clear form in my head. I spend more time imagining my outfits and the dog: a neatly trimmed Scottie, I think. I don't have any idea how to reconcile my fantasy Parisian self (well-dressed, single, faintly ascetic, formidably self-possessed, dog owner) with my current self (nine months pregnant, in elastic-waisted trousers, largely subsisting on Marks & Spencer's chocolate mini rolls).

Conscious of my own ambivalence, I try to motivate myself with remembered trips. My parents, rather touchingly, were keen to make my first time in Paris special. For my thirteenth birthday, despite having been separated for a decade, they decided to take me to Paris together. We stayed on the Ile Saint-Louis, on the Rue Saint-Louis-en-l'Ile, perhaps one of the most perfectly romantic addresses anywhere in Paris, which sets the bar pretty high everywhere. In the mornings, my father would take me on long walks across the city, then after a large lunch, my mother would potter with me around the enthralling stationery shops of the Ile, admiring elegantly clipped dogs and their owners and stopping late afternoon for a Berthillon ice cream. We ate *tarte aux quetsches* in a dark, half-empty restaurant and my parents got happily drunk and maudlin on *eau-de-vie*. Every morning I was despatched mercilessly to go and buy croissants from the bakery across the road (delicious, but the ordering was mortifying) and a perpetually naked man wandered around the flat opposite my hotel room. It was magical and strange, as your first trip to Paris should be.

Later, when I was teaching in Canteleu, I met my mother and sister when, as a result of some devastating gambit in the (largely good-humoured) mental chess match between my parents, they were staying in barely credible luxury in the Pavillon de la Reine on the Place des Vosges at my father's expense. I stayed a night with them and in the morning,

Olivier, whom I had just started seeing in earnest, sneaked in for a free breakfast. On arrival, he looked shifty and somewhat discombobulated. 'A man in uniform has just valet parked my car.' Olivier drove a dilapidated Peugeot of indeterminate vintage, the back filled with a clutter of wood and old blankets, the front approximately eighty per cent rust and Coke cans. After breakfast, I introduced him to my beadily curious mother, we took my sister up the Eiffel Tower, then the four of us sat in a café, ate chips and made slightly stilted small talk. When Olivier left, my mother drew me aside and poked me with mock indignation.

'You told me you *weren't* going out with him!'

'I wasn't!' I protested. 'Er . . . then.' She didn't seem to mind much, satisfied I was in reasonably safe hands.

Soon after we moved to London, Olivier and I took my father and stepmother to the Salon de l'Agriculture. This superlative agricultural show on the outskirts of the city, with outsized cattle, regional produce as far as the eye can see and rabbits in tricolour sashes, is a key feature of the French TV news year and a test of presidential mettle: whether you can glad hand the farmers and admire the cows with sufficient enthusiasm can define a president. Chirac was famously brilliant at the 'hail fellow well-met' bonhomie of it, tasting saucissons, patting cows and drinking everything proffered; Sarkozy got himself into enormous trouble for hissing sour obscenities at a protester. On our visit, Olivier translated gamely for my father as we meandered round the various tasting stations in the wine tent, then admired the magnificently fat cows, all rippling muscles and polished flanks. It snowed and we were staying on the Left Bank, opposite Deyrolle, the magnificent taxidermist. We stared at the stuffed zebras and macaque monkeys as fat snowflakes stuck to our winter coats, then walked down to the Deux Magots for hot chocolate.

My most recent trip was two years previously, celebrating my sister's sixteenth birthday. I was pregnant with Theo and we stayed in pretty Saint-Sulpice on the Left Bank in the eaves of a ramshackle hotel for a weekend of wandering and window shopping. We ate *Poilâne tartines* in the café on the square, walked around the Jardin du Luxembourg and went shopping for cool stuff for my sister and maternity clothes for me. My mother's infallible Rolodex of a memory located several magnificent brasseries she had not visited in decades, where we debated with the waiters several times, for my vegetarian sister's benefit, whether ham can be considered a vegetable. One evening, we took my sister for a cocktail in a mirror-lined bar on the Rue de Rennes to celebrate her nearly being a grown-up and me nearly being a mother and we laughed and took pictures.

My mother came down to breakfast one morning with a bemused expression.

'I had such a peculiar dream last night,' she said.

'Oh?'

'Yes. I was following a bird and it turned round and looked at me and I knew I had seen the face of God.'

'A bird-faced God?!'

'No! A God-faced bird.'

We teased her for a while, then forgot about it as we got

fleeced by a taxi driver who drove us round and round in circles to a destination approximately 200 metres from our starting point.

I have a picture of my sister and my mother from that trip and I locate it as I am sorting out paperwork for the move. They are standing in the Jardin du Luxembourg in the bitter February cold on a raised gravel pathway, near some kind of decorative stone urn, and the picture looks posed even though it isn't. Their bodies are facing towards each other and they are both looking at the camera. My mother's eyes are pink-rimmed from the wind and she's wearing a fuchsia cashmere scarf that I've now brought back with me from York. My sister is in a denim jacket, reddish tendrils of hair whipped across her face by the wind, freckles standing out clearly on her milky skin. She looks about twelve: actually she still looks about twelve now, but in this picture she looks happy. They both do. Behind the camera, I was happy too: we were in Paris, I was having a baby and life was exploding with possibility. It seems a thousand years ago now. I am pregnant again, but it couldn't feel more different. My sister is a hunched little wraith, who drifts almost silently in and out of our life (she is moving in with her aunt in Peckham now the baby is imminent). I feel I have failed her, failed to be any comfort whatsoever and by association failed my mother too. I seem to have nothing to offer.

But move we must, so occasionally I look over Olivier's shoulder in a desultory fashion and make offhand comments. We look at a dark modern cube near Beaubourg, but I don't like it because it's ugly, all smoked glass and 1980s fittings, and it doesn't fit with my image of what a Paris flat should look like. Then we look at a couple of Haussmann-style apartments in the outer arrondissements, one in the 18th and one in the 17th. The small, fuzzy photographs are hard to interpret – they don't seem to have kitchens and the paintwork is straight out of a 1970s prog rock album – but they have the bones of Parisian grandeur, herringbone parquet, mouldings, high ceilings. I do not know Paris well enough to have the city's geography beyond the very centre defined in my head, so we look at a map and try to make a decision: the 17th has the Arc de Triomphe, the 18th, to the east of it, the Sacré Coeur. The one in the 17th is near a park and three stops from La Défense for Olivier to get to and from work, so that, without me ever seeing it, is the one we choose.

Dimly, through my fog of indifference, I perceive the complexities of the process, as Olivier negotiates with agents and owners, heading off to Paris with folders full of paperwork and returning with a muscle in his forehead spasming uncontrollably, but I have nothing to contribute and, eventually, it is done. Our lovely London flat sells swiftly (I feel a genuine stab of sadness at this – it feels irrevocable and I have loved living in Fitzrovia so much) and there is nothing more to do but wait, wait for the baby to come, which it does, finally, late and in a rush in an eerily quiet hospital.

It's a boy and he's angry and angular and strange. I can see nothing poignantly symbolic about him: he's all nose and long, searching fingers, nothing like my mother. He does not look like an old soul, nor does he possess any preternatural qualities of serenity: far from it. He cries a *lot* for the first few hours of his life, furiously, his whole head reddening under his sparse covering of hair. We call him Louis. He doesn't get a middle name: we've run out of names we both like that work in both languages, and all the French names I love and find ineffably romantic – Pascal, Félix, Fabrice – conjure up some loathed school bully or boorish colleague for Olivier.

We look very happy in the pictures in the hospital. I have my head on Olivier's shoulder and my body is misshapen and distorted in a sag of post-partum exhaustion, but I am smiling and so is he. Our angry red bundle is asleep in Olivier's arms, most of his head obscured by an oversized hospital-issue hat. We are, I think, happy. I had worried that giving birth, losing my cosy status as an incubator, might open the floodgates of grief, but holding my furiously insatiable son, it seems that very little has changed. Things feel muted, sort of: the soft pedal is on. I don't understand it – surely this is exactly the time for enormous emotions – but I'm grateful nonetheless.

In the twelve hours we spend in hospital, people come to visit us or send their congratulations with exaggerated jollity, as if we are the long-awaited redemptive twist in a horrible story. Theo comes in with my sister to meet his new brother. He erupts, pink-cheeked and cold, in our tiny boiling hospital room and looks appraisingly at his brother asleep in his plastic crate, etiolated fingers reaching up jerkily at nothing as he sleeps.

'Spider!' he says and it seems to fit, so Spider he becomes.

Then we all go home: Theo, my sister, me, Olivier and Spider to get ready to move to Paris.

Amidst the last-minute packing up and the paperwork, I do not really contribute much: I'm breastfeeding the new arrival, taking him for walks around Bloomsbury in the pram, admiring the blossom and feeling the first blush of spring warmth. Sleep deprivation renders me useless and stupid, which just intensifies my muffled feeling, but the new baby is very easy to love, and taking care of him and Theo is not as hard as I had feared at this stage: my sister comes around often to help and the baby is mesmerized by his busy, funny big brother. I observe and am surprised by the way momentary shafts of happiness inhabit me, as fleeting as the early spring sun. I do one thing, though: I take Louis to meet my mother.

I board a train to York one afternoon with him sleeping on my chest. When we arrive, spring has reached York too: the sun is out and the grass slopes under the city walls are vivid with daffodils, bobbing in the breeze. We cross Lendal Bridge, where the River Ouse is running fast and threatening (yet again) to break its banks, and head down past the Minster, along Goodramgate towards Cemetery Road. In the graveyard, a handsome nineteenth-century wilderness, the rambling lanes are greener than I remember them from the scuffing persistent drizzle of October. The grass is longer, a blackbird is singing and tangled flowering briars block the smaller alleys.

I wonder if I will remember where to go – I have only been here twice, once to choose the spot and once to bury her – but actually it's fairly simple and I pick my way through the overgrown paths and past uneven rows of lichen-green headstones sure-footedly, and make my way into a small clearing ringed with bent willows. I recognize the nearest tombstone ('Sacred to the Memory of Sgt A. G. Davidson, The Duke of Wellington's Rgt, who died on the 12th June 1891 aged 32 years, deeply regretted by his sorrowing widow and late comrades'): we thought she might like a dashing young man in uniform as a neighbour. Next to Sgt Davidson is my mother's grave, unrecognizable from the narrow Astro-Turfed hole of the previous autumn with the tiny coffin being lowered into it. Now it is a small hillock covered with short springy heath grass. No headstone yet, it's a decision too far.

I crouch down and unstrap Louis, still dozing on my chest, then I lie him down on my jacket and sit down next to him to the side of the grave. His eyes snap open suspiciously and he begins to kick and wiggle experimentally, deciding whether to cry.

'So here he is,' I say to the hillock, feeling idiotic. 'I brought him to see you.'

I am not at all sure what I am doing or why. I did not feel anything much at the burial, so I am not sure what I think this daft pilgrimage will achieve. It's not as if I think she's still here in any sense, but then, where else could she be? The whole business still seems unfathomable. I reason, finally, that it is the kind of thing she might have done herself, my mother with her God-faced bird dreams, the stubborn relics of Catholicism, a strain of mystic Quakerism and a belief in ritual. Perhaps that is ceremony enough. I sit for a little longer. The sun is surprisingly warm and my spider baby has decided not to cry. He is kicking his legs decidedly, at high speed, and his eyes are wide open and focusing on, I think, the shifting branches of the willow tree above. He is such a funny little thing, tightly coiled but mainly cheerful, which reminds me of his father. My mother would have enjoyed the puzzle of him and she would have enjoyed his soft little body, his beady, alert eyes and the way he is growing into person-ness, eyelashes unfurling, limbs strengthening. It seems extraordinarily unfair that she can't, and I remember her holding Theo over her knee and gently patting his back, and later feeding him a piece of the terrible cake I made for his first birthday. I cry a little in a choked, hiccuping way like a cat with a furball. I have not had a satisfactory cry since this all happened and I still feel *en sourdine* – muted. There's a Verlaine poem that Fauré set to music called 'En Sourdine' and I think of it now and I think of my mother in her bed on weekend mornings listening to Radio 3 and holding court and a few more tears fall.

I pick Louis up and we head to Bettys, because all emotional journeys in York must end in the city's stateliest and best-loved purveyor of cake and comfort. It's early afternoon when we arrive and the queue for the tearoom is already stretching out of the door and into King's Square, but the shop is relatively quiet, a bustle of women in broderie anglaise mob caps behind the counter arranging Fat Rascals ('it's a cross between a scone and a rock bun and we serve it warm with butter and a choice of preserves,' a school friend could recite for years after a brief sojourn working there).

I hang back for a while, remembering the many hours I have spent in Bettys, when I was tiny, as a teenager and as an adult. Theo had been with us, sitting in a high chair wearing a Fat Rascal bib, while my mother radiated pride and love, presenting her new grandchild to the waitresses who knew her so well. My mother knew everyone in York, the homeless people, the taxi drivers, and particularly the waitresses. Now here we are: baby's first Bettys, another important rite.

Today, the silver trays at the counter are filled with a reassuring selection of springtime treats: neat lines of ginger rabbits, caramel slices, marzipan and fondant cauliflowers. The window is full of Easter eggs (I used to get one every year, decorated with purple and yellow sugarwork daisies) and Simnel cake, the promise of resurrection. I buy two chocolate caramel shortcake slices and three fondant fancies (two yellow, one pink) and take them back to my mum's house, or rather my stepfather's house as I suppose I should start calling it now. I sit at the kitchen table and my stepfather makes a pot of tea in the usual stained yellow pot, then sits it under the usual stained duck-shaped cosy, his every gesture intensely familiar, and I bite into one of my fancies. I eat it quite slowly: cutting it in half first, then nibbling the iced edges before sinking my teeth into the sponge and buttercream and jam. It's another goodbye of sorts.

PART TWO

J'entrais dans une pâtisserie, je mangeais une brioche et je me récitais ironiquement le mot de Heine: 'quelles que soient les larmes qu'on pleure, on finit toujours par se moucher'.

I went into a bakery, I ate a brioche and I recited Heine's words to myself, ironically: 'whatever tears we cry, we always end up wiping them away'.

Simone de Beauvoir, *Memoirs of a Dutiful Daughter*

6

Pot Bouille

A few days later we fetch up in a café on the Boulevard de Courcelles in the 17th near the new flat – Olivier, my sister and me, Theo busy under the table running a small car over its ornamental metal feet, Louis wedged in a corner in his buggy. The sun is out, showing up the smudges on the café windows. We are waiting for the removal lorry to arrive. This is not a part of Paris I know, though the basic street geography – the red neon lozenge of the bar-tabac, green pharmacy crosses, yellow letter box – is utterly familiar: you couldn't be anywhere else.

Our new flat is on a quiet side street, running between two other quiet side streets, tucked away between the Boulevard and the Avenue Wagram. We have had a quick peep inside already. It is on the fourth floor of the block, a solid, classic Haussmann number of pale, regulation quarry stone with iron balustrades and an imposing double door to the street. Inside, a marble-lined entrance hall leads to another set of double doors – glass this time – and beyond that, a tiny creaky lift, with concertina doors that wheeze like leaky bellows as the lift ascends. For those who find the lift too alarming, the alternative is a dark, shallow wood staircase, redolent of furniture polish and old cigarette smoke, the dark blue carpet runner held in place with polished brass rods.

Behind its narrow front door, the flat is huge. It's also a sort of elegant wreck, collapsing and crumbling in aesthetically appealing, but practically alarming, ways. The double-width *salon* still has elaborate ceiling roses and chandeliers, three shuttered double windows with wrought-iron balustrades and original die-cast radiators, but the rotting *point de Hongrie* herringbone parquet gives you splinters if you try to walk on it barefoot. The hallway is lined with full-length gilt-edged mirrors to adjust your hat or check the fall of your bustle, but the kitchen, in keeping with most Parisian rentals, is little more than a grimy tiled cupboard furnished with a set of bare standpipes. A population of small, irrepressible cockroaches occupies the single built-in cupboard.

To the rear, a dark corridor leads to a dark bathroom (peach fittings, mid-1980s, no apparent ventilation) and a lavatory seemingly as old as the building itself, with tarnished brass fittings and massive porcelain ware crazy-paved with cracks. When I pull the chain, the pipes roar and tremble until the whole flat seems to vibrate. One bedroom, as the fuzzy estate agent's photographs hinted, appears to have last been decorated in 1979 under the influence of powerful hallucinogens, possibly using fingers or some other body part to apply the turquoise and violet paint. The others are fairly ordinary in comparison, though the one that will become mine and Olivier's is more of a corridor than a bedroom and it is set at an angle such that our window, which faces the rear, overlooks a messy patchwork of nearby windows, pipes and roofs, quite different from the neat façade to the front. It is the kind of view that can feel quite romantic when you are on a budget city break in a two-star hotel somewhere, a glimpse into a whole set of other lives. There are serried ranks of dusters and wrinkled American tan pop socks, a whole ledge of cactuses and in one curtainless window, ominous to contemplate, a drum kit. From the living room at the front, the view is very different: we over-look the austerely perfect *salon* of the people opposite, furnished with expensive-looking antique rugs, upholstered Directoire chairs and a baby grand piano.

Soon after we finish our coffee and walk in awkward convoy back to the flat, the movers arrive and install an external lift from the lorry to our window and our things start to ascend, wobbling alarmingly. I am standing in the corridor trying to work out what each hastily assembled box is when there is a knock at the door. Olivier opens it: a small woman in her fifties or sixties in a blue housecoat. He starts to formulate a pleasantry, but she cuts him off.

'Is that your pushchair downstairs?'

'Yes, but . . .'

'You need to move it.' There is no token welcoming preamble; it is despatched like a whistling ace in the first point of the first set of a tennis match, to send a message.

This, then, is the concierge.

I can't help but feel a thrill at the thought we have a concierge; I feel like you can't be a proper Parisian without one. I know this from a thousand films featuring officious women in housecoats in very minor roles. Proust writes to his concierge: complaints about noise ('I would be grateful if you could find out what is going on in Dr X's . . . where there is now banging all the time') and recriminations about grievances he has heard of second-hand. In Simenon's Maigret novels, concierges are watchful, used-up by life, ugly, like in *Les Fiançailles de Monsieur Hire*: 'She was thin. Her clothes hung around her like they hang around the crossed sticks that serve as a scarecrow's skeleton and her nose was damp, her eyelids red, her hands chapped by the cold.'

They are also a mine of information, officious and gossipy, prurient and ever alert: they know when their tenants go out and when they return, how their fortunes are faring and who they meet. Madame Jeanne in *L'Enterrement de Monsieur Bouvet* is disappointed by life, almost effaced from it even, but the death of Bouvet, a tenant for whom she has a real affection, galvanizes her into activity, laying out his body and preparing his funeral, chivvying the other tenants to pay their respects.

Our concierge shows no particular interest in the lives of her tenants: she would happily leave us to rot until someone complained rather than arrange our funerals and she is devoted to one thing and one thing only – the lift. She treats it with tender solicitude like a fragile, much-loved family pet. Her flat is right next to it, so that she can keep an ear out for incidents of mistreatment. Inside the lift, which smells strongly of Brasso, there are sheets of instructions pinned to the wall about the correct treatment of its door, the maximum number of persons and objects it should be required to accommodate and whom to call if it is indisposed. The walls are also often the forum for frosty, anonymous tenant-on-tenant interaction, from pinched-lipped circuitously phrased remarks ('will the person who uses their washing machine after 11 p.m. on the fifth floor please be kind enough to have some consideration for other residents') to full-on ranting when someone just seems to have snapped after months of resentment.

'The lift buttons, *Madame*,' the concierge says to me early in our tenure, materializing as if from nowhere in a puff of bleach and suspicion and starting to speak, again without preamble. Her eyes are glinting in the gloom and her small form bars my route out of the building.

'Yes?' I smile back, naïvely expecting some piece of advice on how idiosyncratic they are.

'There are FINGERMARKS on them.' She turns her gaze to Theo, waving a rapidly browning slice of apple around cheerfully, his feet swinging in the pushchair. Lowering her eyes, she takes in the filthy tangle of knotted yarn that is his comfort blanket. It is absolutely disgusting; an insanitary clump of tendrils.

'Oh!' I do not have the presence of mind to ask her which part of one's anatomy one is supposed to use to touch the lift buttons.

'Dirty fingermarks,' she continues. 'Small ones.' Her gaze does not leave Theo. I notice a small blob of cereal adhered to his collar. His top is wet with dribble.

'Please ensure your son does not treat the lift buttons as a toy. They are for adults.'

I open my mouth, then close it again as she has already dematerialized, shutting the door to her flat behind her.

The concierge sets the tone: it is soon apparent that most of the other residents hate us.

Heavily silent during the day, at night, the block rustles with the muffled second-hand impressions of other people's lives. The smell of *choucroute alsacienne* or a burnt Monoprix pizza, cigarette smoke, raised voices, the eight o'clock TF1 news playing simultaneously on four or five televisions. Later comes a round of creaking plumbing noises and finally in the early hours, when the heavy silence has settled once again, Louis wakes.

There is a particular kind of promiscuity and a relationship to that promiscuity in Parisian apartment blocks which is well explained by Jonathan Conlin in *Tales of Two Cities: Paris, London and the Birth of the Modern City*. In the seventeenth and eighteenth centuries Paris grew upward while London grew outwards. Parisian housing took on a highrise, high-density character still recognizable today (though worse then), while Londoners spread into the surrounding country, preserving lower-rise, more self-contained housing stock. These contrasting urban geographies nourished two quite distinct notions of home: the Englishman's home became his castle around this time, a private and precious bulwark against the savagery of the street. Parisian life, in contrast, both facilitated and tolerated a more fluid barrier between 'home' and other. Baron Haussmann's nineteenth-century city planning and renovation profoundly altered the shape of Paris, addressing overcrowding, placing a limit on building height and carving vast new boulevards through chaotic and sinuous alleyways of the central arrondissements, but that fluidity, and the difficulties proximity brings, remain.

Proust's room on nearby Boulevard Haussmann wasn't cork lined for aesthetic reasons: it was cork lined because life is *loud* in Haussmann blocks. A cache of letters written by Proust to his neighbour, one Madame Williams, came to light recently and they are full of delicately worded references to noise. 'A series of light taps on the parquet above me were so precise that veronal was useless,' reads one, later lamenting: 'What bothers me isn't continuous noise, even if it is loud, but *banging* on the parquet . . . and everything which is dragged along or falls or runs on it.'

You can get a more visceral account of life in a Haussmann block in Zola's *Pot Bouille*. *Pot Bouille* – the title means something like 'melting pot', a sort of unsavoury, chucked-together stew – is an unflattering downstairs, upstairs (the servants are in the eaves in this set-up) look at the life of a classic Haussmann block in the 1870s, viewed partially through the eyes of new arrival, provincial youth, Octave Mouret. Peeling back the elegant façade, Zola gleefully lifts the lid on the cupidity, lust, petty jealousies and grinding, constant machination that hide behind the rigid proprieties and politenesses. There's ghastly Madame Josserand, a Gallic Mrs Bennett, desperate to marry off her daughters to anyone, at any cost. Madame Campardon has suffered some gynaecological unpleasantness in childbirth, which is whispered throughout the house, and is an invalid

– her husband has moved in her cousin and the three live in an uneasy *ménage à trois*. Callow Trublot, who disdains all the so-called respectable women of the house, molests the servants with impunity and Mouret himself is far from a wet-behind-the-ears innocent: he's calculating and cynical, throwing himself wholeheartedly into a campaign of seduction and personal advancement with no less than four women in his entourage. The prevailing sense in the book and the building is of an oppressive undesirable intimacy. There are a lot of smells: sour breath, sweat, powder, cooking odours, damp skirts, mouldy cellar, dirty sheets, 'the fatty scent of a poorly maintained sink'. 'The walls between the servants' rooms are as thin as a sheet of paper,' says Trublot, feigning disapproval, 'it's hardly moral.' Rubbing shoulders this closely, you simply can't maintain the façade of civility and everyone knows far more than they could ever wish about the habits of their neighbours. It's stifling, ugly and utterly human.

In our block the promiscuity of collective living is less a conduit for immorality than a resented source of constant conflict. Everyone wants peace and no one can have it, so we peck at each other mechanically, like battery chickens. As the new chickens on the block, we draw a considerable amount of the available ire.

First, we mark ourselves out as undesirables by having children. Next, unforgivably, we get the lift wrong. I know this because a smartly dressed middle-aged couple knock on our door, brimming with outrage, to tell us so. Apparently, by failing to close the creaky concertina door correctly, we

have blocked the lift on our floor. Finding the lift incrim-
inatingly stuck here, this couple have identified us as the
culprits.

'IT IS UNACCEPTABLE,' says the man, putting his
face, which has become puce, very close to mine. He is
wearing a dark red paisley scarf tucked into a fine dark
tweed jacket and he smells of deliciously expensive aftershave. Probably Guerlain, I think, and start wondering what
it is, but my reverie is interrupted by his wife, who looms
over his shoulder in patent heels, a short, tight Catherine
Deneuve-style skirt and a cloud of disapproval to add 'SO
inconsiderate!'

'I'm sorry, I had no idea,' I try to reason, half bemused
and half ashamed. 'We only moved in recently, so . . .' I shift
the baby on my hip, hoping he will serve as a 'get out of lift
jail' card. I could not be more wrong about this: having small
children is the worst thing you can do to alienate your neighbours.

'I couldn't give a shit!' says the man, incensed. It sounds
quite shocking out of the mouth of someone in tweeds and
mustard cords. The two of them stalk off angrily and I close
the door.

When Olivier gets home, I try to tell him without sounding pathetic. He has started work and goes off to his tower
block in La Défense each morning. When he returns in the
evening, I am usually either in tears or in a rage, or both.

'They were *horrible*,' I say, but he shrugs.

'It's just a game.'

'A game? What do you mean?'

'I mean, you can't take it seriously. It's not personal; that's just the way it works. What you need to do is find something to complain about back. Fight fire with fire.'

'The only thing I could complain about is that THEY WERE HORRIBLE. And possibly that he was inexplicably dressed like a pre-war country squire.'

At night our unpopularity is compounded by Louis's appalling antics. He goes down at 8 p.m. with every semblance of one tired after a full and frank day of kicking his legs and chewing things but at four or five – and on bad nights at three, then four, then five – he wakes, inexplicably furious, demanding comfort and company. There is nothing wrong with him: he is well fed, neither too hot nor too cold and there is no noise that wakes him. We need to let him cry it out, but I don't dare; it seems an outrageous breach of the fragile social contract.

Worn down, we decide we must give it a try. I buy some earplugs, beige foam slugs, and when we go to bed, I put them in and fall into a deep, near-instantaneous sleep. It feels like only minutes later that I am woken by Olivier shaking my shoulder.

'What?' My mouth has difficulty shaping the words; I have been dragged to the surface at the deepest point of my sleep cycle. I take out one earplug.

'He's crying.'

I frown slightly, my eyes still closed. If I keep my head completely still, perhaps I can just sink back into sleep? I try to formulate my thoughts into as few words as possible.

'We were going to leave him tonight.'

'Yes, but listen.' Olivier puts his hand on my shoulder and squeezes. I open my eyes; he has his head cocked to one side. I sigh and listen, emerging regretfully from the delicious emptiness of deep sleep. Louis is crying, this is certain, on a rising pitch of fury. But here is another noise: a rhythmic *thump, thump, thump*.

'What the fuck is that?'

'It's coming from upstairs.'

'What, the old guy? The ex-footballer?'

'I think so.'

We've spoken to this man a couple of times. He is about seventy, with a handbag-sized white fluffy dog. Every time I see him on the stairs he tells me he used to be a footballer. This is the full extent of our conversations, but I have been thinking of him as an ally of sorts, since he hasn't actually formulated any complaints.

I listen for a little longer. The pitch of the banging seems to be rising both in volume and frequency. Unsurprisingly, this is not having a soothing effect on Louis.

'Jesus.' I force myself into a sitting position, then drag my unwilling limbs out of bed and trudge to Louis's room. Through the gloom I can see him thrashing around in his cot. His legs are imprisoned in a baby sleeping bag, which he keeps lifting jerkily into the air, bashing into his mobile and sending red and yellow plastic giraffes shuddering. The noise seems to be coming from directly above his room and it's hard, wood on wood. A walking stick, perhaps.

I lift Louis from his cot and hold him against my shoulder, still listening. He doesn't even seem to be awake, not really: his eyes aren't even open. He snuffles into my neck, sobs slowing to hiccups and then finally silence. From above, there is one last, resonant thump, then silence.

I carry Louis back through to our bedroom, treading carefully, conscious of the risk of splinters. His body is soft and relaxed now, his cheeks cooling. I sit down on the edge of our bed and sigh. Olivier has put a pillow over his head. I glare at it.

'Now what?' I ask. 'What are we going to do if we can't let him cry?'

There is an indistinct noise from under the pillow.

Two weeks later, I am scratchy with fatigue. As we sit in front of the television watching a television chef berate a teenager for the state of his work surfaces, a single fat tear pools in the corner of my eye, then another.

'What is it?' Olivier does not actually sound like he wants to hear the answer but I am too exhausted to care.

'I'm so tired.'

Even when Louis goes back to sleep, I don't. Night after night I find myself sitting on the hall floor, looking at the shadows of the balustrades cast by the yellow light of the street lamps. Sometimes I send a plaintive text to my insomniac friend Kate in the selfish hope she might be awake and sometimes I get an answering echo, a steady, funny few lines of comfort. But mainly it is silent and lonely and I am done, done with it all.

'There, there.' Olivier gingerly pats my back with the flat of his hand with all the assurance of a man left in charge of an unexploded landmine. 'Let's try again. Another few nights?'

'But what about ceiling bastard?'

'Fuck him.'

'Fuck him' isn't really my style, and the thought of deliberately (well, tangentially but still consciously) provoking the ire of our neighbours appals me. I hate being antisocial; it jars me to my English core. But I don't have any better ideas so that is what we do.

On the very first night Louis wakes around 3 a.m. and wails continuously for five minutes, not weakening for a nanosecond. At this point, someone starts thumping on our door.

'Oh GOD.' I jump out of bed wide-eyed and stare at Olivier. He squints back at me, then rolls his eyes at my panic. I get up, run to Louis's room and snatch him from his cot, then I go and shut myself in the bathroom. I can hear Olivier speaking to another man. Their voices are raised, so I run the bath tap to try and drown them out. I know this isn't quite sane, but I just can't bear to listen. Louis is silent now, eyes wide open in the dark like a bush baby, the perfidious shrimp.

Some time later, Olivier opens the bathroom door. His expression is difficult to read, there's amusement but also fury. He doesn't look entirely stable.

'What?'

'Well!' he says, with a deranged twinkle. 'It was that tit from downstairs.'

'What, who?'

'The kid with the big hair and the scarves. Lives in mummy and daddy's flat.'

'Oh yes. What did he say?'

'Oh, you're going to love this.'

My stomach flips.

'He said, "It's not normal that your baby cries like that and I'm going to report you to social services."'

'WHAT?' Louis jumps, startled, on my shoulder, the light sleep into which he has fallen disturbed.

'Calm down. He's just being a dickhead.'

'But, what if he does it? What will we do? I can't . . .'

'Calm down and let me finish. So I said to him, "Oh, so do you have a lot of experience with babies? Because obviously we could do with your expertise."'

'And what did he say?'

Olivier smiles mirthlessly. 'He said it was *inadmissible* to let a baby cry like us. So I asked him if he wanted a go. "Here," I said. "He's just through here, why don't I go and get him for you?" Then he said, "I don't want your baby."'

'Right.'

'So I said, "Yes you do! You should definitely help us with your vast knowledge of babies, just stay there and I'll go and fetch him." Then he just called me a *connard* and left.'

'You seem quite happy with this outcome.'

Olivier cocks his head to one side. 'Well, I *was* happy with it. But now I wonder if I should have encouraged him to report us. It might have helped us get a *crèche* place?'

7

La Curée

If you turn right out of our front door (brasses polished to an unimpeachable sheen by the concierge to discourage the unwary from touching them with their filthy animal hands), past the tiny man with the giant wolfhound who is dragged up and down our street at regular intervals ineffectually calling 'Wolfie! Wolfie!', you hit Haussmann territory. Wide, grey boulevards stretch out at precisely triangulated angles towards other parts of Paris, in one direction to the Arc de Triomphe and the Champs-Elysées and in the other to the Sacré Coeur. In the early days I walk along each experimentally, observing the pattern of shops and buildings. Imposing grey stone apartment blocks like ours alternate at regular intervals with pharmacies, bakeries, dry cleaners and bars. Now and then there is a tiny square of gravel and neat grass where smartly topiaried dogs do their business, ignored by their smartly coiffed owners. Everything is tidy and it is not especially welcoming. The curlicued railings and ornamental stonework seem designed to deter riff-raff and I always look the wrong way as I cross the fast four-lane boulevards, drawing a hail of honking.

If our arrondissement feels austerely unwelcoming to me

with its wide grey boulevards and formidable architecture, I know it used to have a very different reputation. In the nineteenth century this was the epicentre of new money, a place of bling and exhibitionism and louche display in salons with not particularly rigid morals. It's the place that Edmund de Waal describes in *The Hare With Amber Eyes*, a glitzy enclave of railway barons, industrialists and bankers and the kind of place where Maupassant sets his *mondain* stories. Imagining how it must have been, I can't help but think of the dreadful mini-series we watched at university called *Belle Epoque*. Sample dialogue: 'Why *bonjour*, M. Proust! How surprising to see you out of your famous cork-lined room where you write your intricately detailed auto-biographical novels! Can I introduce you to M. Eiffel? He is involved in a most intriguing project using the ingenious new technologies of our age . . .'

Most of what I know about the 17th arrondissement comes from my old friend Zola. *La Curée* (The Kill), which is the second novel of the Rougon-Macquart cycle, takes on the particularly hot topic of property speculation in the 1860s, right in our neighbourhood. The novel deals with speculation in both property and human chattels. It's a story of rapid enrichment and moral turpitude at the height of Haussmannization. The 'Kill' of the title describes the hunt for and acquisition of quick and easy fortunes by preceding Haussmann and buying up housing that would then be compulsorily purchased by the state at an inflated price. It also evokes the callous way Aristide Saccard (the speculator at the heart of the story) treats people as strategic collateral in his ascension. Both in the novel itself and, even more so, in Zola's preparatory research (he would spend weeks in the field making minutely detailed notes before commencing a project), the newly gentrified Plaine Monceau area where we live is described vividly and it's almost trashy: loud, bright and garish. Gold, the colour of new money, is omnipresent: Zola doesn't do subtlety where there is scope for an avalanche of the bleeding obvious. In the new house overlooking the park occupied by Aristide Saccard, there are gilded railings, gold panelling, vast mirrors, gold upholstery and gold ceiling roses. The descriptive passages are constant, heavy and filled with so much gold you feel almost assaulted by it. I find myself imagining a sort of nineteenth-century version of Roberto Cavalli's yacht, all life-sized gilded porcelain panthers and circular beds covered in animal pelts on an inlaid Carrera marble floor.

Leached of its original *nouveau riche* glitz, the Plaine Monceau feels chilly to me, even in the warmth of spring, even under the blossom-heavy trees in the park. Because if we turn left out of the front door and walk for two minutes, which we do most days, we reach the heart of the Plaine, the Parc Monceau, which is the reason we chose the flat. The park entrance is marked with a slate-topped rotunda and vast black and gilt gates, and beyond the gates is classic Parisian park territory, dusty gravel paths and neat flowerbeds, the lawns mined with sternly worded notices about what is and is not acceptable. There are two children's playgrounds, a sand-pit, a string of fat ponies who walk slowly up and down the central alley bearing tiny children, a carousel, a pond full of overfed Barbary ducks and a kiosk that sells sweets and balloons and crêpes. It is a wonderland of delights and we go almost every day. Within a couple of weeks I loathe the place with the heat of a thousand suns. When I find out it was used for mass executions in the repression of the Paris Commune revolt in 1870, I just nod, with a complete absence of surprise.

The Parc, which also contains a profusion of weird statuary and follies, was originally designed by Philippe, Duc d'Orléans, the aristocrat whose passion for the Jacobin cause in the Revolution caused him to change his name to 'Philippe Egalité', sit in the revolutionary National Convention and vote in favour of the execution of Louis XVI. For all his republican fervour, Philippe was unable to escape the implacable, twisted logic of the Terror and faced the guillotine in 1793. Sometimes, on my gloomier days walking the sandy alleys and dodging the uniformed guards when Theo escapes onto the outlawed lawns, I think about Philippe Egalité, complicit in, furthering even, his own downfall. Loving Paris feels a little like this at times.

It is a warm spring, but there is no warmth, either literal or figurative, in the playground, which catches the wind and makes me anxious. We don't fit in. I thought Theo's yellow oilcloth Petit Bateau coat was perfectly Parisian, but all the children here look like they have escaped from a nineteenth-century etching: they are exquisitely dressed in Bonpoint poplin and tweed and none of them is coated in drool or breakfast. Their games are quite neat and orderly: they go the right way up the slide, then slide down, then do it again, and they make neatly levelled sand pies. Theo is anarchic and fanciful and he tries to talk to them in English: none of this wins him any playground points and he ends up alone and frustrated most of the time. I have the advantage over him in speaking French, but I am wearing Gap jeans, an old winter coat and trainers. I don't even know where my make-up is: did it even make it through the move? It's not as if I need it. I have two tiny children and it's the playground, for god's sake, not a catwalk show, but Paris is worse than Leeds for dressing up, it turns out. Everyone has their face on, shoes are shiny, the West African nannies are draped in immaculate outsized fake Louis Vuitton and Chanel shawls and no one, not even the grandparents in green loden coats reading *Le Nouvel Observateur*, ever talks to me. The only consolation is that they do not talk to each other either. Usually my only interactions are in negotiating the return and fair distribution of toys, which all the other adults ignore entirely. Once, though, a grandmother snatches back a spade Theo has picked up from the sandpit and slaps him smartly across the wrist.

'It's not his. He needs to learn,' she says to me decidedly as I turn open-mouthed to try and remonstrate. Words fail me: what I really want to say to her – touch my child again and I'll report you to the police, you *hag* – only comes hours later.

Sometimes after, or instead of, the playground, we go to the carousel, the *manège*, which has cars and lorries and fire engines and bright flashing fairground bulbs. On our first few visits Theo is desperate to have a turn, but as soon as he is seated in a small car, rudimentary seatbelt fastened, he finds it terrifying and screams to be removed. This panto-mime happens several times before he works up the courage to stay on, face furiously concentrated, ticket clutched in his hand. The atmosphere around the *manège* is surprisingly serious, for something that is supposed to be fun. The *manège* man doesn't exactly exude bonhomie or job satis-faction and the children rarely smile: they are grave-faced, small hands tight on steering wheels, or ready to press a button or anticipating the important handover of the ticket. Once the *manège* starts to move, they spin, stately slow, faces blurred, ignoring the waves and encouragements of parents and nannies. Sometimes someone breaks down and cries, a red, crumpled face flashing past with the others. Depending on the degree of parental stoicism, this might be met with a jolly exhortation, or in the last resort, the long legs of the *manège* man, striding over tiny cars and horses to whisk the wailing infant to safety. It has a strange, U-rated sense of peril that attracts and frightens the children all at once.

Parisian parks and public spaces are supposed to be emblematic of French childhood: they are the theatre of its pivotal events. As a sickly child in *Du Côté de Chez Swann*, Marcel's outings are limited to trips to the yellowing, also sickly, lawns of the detested Champs-Elysées, but it is there, bored of playing next to the wooden horses and seeking dis-traction, that he spots Gilberte for the first time, making each return trip an agony of anticipation. Will she be there? Will rain thwart him? The Champs are transformed by the intensity of his longing and expectation into a shimmering wonderland of possibility.

In Simone de Beauvoir's account of her very proper Parisian childhood, *Memoirs of a Dutiful Daughter*, 'le Luxembourg' is so much part of the quotidian that it doesn't even merit its full name and becomes almost a character in its own right. It returns again and again as the arena of so much formative memory: it is the place where she experiences her first crush on another girl, the place where she 'marries' her cousin and where they have their honeymoon on the carousel, where she takes twilight walks with her father, spies on courting couples and spends her first solo outings reading near the Medici fountain. In the 'perfectly domesticated', orderly landscape of Catholic schoolgirl Paris, the park represents a tiny taste of freedom. As I watch Theo clamber into Monceau's fake grottos, collect leaves and run cars along the base of the statues, it seems a small kind of freedom compared to my childhood in the empty expanses of the Yorkshire moors and dales, but when you're as little as he is, perhaps even this is enough.

More often, though, I think about how much longer we need to stay for Theo to be tired enough for us to have a relatively calm evening or whether Louis is about to explode with furious hunger and whether I have time for a crêpe on the way home. The crêpes are so good. They come scaldingly hot from the iron grid in the park kiosk, handed over by the unsmiling man behind the counter. They are pale and a little floppy, but with a crunch of sugar crystals, the outside speckled with darker brown, wrapped in a tight fold of white waxed paper. This momentary sweetness is the high point of many afternoons.

The thing I like best about the neighbourhood is unsurprising: it is the bakeries. The bakery windows are a burst of forgiving colour: they are instantly identifiable by the wash of warm yellow light that emanates from within them, punctuated with vivid points of glossy red and chocolate brown. Often, you can smell them before you see them: the best ones exude a yeasty, buttery promise that cuts through the ambient grey.

I like how predictable French bakeries are: these ones are just the same as the bakeries I haunted in Normandy and on holidays, they have a clear physical vernacular that everyone recognizes and respects. Big cakes are displayed in the front window facing the street: glossy glazed strawberry tarts or neatly overlapping apple slices; moussey creations for six or eight with an impressionistic swirl of colour on top. Inside the glow continues, coming partly from the soft strip lights on the underside of the sloping glass-fronted counter, which draws your eye to a deep bottom shelf, filled with rows of éclairs and *religieuses* in paper cases, golden brown icing-sugar-dusted *millefeuilles* and individual tarts, perhaps plump, neatly aligned raspberries or chocolate, dark and thin-crusted with a tiny flake of gold leaf on top. On the upper shelf of the counter are smaller things: *macarons* neat like buttons in a haberdashery store or *financiers* (little rectangles of almond-heavy sponge) or *canelés*, dark ridged domes, mysterious and as unappealing to look at as shrunken heads.

The counter is usually on a slanting angle from the front door to the till to maximize queuing space, and so as you inch along the Sunday morning queue you can examine the stock, checking anxiously whether what you have come in for is still available. Baguettes are behind the till in racks or baskets, next to shelves of other bread, round and square loaves, to be put through the slicer.

We have three bakeries within a couple of hundred yards of us, but the one on our street is a disappointing washout, with scorched baguettes that taste of bleach and a couple of flabby quiches. A little further away is the Boulangerie du Parc Monceau, which has a Seventies gilt and smoked-glass front window, a pile of old copies of *Le Parisien* in a rack behind the door and a handful of tables. It is slightly better. The women behind the counter in blue-striped blouses are predictably unfriendly but not actively hostile (unless Theo puts his whole sticky face against the glass of the counter cabinet, which he sometimes does) and they will warm up a crêpe from the pallid pile near the till and sprinkle it with granulated sugar for us. I often take the boys in for a quick afternoon break: it is next to a good, busy intersection for Theo to observe cars and Parisian dogs squatting and straining on the pavement. It also has a tricky *priorité à droite*, which means that we are perfectly placed to observe vicious altercations between motorists, which are numerous. Olivier sometimes comes with us for coffee on weekends and is particularly tickled by one such incident, where the person in the wrong gets out of their car in fury and shouts:

'Just because you have right of way, it doesn't mean you have to TAKE it, *connard*!'

At a safe remove, with a cake, it makes for an entertaining interlude in our afternoons.

Better still is Aux Enfants Gâtés (The Spoiled Children) at the end of our street. Aux Enfants Gâtés is a *pâtisserie*, not a *boulangerie*, so there is no distracting bread production to worry about and it looks like something from a Jean-Pierre Jeunet film, somewhere Amélie Poulain would come to buy a beautiful tart for some lovelorn neighbour. It is dark and ornate and as well as cakes there is a small counter of also dark, oversized chocolates. What I really like there, though, is the *flan*.

Flan is my thing; it is my cake. I knew I had been accepted into Olivier's family when a *flan* started to appear in the box of mixed cakes his father would bring back from the bakery for Sunday lunch, next to the coffee éclair (Yves) and the chocolate-flecked cream meringue (Olivier) and the fruit tart (Jacqueline). You get assigned a cake early in their family and that assignment is impossible to shift; ten, twenty years later you will still be getting that cake for your pudding. It is pointless to protest that you haven't liked meringue since you were fourteen, because in front of the bakery counter, that is the thing they will remember. Thankfully I *do* like *flan*, which is a plain, set custard usually in puff pastry, sometimes with a shiny glaze of apricot jam on the top. It is the most perfect of comfort foods: undemanding, simple and sweet.

I start to carve out a tiny nugget of routine in my aimless, baby-dominated days. My sister comes round and minds the boys during their lunchtime nap while I dash out and buy us both a salad, and me a *flan*, wrapped up in a neat hospital corner of white waxed paper.

My sister doesn't like cake. I realize quite early I don't really know what she likes, or if she should even be here. She is staying in a rickety one-room sublet, which Olivier has found for her ten minutes away. She has opted to stay in Paris for a couple of months, because she does not want to be in York and she has decided not to go to India (her original gap-year plan before Mum died). It's an uneasy arrangement for both of us (though not for Olivier, who has the most basic and inclusive attitude to family: of course she must come, there is no debate). We're family, in that fundamental, instinctive way Olivier responds to, but we aren't intimate. There are ten years between us and I left home when she was in primary school, so how could we be? That impulse to keep one another close has been powerful and I'm glad she's here, but I can't shake the feeling that it's not helping. I mean, she's helping me with the practical side of looking after the boys and that's a precious lifeline, but I'm not helping her: I don't know what to say or what comfort to offer, so I don't say anything, most of the time. All I have to offer is the babies, the basic animal consolation of small children and their simple needs.

So my sister takes Theo out to the park and plays games with him, or stays at home and amuses him while I go out to sort out some piece of paperwork. She's completely lost, in a strange country, and all I do is sit around and eat cake. I look at her sad, lost face and I just feel helpless, so I sit and eat cake guiltily, at greedy speed, in the uneasy silence of nap-time. Maybe there's nothing to be said? The Enfants Gâtés *flan* is small with a dark caramelized top and it is barely set, extravagantly trembling when you put a spoon into it. It is pure comfort, the regressive comfort of beige, nursery food before someone tucks you up in bed with a brisk kiss on the forehead. I wish I knew what would comfort my sister in this basic way. I wish, really, that she liked *flan*.

8

Esprit d'Escalier

Outside our handsome building full of people who hate us is all of Paris, gorgeous dreamy Paris, the city of all my childhood dreams. Unfortunately everyone there seems to hate us too.

Perhaps hate is too strong; it's more that they find us tremendously irritating. My mere existence seems to be an affront to much of Paris, which is a serious blow to my belief that I am a French person trapped in an English woman's body, just waiting for the opportunity to emerge, ice cool, uncompromising and unapologetic.

Day after day, walking to the shops and the market, I am subjected to a surprising – to me at least, used to the blanket indifference of London – barrage of criticism. I thought the social contract of capital cities (you leave me alone, I leave you alone) was the same everywhere in Europe, but it appears I was wrong. Strangers, passers-by, stop to tell me I am walking too slowly or in the wrong place, that my toddler needs to stop shouting or that his sticky fingers have no place on that shop window. The baby attracts a particular brand of ire, which is mainly directed at how he is dressed. Why, women ask me, incensed, is he not wearing a hat (it is May and 20°C)? Where are his socks (he has probably taken them off and dropped them)? Why have I not brought a blanket (see above, May, 20°C)? The way I dress him is taken as a personal affront.

Olivier thinks I am being over-sensitive. 'It's just a game,' he explains, again, weary and crumpled in his good work shirts after a slog along the RER A line. When he gets home I meet him at the door and unload my grievances, pink-cheeked and indignant. I find his arrival in the evening confusing. I wait for this moment all day and when it comes, I am relieved of course, and happy to see him. The cavalry have arrived and I can pee, drink a glass of wine or read my book for ten minutes. But at the same time, this is when all my resentment comes out. He has an independent existence with colleagues and a desk and a lunch break. He even gets packets of luncheon vouchers, €7 a day to spend on Paul sandwiches, and when he gets home he smells of the outside, of elsewhere and other people. I have nothing to show for my days but a series of mundane grievances and some kind of purée smeared on my sleeve. I unload, daily.

'The dry cleaner shouted at me because she only takes cash EVEN THOUGH there's a Visa sign on her door,' I tell him one evening. 'She said I was wasting her time.'

'*Salope*,' he says reflexively, with a shrug. Bitch.

'She was *horrible*! I was totally polite and she was just gratuitously mean.'

Olivier walks into the kitchen and looks in the fridge. This is a doomed endeavour, because I am too scared to buy any real food due to everyone being horrible all the time. Apart from cakes, all our food comes from Picard, the superlative frozen goods shop. I love Picard. The aisles are quiet and free of violently inclined old ladies, and the people on the till process your shopping in capital city-appropriate silence. Picard is reputedly where Parisian women buy pre-prepared morels and scallop dishes to cheat at dinner parties. It sells delicious meals, pasta gratins and seafood *tourtes* and things with '*sauce vierge*' which are far better than anything I could make using real ingredients. Nowhere in Paris sells any of the things I normally bought in Marks & Spencer anyway: neatly trimmed vegetables, pre-packed stir-fries or breaded cod fillets; food for children and the culinarily timorous. Monoprix is nothing like Marks & Spencer, though you would think by rights, this being Paris, it should be better. Our nearest branch is in a dingy basement and it has terrible lighting and luridly pink vacuum-packed meats. Franprix is far, far worse: even the crappiest Tesco Metro beats Franprix (although I concede that the selection of yoghurt is extremely comprehensive).

Giving up on food, Olivier finds some wine and pours himself a glass.

'You just have to be rude too. They're rude, you're rude back. The best way to react is to say that not accepting cards is totally unacceptable and she deserves not to have any customers.'

'I can't do that. I just couldn't.'

'You need to try. It's not personal, they're like that with everyone.'

'But it really feels personal! Because when someone is incredibly rude to you, it kind of *is* personal, isn't it?'

'No, you don't understand.' He frowns, struggling to explain. 'It's just . . . what you do. It's a bit like a kind of dialect. That's just how people talk.'

Unconvinced, after two months I tally up my street incidents to try and decide whether I am over-sensitive.

I have been:

Shouted at by the dry cleaner for trying to pay for my cleaning with a credit card.

Shouted at by a woman on the till at Monoprix for loading my shopping wrongly onto the conveyor belt.

Shouted at by the woman behind me in the Monoprix queue for unloading my shopping too slowly.

Shouted at by a woman on the till at Monoprix for trying to pay for €27 of shopping with a €50 note.

Shouted at for blocking the pavement with the pushchair, about ten times, by motorists, old ladies, other pushchair pushers and once by a handsome young man in a navy quilted jacket, who seems far too young to care about such things.

Shouted at by old ladies at the market for taking up too much space with pushchair three times.

Shouted at by market stallholders variously for touching – not squeezing – an avocado, for dithering, and for asking for fruit at the vegetable till.

Poked with a walking stick for blocking an old lady's ingress to Paul once. I am still reeling at this one: I never expected things to get physical. She looked so sweet and vulnerable too, with fluffy white hair and frail, blotchy legs in patent leather mid-heel court shoes, but she just jabbed me in the ribs and hissed at me.

One afternoon, as I leave the Parc Monceau, someone shouts after me. I turn, assuming I or one of the children must have dropped something, expecting to meet an extended hand proffering a toy or sock. Instead, three nannies, each with a child in tow, surround me.

'You need to do something about your jeans,' one says, gesturing at my bottom. 'They're falling right down.' The other two stare, eyes narrowed. This is not friendly advice, it is admonition.

My mouth sags open. My jeans are riding quite low, but I'm a long way from round the knees gangsta pants. 'I'm carrying a baby and pushing a buggy,' I say. 'I don't have a free hand to pull up my trousers.'

They raise their eyebrows and walk on.

Later, in bed, after all these incidents, I think of the clever and cutting things I could have said to them. 'Oh!' I say, witheringly, in my head. 'I didn't realize there was a dress code for the sandpit!' Or 'The next time I want fashion advice from a woman who thinks stonewash is still a thing, I know where to come, thanks.' There is a reason *esprit d'escalier* is a French expression, I think.

Surely this can't be normal. What is going wrong? It is not that I am failing at the basics: I know to say hello, properly, when I go into shops or meet the concierge. But what I gradually discover is that I am only speaking half the language: the rest is all about appearance, body language and tone.

Clearly, I am not doing myself any favours aesthetically: I know this from the looks I get in the Parc Monceau. Years of living in London have left me believing I can leave the house in anything: in my post-natal wreckage phase, I walked around Fitzrovia and Soho in men's tracksuit bottoms, a giant fleece and what were essentially slippers and no one even glanced at me. Here, that's simply not an option. I do understand that the way I look is genuinely affecting the way I get treated, but I can't quite get it together to do anything about it. With Louis's nocturnal habits, just getting up is already a struggle; the idea of dressing up is simply absurd. Worse, stuff has a habit of adhering to me and I am seemingly incapable of getting through a day without acquiring a squalid full body coating of crumbs, dust and coffee.

In normal circumstances I love clothes. I love agnès b shirts and Margaret Howell trousers and anything that promises to make me look ice cool and insouciant like Inès de la Fressange or *désinvolte* and boyish like Jane Birkin. It doesn't work at all – I am short and curvy and I look like a prison warden in buttoned-up white shirts and blazers – but until now that has never stopped me trying. I suppose my current dirty Gap jeans and T-shirts are a sort of mourning; an external expression of that feeling of being undone on the inside. Even so, I'm confounded by my own inability to measure up: this is *not* the Parisian image I had imagined for myself in my teenage dreams. There's a difference between being Birkin casual and slatternly, and I am far, far over the wrong side of this divide. My lack of effort is viewed as disrespectful on some level and I am paying the price.

My problems go far deeper than the merely sartorial, though. My real problem, it transpires, is that I actually *am* English. I am so, so English. There is no French person inside me trying to get out; there is just a bottomless well of Britishness, stewing like tea in a WI urn. This is revealed most strongly by my enslavement to the apology. Kate Fox describes what she calls the 'reflexive apology rule' in *Watching the English* and every day on the streets of Paris, I demonstrate it. I can say sorry about almost anything and sorry is almost never what I actually mean.

'*Pardon,*' I say automatically when someone stands on my toe in the métro. I mean 'sorry' here in the British sense of 'you have invaded my personal space and I wish to make you aware of this fact so that you desist. However, I do not want this exchange to escalate into unpleasantness or embarrassment for either of us.' I am usually ignored.

'*Euh, pardon?*' I squeak indignantly when someone barges in front of me in the bakery queue without any apparent awkwardness. I mean 'What the fuck do you think you are doing, you ANIMAL, is nothing sacred?' but that is not how it comes across.

'*Je suis désolée,*' I say apologetically in Monoprix with a smile, handing over my €50 note, but when I do this, I actually make things worse.

'*Pardon!*' I protest when elbowed out of a shop doorway as I try and open my umbrella, or jostled in the Post Office (god, I hate the Post Office. Everyone in there is furious all the time).

None of these is a real 'sorry': I firmly believe myself to be in the right. Olivier doesn't have this impulse to apologize for everything. He is not particularly enjoying life in Paris, but this part of it – the counter-offensive and the quicksilver reaction – seems to come instinctively to him. On weekends, I watch, lost in admiration as he negotiates our way through the city with steely resolve.

On top of the apologies, there's something wrong with the way I express myself. It's not, strictly speaking, the language. I have a good ear and a natural facility and I am fluent in French: until now, I have always enjoyed how good I am. But now, I am starting to realize, I am not *myself* when I speak French. I'm not funny or clever or fast. I don't know how to make the kind of jokes I make in English – black-hearted, self-deprecating ones – and on the odd occasions I have tried to make a joke it has been received with such blankness, I have stopped trying. I am diffident, wary, slow to voice an opinion. I don't play with language or enjoy it any more: I just want to pass. This makes an idiot of me: a boring, monotonous idiot.

Faced with this unedifying image of myself and with the unremitting disapproval of most of Paris, I find myself thinking more sympathetically about expats, the kind of expats who live in an insulated bubble of Marmite and Robinson's Lemon Barley Water, *The Archers* on long wave and week-old copies of *The Times*.

I have always felt rather sneery about this kind of expat life – what is the point of living abroad and pretending you don't? – but I am starting to see how you could draw some comfort from preserving or recreating elements of home. It need not be all about a myopic insistence that your way is better, or a deliberate, proud display of ignorance. Perhaps, instead, it can be a way to bolster your eroded sense of identity? The idea that the expat you is a lesser thing – less articulate, less able, less powerful – is hard to avoid, and if you can feel more yourself by surrounding yourself with the familiar, who am I to question that?

I get a chance to see for myself, when I make a British friend of sorts.

Jill is the first, the only, person apart from the grass-monitoring guards to talk to me in the Parc Monceau. I am walking slowly along one of the alleys in Theo's wake as he picks up small stones and keeps up a perplexing monologue about dragons, Louis strapped to my front, when I hear someone speaking English. It is a woman of about my age, short and dark, with a little boy who must be about Theo's age, and a baby in a pram. It's a bit like looking at myself, except she's Scottish. I sidle closer and start speaking to Theo quite loudly in English, hoping she'll overhear.

When she looks over, I smile, tentatively.

'Are you English?' she asks me.

'Yes!'

And just like that, I have an ally.

It's not that Jill and I become great friends: we don't have that much in common and we're both at the frayed, desperate end of our tethers with very little to offer, but there's a sort of comfort in that. Jill lives with her kids in a chaotic, messy apartment round the corner from my chaotic, messy apartment. She is married to a French engineer, but he works in Toulouse and only comes back every six weeks or so. She has been living in Paris for four years already, but she does not seem much more integrated than I am, which is worrying.

'So, do you know many people round here?'

'Just the ones in the building, really.'

The inside of her flat is as English as an embassy staff lounge. The boys watch videotapes of CBeebies her parents send across from Aberdeen every week and the coffee table is spread with copies of *Heat* and *Hello!* When she makes me a cup of tea, she pulls out a packet of chocolate HobNobs with a flourish, like a conjuror bringing out a rabbit from a hat.

'Shall we watch *EastEnders*?' she asks me one day when the boys are busy with a game. I agree, and we sit on her saggy sofa and watch Den and Chrissie slog it out on screen as we nurse mugs of PG Tips. It's very weird, but undoubtedly comforting.

Jill has dabbled in the expat community, the coffee mornings, NCT groups and bake sales, but she tells me they all happen in the interior-decorated apartments of American bankers' wives over on the Left Bank, a tricky multiple métro ride away, and anyway they aren't places she feels welcome or at home. I understand that and can't imagine wanting to join in this world of matching china and playdates, so we form an alliance of convenience. I call her when we are heading to the park and she does the same, then we walk together and chat desultorily about developmental milestones or where to buy jelly. This isn't how I ever imagined my social life in Paris but, it turns out, I'm extremely glad of it.

« 9 »

Am Stram Gram

Stopping work barely registered at the time: there was so much else going on, it seemed largely irrelevant, but now, with Louis approaching six months, this is new territory for me. By the time Theo was this age, I was back in the office, eating canteen cereal at my desk in the mornings, billing hours of spreadsheet crunching tedium, exchanging half-hourly emails full of gossip and moaning with my favourite colleague Laurie and, most importantly, earning money.

I had no idea earning my own money was important to me until now, when I have none. Nothing we have is mine: I do not even have a bank account of my own here so everything I buy – socks, deodorant, cakes for lunch – comes from Olivier's salary and it feels like another part of my identity is being chipped away. It turns out it is very easy to claim that you are indifferent to money when you have enough of it. I hate not having any: it feels shameful and a bit pathetic.

The temptations to spend money are not that numerous – I am too scared – but my real weak spot is food. At week-ends Olivier and I go out down to the beautiful market on the Rue Poncelet. The market is five minutes from our flat, and I walk through almost daily. It starts off with a trickle of

good-looking food shops. There's a flouncy gilt-fronted traditional bakery with queues out along the street, an Austrian
deli-café with a window full of strudel and sachertorte, a
coffee roaster, and the hymn to mould that is the Aléosse
cheese shop. After that the market starts in earnest with
stacks of fruit and vegetables: traffic light bright mandarins,
velvety purple artichokes, long pale tendrils of frisée and
fat green grapes. Round to the right in Rue Bayen are three
huge fish shops tended by wisecracking men in waders and
floor-length blue-and-white striped aprons, fussing at their
iced display of pink prawns and inky sea urchins or tending
to tanks of crabs and lobsters (spiky prehistoric spider crabs
and smooth blue colossi) with claws secured in rubber
bands. Opposite the fish shops are a couple of open-fronted
traiteurs, selling roast chickens and quail and racks of spare
ribs, round yellow sauté potatoes and giant terrines.

On my own, I never buy anything. Partly because it
intimidates me, but also because everything is terribly expensive: it's Selfridge's food hall in disguise. This means that on
weekends with Olivier, I am desperate to go and get lovely
things and this leads to a kind of stand-off.

'Couldn't we make our own?' he says, blanching at the
prices of lasagne in the Italian deli as we walk through the
Saturday morning shopping crowds, and I narrow my eyes at
him or go all coldly polite. I want nice things now and again
and perhaps even more than that, I want acceptance from
the snotty local shopkeepers. Olivier wants us to live within
our limited means. A fog of unspoken tension sits around us
and I can see only one solution: I need to get a job.

This should not be impossible. The whole point of doing European law was so that I could be employable in places other than England, and Paris has plenty of firms doing the kind of work I specialized in. But my sister has gone back to the UK to prepare for starting university, so before I can even start looking, I need to arrange at least a few hours' childcare a day. I'm confident this will not be a problem. French pre-school childcare is famously wonderful, isn't it? Universal schooling from age two, exquisite three-course meals for toddlers, smocks, quaintly shaped cursive script.

It isn't like that for us. French state nurseries are indeed a nirvana of low-cost high-quality full-time childcare, but in Paris the demand for places outweighs availability by a factor of ten to one and draconian civic regulations mean there is virtually no private childcare provision apart from *nounous*, nannies. We know people who have campaigned daily, at the town hall, for months on end to try and wangle a nursery place. Olivier's friend Eric is one of them and has secured prized places for his two children at the nearby Étoile *crèche*. 'You need,' he says confidently, 'to make their lives hell.'

I certainly have the time to do this, if not the temperamental suitability, so I head off to the town hall, the *mairie*, with a file of birth certificates, proofs of residence and health insurance documentation.

The *mairie* is an ugly 1970s concrete monolith. Inside, it smells of dust and disinfectant and promises the systematic abuse of microscopic amounts of power. I follow some approximate signage for the '*Section Petite Enfance*' and end up in a dark corridor with a green linoleum floor and large empty offices on either side. I walk, tentatively, from office to office, looking at the signs on the doors, trying to find the right official. Finally, I track him down to an almost empty open-plan space at the end of the corridor. The desks are oddly configured in a sort of square, with a high, front-facing counter at which the supplicant (me) stands. I can barely see over the top, but behind it is the top of a dark-haired head, bent over a pile of paper.

'Hello?'

No movement. Chastened by my months of reprimands, I wait, meekly uncomplaining. Eventually, after what feels like several minutes but is probably barely thirty seconds, the head lifts slowly, emerging from a brown roll-neck sweater in the manner of a tortoise cautiously emerging from its shell. It is a middle-aged man looking at me. I smile; he does not.

'*Bonjour, monsieur.*'

Olivier has impressed on me that this is our big chance to win sympathy and to position ourselves as deserving of the arbitrarily bestowed bounty of a *crèche* place.

'I would like to, er, enrol my son on the *crèche* waiting list. Is this, er, the right . . . ?' My voice trails off.

Without speaking, the tortoise extends a hand to the grey filing cabinet that fences him in on the right, opens a drawer and extracts a wodge of papers. With a light slap, he places them on the counter, a lidless blue Bic on top.

'You must fill these in.'

'Great!' I sound nonsensically happy with my forms, like a simpleton. 'Can I stay here to do it, or . . . ?'

The tortoise waves a weary hand in a gesture I intuit to

mean that if I so please, I can stay. Whatever floats my boat. The head retracts back into the polo neck, out of sight.

I start to fill in the boxes. I am fully prepared, with my file of supporting documents, to provide the required information on my maternal grandparents, blood group and immigration status, removing each document as required and filling in the relevant box with nerdy satisfaction. I am conscious, however, that I am not actually doing what I promised I would: pleading our case. I need to man up.

'This is, erm, very important to us because I need to return to work. I am a lawyer.' ('*Je suis avocate*' sounds great in French. It speaks of eight years of spectacularly dreary study, black gowns and white pleated collars. Of course, in the UK I spent a single year cramming for a set of open-book exams, then two years wrestling spreadsheets for my own title, but no one need ever know that here.)

It is unclear if the man behind the desk has heard me. If he has, he shows no sign of acknowledgement. I continue writing and try again.

'We moved here recently after a very difficult time. My mother died in an accident while I was pregnant with my second child, I am responsible for my younger sister and I do not know how we will cope without a *crèche* place.'

I feel embarrassed for myself.

There is still no response from behind the desk. The tortoise turns away on his wheeled chair to reach for another pile of papers.

'There, finished.'

I pass the form across the high desk. The tortoise takes

it and flicks through without interest as I watch. Then he pulls open the top drawer of the desk, removes a stamp and stamps the form with a loud flourish, scribbling a biro initial in the centre of the stamp. Finally he gets up, walks to the photocopier in the corner of the room and copies the documents. From the back he looks quite vulnerable, stooped and skinny, his cords hanging off his waist.

On his return he hands me the photocopy.

'*Voilà.*'

'Thank you!' I give him my best shot at a thousand-watt smile. 'So, what happens now?'

'You will find out in writing in September whether your children have been accepted.'

'Thank you. And in the meantime?'

He looks at me for a second, the first eye contact we have established. I feel a nanosecond of connection. It's not openly hostile, but there might be a touch of mockery there. I can't even trust myself to interpret it right.

'Nothing, *madame*. You wait.'

I feel like I have failed, but there seems to be nothing else to do for the moment.

'OK. Thank you. *Bonne journée.*'

His head is already bowed over the desk as I turn away to walk out.

Without any real hope of accessing the Republic's finest childcare, we turn to what the private sector can offer us.

For Louis, this is a couple of hours each morning with Charline. We find Charline through a babysitting agency. She has no childcare experience, but when we speak to her, kindness and good humour radiate off her in waves: she is smiling, solid, sensible. She is also a Seventh Day Adventist and attributes almost everything to the Lord, but if the Lord is telling her to come and work for us, I am fine with Him. I love her. Nothing is ever a drama with Charline: she enjoys Louis and finds him funny, enjoys playing with him. Unlike me, she doesn't get twitchy if he won't nap or spends the morning grizzling, and in her presence I relax a little too. Sometimes, if Louis is particularly good-humoured – and he often is with her – she makes lunch for the three of us. She is a terrible cook, but I don't care, it feels like such an act of love that I eat up her singed cubed chicken tearful with gratitude.

For Theo, it is a *halte-garderie,* a sort of morning drop-in centre. The one we find is called Am Stram Gram.

Am Stram Gram is named for a counting rhyme (a French 'eeny, meeny, miny, moe') and it is a primary-coloured surprise on a narrow grey street named after Aléxis de Tocqueville, the French historian whose dry as dust prose I endured for several long months of my first year at university. It takes us twenty minutes to walk there in the mornings, along the wide anonymous boulevards north of our flat in the direction of the *périphérique,* the ringroad.

Behind the front door is a reception area with coat pegs and baskets for shoes. The idea is that parents deposit their children in this entrance, despatching them with a brisk kiss at the red wooden gate and leaving both parties to get on with their morning. Beyond the red gate, I discover when we are shown round, is a wet room, a messy room, an 'art' room and a fish tank. There is also a slide and a heap of cushions. At the start of the day a bell rings and children move from one organized activity to another, for allotted times in allotted groups. At the end of the morning, parents are presented with a completed sheet of paper detailing the 'theme' of the morning ('Ancient Egypt', 'the secrets of the mountains', 'life in a medieval castle') and what activity each child has participated in ('paint', 'chalk', 'stories', 'play-dough'). The assumption is that new arrivals should slot in without any special attention.

This is explained to me by Monique, who is in charge. Monique has a cast-iron range of a bosom and winged spectacles, like a matron in a Gary Larson cartoon. She is not particularly friendly – by now I am well past the point of expecting friendly – but she is reassuringly certain about everything. Theo will settle in swiftly, she says, if I show sufficient confidence.

'It is up to you,' she says, 'to show the example.'

My example is a bit wobbly. I do not, initially, leave Theo: I am not confident. I find I am unwilling to leave him to fend for himself after the chaos of the past few months, so I craft an elaborate version of our sob-story and obtain permission – exceptional, short-term, on sufferance, Monique stresses, eyes narrowed in disapproval – to come beyond the white-painted picket fence for a week or so to help him acclimatize.

I don't know about Theo, but I certainly acclimatize quickly. I find the minutely organized routine immensely comforting: there is a time and a place for everything, in-structions are clear and clearly explained and nothing is left to chance. After the painting or the water play, after stories and sliding, the morning ends with song and snack time, which is, of course, also signalled with the bell. I crouch happily on the floor with the tiny children (Theo is less enthusiastic), shuffling to the back so everyone can see past me, and learn the tunes and the actions to songs and rhymes that every French child knows: 'Mon Petit Lapin' (waggle your rabbit ears, hide under a cabbage), 'Les Marionettes' (*ainsi font font font les petites marionettes*, with a twisting wrist gesture to represent puppets), 'La Baleine Qui Tourne' (my favourite: a whale eats some boats, but then regrets his actions) and 'Les Petits Poissons' (Am Stram Gram friendly message: small fish can swim as well as big ones). At the end of song time – which is signalled by a second rendition of 'Mon Petit Lapin' – a plate of halved Petit Beurre biscuits or apple slices (or, when there is a birthday, a dry cube of chocolate loaf cake) circulates.

This is all balm to my conformist soul, and I would happily spend every morning colouring in medieval craftsmen then taking part in song time. I love the feeling of knowing what to do, for once, and having precise instructions to follow. But all too soon my time is up and Monique insists Theo needs to go it alone.

The first day is awful. Theo does not understand why on earth he has to stay by himself – which is reasonable, given I have been accompanying him for the past week – and he is furious: puce and hysterical, small fists grasping desperately at whatever part of me he can grab as a breezily determined Am Stram Gram staff member detaches him, finger by stubborn finger. 'No, *Maman*!' he shouts. 'NO. I don't like it!' I leave to the sound of his wails, and walk the streets in a guilty, unhappy daze. I get a *palmier*, one of those big dry flaky pastries, from the bakery opposite, cram it into my mouth as I stand on the railway bridge down the road, and chew, compulsively, wondering what is happening behind the white gate. '*Bon appétit*,' says a passing youth, sarcastically. Eating on the street is of course absolutely beyond the pale in Paris but, momentarily at least, I am past caring.

I walk around for the allotted two hours. The streets are quiet on this weekday mid-morning and I walk fast around the Boulevard Pereire and all the way down the Avenue Niel and find myself at the Arc de Triomphe. The bloody Arc de Triomphe is our arrondissement's only real monument and as a piece of civic architecture I find it a serious downer. I do not like its triumphal vastness nor the creepy eternal flame, which looks like something from a high-tech crematorium. Everywhere I go, the damn thing seems to be visible: it's following me. The Arc is new to me: this whole western swathe of the city has been a discovery. It's a part of Paris shaped by industry, curved around the emerging railway lines, initially peopled by the engineers and investors and entrepreneurs whose wealth gilded the railings and whose names are immortalized in the wide grey boulevards. Where are my wrong but romantic heroes here?

When I get back to Am Stram Gram, I can hear Theo before I see him: he is totally spoiling 'Les Petits Poissons' with a vigorous chorus of 'NO NO NO.' Peering cautiously over the fence, I can see him, arms folded, right at the back.

He isn't crying, he's just furious, which seems about as much as I could hope for.

Gradually, haltingly, we develop a sort of routine. Around eight, I put Theo in the buggy and walk him along the avenues busy with commuters and schoolchildren up to Am Stram Gram. We start a story on the way, a rambling shaggy dog story full of peril we compose between us. I leave him for a couple of hours and try and look for jobs. On the way back, we finish the story and go home for lunch and a nap.

In the afternoons, we go – all three of us – to the Batignolles park.

The Square des Batignolles is much nicer than Monceau. It is a pretty, sloping, watery affair with an old fashioned *manège* (swans, bi-planes, an omnibus). There is a small lake, framed by a collection of plane trees that predate the construction of the park, and a glass folly on a hillock that is open for small children to run in and out of, inventing stories. It is home to a population of exotic ducks which it is strictly forbidden to feed (everyone ignores this) and a population of aggressive chaffinches. Most of the time Theo ignores all these attractions in favour of the main one in his eyes: the trains.

Theo loves trains, and from the low wall on the westerly side of the square, you have a perfect view of the curving sweep of ten or twelve sets of train tracks that run out of the Saint-Lazare station and sweep up, under the Cardinet bridge and out towards the western suburbs. This is the heart of Parisian rail history: trains shaped this arrondissement.

It was from here that the Pereire brothers, Isaac and Emile, ran the first passenger line in the city, out of Saint-Lazare and west to Saint-Germain-en-Laye twenty kilometres away. No one was quite sure it would work until the line opened – the tunnel through the Batignolles hill was a terrifying 331 metres long and contemporary commentators feared the temperature within might reach 45°C and kill everyone – but after a successful maiden voyage the line enjoyed instant popularity, with 18,000 visitors on its first day open to the public.

The trains found their way into the art and literature of Batignolles, then a cheap place for studio space (that famous Fantin-Latour group portrait of the Impressionists where everyone is standing around, grave and bearded, is called *Un Atelier Aux Batignolles*): this is where my romantic heroes hung out (and I'm a bit wistful we don't live here). The local creatives observed and absorbed their trains. Monet's Saint-Lazare series is the best known, but Manet's *The Railway* is also a vision of Saint-Lazare, with his favourite model, Victorine, sitting by the railings with a young girl, apparently fascinated by the clouds of steam emanating from within. Caillebotte painted the nearby Pont de l'Europe, a popular place to watch trains, with its network of rails. Zola, too, liked a train. Of course he did; no contemporary phenomenon was safe from his pen. *La Bête Humaine* – a violent, claustrophobic tale of murder and revenge – takes place along this same railway line from Saint-Lazare to Le Havre and the engine in it, *La Lison*, is a character in its own right, valiant but dangerous. When the engine lies wrecked following a derailment, Zola describes its demise in these affecting, haunting terms:

'The poor *Lison* only had a few minutes left. She was cooling, the embers in her hearth were collapsing into ash, the breath that had escaped so violently from her open flanks had dimmed to the soft complaint of a crying child.'

La Bête Humaine is full of people looking at trains, just as Manet did in his studio in the Rue de Saint-Pétersbourg, or Zola did in his garden in Médan, and every afternoon, we sit too and watch the ballet of rolling stock for as long as Louis will tolerate. I lean against the wall and hold Theo safe as the late-afternoon commuter trains increase in frequency, heading out to Saint-Germain, Le Pecq or Vésinet, and listen to his commentary.

'Train!'

'Yep.'

'That train is FAST.'

'It is, isn't it?'

'Train!'

'Oh yes, another one.'

'It's full of people. Hello, people! You're in the train!'

'Indeed they are.'

'Bust my buffers! Careful of the bridge! Oh no! Watch out!'

This last is in homage to Thomas the Tank Engine. I don't know if Theo likes trains because of Thomas or if he likes Thomas because he likes trains, but either way, the little blue engine dominates our days. The flat is full of winding, elaborate wooden tracks and Thomas-branded trains, wooden faces painted in exaggerated expressions, linked together by their magnetic buffers. We have bridges and signals and cranes, cackling trucks and ersatz TV tie-in locomotives. The trains run across the table at breakfast time, line up neatly on the sofa, covered with Theo's comfort blanket to watch television, and go on occasional outings, carefully clasped in his hands, ready to enact new catastrophes.

Because Theo and his trains are all about disaster, thanks to Thomas. His play is a litany of perilous incidents watched and then replayed and amplified: chains break, loads drop, there are crashes and fires and derailments. Theo re-enacts it all in lurid detail day after day: collapsing bridges, sheep on the line and mechanical failure. He is particularly drawn to – and terrified of – an episode in which a giant boulder pursues an engine around the Island of Sodor, wreaking destruction and terror. He feels compelled to revisit the trauma often, discussing 'Boulder' in hushed tones, retelling and replaying the worst moments obsessively. In some moods, an inadvertent reference can trigger a sobbing fit and for a few weeks, Theo's first thought on waking is the risk of being crushed by a gigantic rolling stone in the streets of Paris. 'Boulder coming to squash you,' he says, gravely pointing a finger at me, his words heavy with the weight of prophecy. As I put him to bed, he takes hold of my wrist for a last, urgent check.

'Boulder coming?'

'No, Boulder is definitely not coming. It can't fit in the lift, and it can't roll upstairs.'

'Where is Boulder?'

'Far away. On holiday, perhaps.'

As we travel to and from Am Stram Gram, our stories are full of rail-based catastrophe, though mine are a little more fanciful than the Reverend Awdry's, with trains waylaid by escaped dragons or herds of buffalo, sprouting wings or being carried away on rockets. Even so, each day, the pattern is the same: I try to tie up each tale with a neat rescue and resolution and Theo refuses, insisting on further and more perilous adventures. Engines are forever falling down holes on their way to parties, and the spectre of Boulder is never far away.

'NO,' he says, at any hint of a positive twist to the story, eyes flashing with displeasure, ''cause the lion ATE the wheels.'

'Aha. Right. OK, well, the lion ate the wheels but they gave him a poorly tummy so he had to sick them back up again. And Percy took the wheels and gave them a rinse in the pond, then put them back on and raced off just in time for the—'

An imperious raised hand cuts me off. 'No but THEN Percy 'sploded.'

Sometimes I try and fight back.

'No, it wasn't an explosion. It was just . . . um . . . a firework in his boiler? What a surprise!'

Theo is intransigent. 'No. He 'sploded.'

Any happy ending I can wrest from him is hard won and grudgingly conceded.

I wonder, sometimes, if this fascination with terrible things happening has anything to do with Mum. I have never been straight with him, never insisted on getting his butterfly attention for five minutes during that confusing, awful time: to say 'Granny died.' I wonder what it was like for him to live in the slipstream of all that shock and unhappiness, the weird upheavals, trips to York and back, hushed conversations and crying adults. He never asked, but I know that's no kind of excuse. Bossy Monique at Am Stram Gram has already taken me to task about it.

'You must explain to him, it is vital for his development,' she tells me with an accusatory glare, but I still can't, it feels so harsh and so final. I think I fear too, that it won't actually mean anything to him at all now and that would almost be worse than him being sad. It has been months after all, would he even remember her? I can't bear the thought of her forgotten, but he's so little, almost half a lifetime has passed since he last saw her.

Perhaps Thomas – bossy, harsh Thomas – helps? I see the way Theo flirts with catastrophe, peeping into the abyss and challenging me to find a way back over and over again and I feel as if it gives me a convoluted way of making good my failure.

So our stories meander on as we walk to and from Am Stram Gram, disaster, recovery and disaster again. Every day, the drop-off gets a little easier and soon, within six weeks, Theo has entirely acclimatized to Am Stram Gram's orderly world, hurrying to put his shoes in the basket as the bell starts to ring, anxious to be on time. Excluded from song time, I glean what I can from the completed report sheet I get each day and a handful of 'artwork': carelessly crayoned print-outs of mushrooms or skiing gendarmes, Theo's 'take' on life in a fortified medieval castle (a brown line scrawled across a photocopied blacksmith), a dried-leaf collage or a potato-print spider. He never wants to talk about his activities; the story comes first, whatever perilous cliffhanger our engines are currently in must be resolved. But the evidence seems clear: he is starting to develop a life independent of me.

« 10 »

Kings of Pastry

Now that I have childcare, at least a little of the time, I can concentrate on getting this job.

First, I find and arrange a meeting with a legal recruitment consultant, who I select randomly on the Internet. Her office is in the 8th arrondissement on a back street near Boulevard Haussmann – recruitment people here don't meet you over a latte in Costa like they do in London – and it is serious and dark and imposing, with a lift with a vast iron door I need two hands to open and close. In contrast, the consultant herself looks like a stock photo of a young executive, with swishy hair and a neat scarf and a dark suit. Her make-up is lovely. I am uncomfortably squeezed back into one of my work trouser suits and my blouse feels too tight. I am a bit sweaty, unused to proper clothes, but I have put on some eyeliner and dredged up a vague memory of how professional people behave with each other. I am sort of excited as well as nervous: this is really my first grown-up, non-child-related encounter in Paris (we have also bought a sofa, but that doesn't really count; also, I think we made a terrible choice so I am trying to forget the sofa).

'Well,' says the recruitment lady when we are both seated at her large, dark-wood conference table with black coffees, like the proper grown-ups we are. 'You have an excellent CV, great academics, a top tier firm . . . We should have no difficulty placing you.'

She is probably just being nice, but I feel a little glow of gratification.

'Thank you, that's great news.' I pull out my extra-perfect French accent for her.

'So, what are you looking for? Another role in private practice? Or in-house?'

'Well, potentially I'd be open to either, but it really needs to be part-time.'

The consultant frowns. 'Part-time?'

'Yes. I have two very young children . . .' I trail off as she makes a face, then puts down her pen.

'The problem is . . . Well. I only know one person in your sector who works part-time. One. In my twelve years in the job.'

'Really?' I find this very hard to believe. Plenty of people work part-time in my sector back in London. Well, plenty of them work four days a week and a few more part-time. I sip my coffee anxiously.

'It's just not part of the culture. I really think you will struggle to find a part-time role. They just don't exist.'

I don't really know what to say to her. 'So . . .'

'Perhaps in-house would be easier with your responsibilities?'

'Um, yes, I suppose so . . .'

We agree she will have a look around and get in touch if she hears of anything suitable.

As I leave, deflated, I think of all those Parisian mothers at Am Stram Gram, dispensing a single no-nonsense kiss and leaving swiftly in a cloud of expensive scent. They all work: France, with its tax breaks on childcare and priority *crèche* spots for kids with two working parents, assumes they will. So they get up early and put their make-up on, leave their children with their nannies or take them to nursery, then they work all day. When they get home at seven, they supervise homework and bedtime, eat the dinner the nanny has prepared or make it themselves (possibly assisted by Picard). After a serious conversation about Palestine or the stock market, they have sex with their husbands. Or so I imagine. I feel cowed by their reserves of efficiency and competence. What, actually, do I do? I drift around the city nervously, read books, get upset multiple times a day and don't even cook proper meals. In the evening we watch overwrought cooking shows and then I fall asleep, wearing earplugs, purple tracksuit bottoms and my father's moth-eaten cricket jumper. I am not up to Parisian womanhood by any stretch of the imagination. I can do my job, the one I used to be paid for, and I can – more or less – look after my children. But both together *and* sex and current affairs? Realistically, no.

But the weight of expectation is definitely there. One of Olivier's friends has been complaining to him about his wife, a clever accountant, who has expressed a desire to give up work after having her second child. 'That's not the woman I married,' he says. 'I don't want to be with a *housewife*.' I can't decide if this is admirable or appalling.

Despite my worrying lack of a work ethic, the recruitment consultant finds me an interview a few weeks later, for a pharmaceutical company on the very outside border of the 15th arrondissement, to the south of the city. I read up on intellectual property law and parallel trade and grey imports and locate some more work clothes in the bottom of a box, then I take myself off one morning in a too tight skirt and shoes that rub. Charline looks me over before I leave and declares me '*très pro*' which seems unlikely, but buoys my confidence. I arrive too early and have to spend twenty minutes hanging around in a bookshop getting progressively more and more nervous while pretending to read an Amélie Nothomb novel, and when I am finally shown into a huge, dimly lit boardroom to sit opposite the HR director at a table that would easily seat thirty, I am barely functioning with nerves. It shows. I don't quite know how it all goes wrong, but apparently my interview is so epically disastrous that after about twenty minutes my interviewer holds up a finger and stops me in mid-flow, to make a call cancelling the planned second stage practical part of the process. After this, the recruiter stops calling me.

Out of ideas, I email the partners at my old firm's Paris office, who invite me in for interview. Their offices are in a beautiful eighteenth-century villa just off the Champs-Elysées (at least the job search has got me out of the 17th, however briefly). Reception is brutally air-conditioned and the main desk is staffed by a gaggle of beautiful, haughty women dressed in the firm's colours with matching hair accessories in their chignons. The collective effect is ultra-high-class air hostess, except none of them offers me a gin and tonic and a packet of peanuts. All the surfaces are glass and I feel anxious when my fingers brush against the table in case I leave dirty fingermarks (the concierge has me well trained by now).

Two partners interview me: the male one is small and neat and terribly patrician, and the woman is simply terrifying. She is sort of tomboyish, in an ultra-stylish kind of way, in a slouchy trouser suit and Superga plimsolls and her expression in repose is the purest Parisian scorn. If she came anywhere near me in Monoprix, I would hide in the nappy aisle until she went away again. Thankfully, she doesn't speak at all for most of the interview, doodling instead on her notepad as I stumble my way through a very polite grilling.

For all my nerves, I must make some rudimentary sense, because they call the next day to offer me a full-time position, albeit for considerably less money than my previous role. Of course, that is still considerably more money than my current salary of 'nothing at all' and I am really happy that *someone* wants to employ me. I start to imagine myself as one of those Parisian women, with a wildly demanding job. I think about new shoes and handbags. I am mentally stalking through the office in Robert Clergerie heels, on my way to a high-stakes meeting with fantasy clients who look like Daniel Auteuil and want me to help them with their luxury fashion businesses.

A friend from the London office calls.

'So they offered you a job?'

'Yes! I'm really pleased.'

'This is going to sound bizarre, I know, but . . . I don't think you should take it.'

'Oh. Really? Why?'

'I just don't think it would be right for you at the moment. It's really demanding, you know.'

I am a bit bemused, but as I hang up, doubt gathers. Could I cope? I don't know. I don't really know what is going on in my own head at the moment; everything is so foggy. I don't feel grief or anger or fear, at least not in any way that I recognize. I just feel stalled, sitting lost in my own life with no idea how to get restarted. Surely a job is the way forward? I will meet people, at least? I need to get a foothold in the city somewhere other than Am Stram Gram and the expensive paediatrician's office (they have an almost full-sized replica Cadillac in the waiting room; I can't help feeling I haven't found the most economical option for the constant sore throats and rashes). Who am I in this place without work, even work I don't much like? My mind wanders to Simone de Beauvoir, an evangelist for the importance, the salvation, of work.

'Earning your living is not, of itself, a goal, but it is the only way to attain solid internal autonomy,' she says, even when she is teaching indifferent teenagers in a Rouen lycée, and I know she's right.

And yet, and yet. My colleague has spooked me, and on reflection, I think he's right. In my old job in London I had been pregnant and coasting more or less since I had qualified; here there would be no slack whatsoever. I can't see how to shoehorn eighteen-hour days and constant availability and foreign travel into our life and, quite honestly, I'm a bit scared. What if it makes everything worse? I just don't see how we'll cope.

So I turn them down and I feel like a pathetic failure. But since I no longer need my mornings for job-hunting at the moment, I can at least turn to what I am really, really good at: cake.

Because if anything, anything at all, has made me happy in Paris, it is cake. I know where I am with patisserie, with the lovely familiar geography of the French bakery window: this is how I started to explore and months later, it continues. I navigate the city via more and more bakery windows, appraising *Saint-Honorés* and *Paris-Brests* and comparing éclairs. I start out in our local bakeries and then gradually widen the perimeter. The bakery by the Batignolles gardens does fat gooey puff-pastry twists with warm pistachio crème pâtissière and dark chocolate. There is the bakery that makes loaves in the shape of hedgehogs and crocodiles down by the Boulevard Malesherbes. In the Rue de Lévis there are three good bakeries and I walk between them, gimlet-eyed, trying to decide whose *flan* looks better. When I have a little longer I can go further afield, down to the Place de la Madeleine, where I cruise around the windows of Fauchon and Ladurée, admiring perfect *macarons*. I measure out my days in waxed-paper parcels. They are an indulgence, but I get so much pleasure from so few euros with cake, it feels like a thrifty solution to my gloom.

There is something utterly reassuring, too, in the unchanging canon of French patisserie. It has its own beautiful language, a gorgeous rolling poetry reminiscent of Paris métro stations: *Tropézienne, Opéra, Tarte Bourdaloue, Kouglof, Divorcée*, instead of *Crimée, Stalingrad, Poissonnière, Mouton-Duvernet*. No Francophile can be insensible to this. French cakes have not only a name but also a history and a set of rules attached. A *Paris-Brest* is piped praline cream in a choux doughnut, and it is wheel-shaped in honour of the Paris-Brest cycling race. On a *religieuse* (a 'nun'), a small choux bun sits on a larger one and they both have the same-flavoured fondant icing – traditionally chocolate or coffee – while on a *divorcée* the smaller bun is coffee and the larger chocolate. I like how everyone knows this and I like the fact that I know it too: it's easy and accessible and it thrills me how easy it is to fit in in bakery world. If someone says *Mont Blanc* I immediately visualize a domed nest of piped chestnut and vanilla cream and if they say *Opéra* I know there will be thin layers of chocolate, coffee cream and genoise sponge. Even a marzipan potato (and who could possibly want such a thing? I would rather eat a raw real one), brown, squat and profoundly lacking in charm, has a 'right' composition and appearance.

The rules are a reminder: French patiserie is a serious business, at least as much about skill and display as pleasure or indulgence. If pastry became a weapon of statecraft in the second half of the sixteenth century under Catherine de Medici (Catherine imported Italian techniques with her Florentine cooks, bringing nougat, *macarons*, frangipane and ices to France) it reached its apogee in the era of Carême and the *pièce montée*, at the end of the eighteenth and beginning of the nineteenth centuries.

Antonin Carême – foundling, monster of ambition, culinary auto-didact and patisserie 'architect' – was not a man to sell his chosen occupation short. 'There are five arts,' he wrote in one of his many distinctly unhelpful works on patisserie, 'painting, sculpture, poetry, music and architecture, of which the principal branch is patisserie.' Anyone wishing to pursue that art form would be well advised not to rely on, for instance, *Le Pâtissier Pittoresque*, which contains instructions for constructing a forty-four-columned Gothic pavilion out of sugar paste that extend to only eleven lines, with such helpful information as: 'the decorative details should be pale violet and darker purple. The bridge should be white.' The introductory chapter is barely more informative: readers are instructed to go to their druggist and ask for four of a mysterious unit of measurement of '*bol d'Armenie*', a type of clay, and the same quantity of ammonia. Another favourite instruction is to 'keep the almond paste in a big, oval porcelain dish of the type used for making poultry and truffle terrines, *façon Nérac*', the kind of item any well-stocked kitchen should surely have to hand.

Carême started from nothing and built a stellar career on choux pastry and single-minded ambition. Ian Kelly's lovely biography, *Cooking for Kings*, describes how, when apprenticed to a pâtissier in the Palais Royal, Carême would spend his free afternoons in the Bibliothèque Nationale studying classical architecture, which he would then translate into sugar and pastry and marzipan. His creations were edible, but that was not really the point. Rather, they were intended to dazzle and astonish the observer and it was this that attracted Carême's later employer and patron, Talleyrand.

Charles-Maurice de Talleyrand-Périgord was a career diplomat who floated unscathed through fifty of the bloodiest years of French history right at the heart of power, shifting and swerving and body-checking his way to the top, and he saw in Carême a man with ambitions and abilities to match his own. For twelve years in Talleyrand's service and on loan to other European potentates to oil the wheels of international diplomacy, Carême created patisserie designed to shock and awe. He made a Welsh hermitage and a copy of the Brighton Pavilion for the Prince Regent, a banquet featuring fifty-six separate desserts for Tsar Alexander, even a Venetian gondola for the birth of Napoleon's son Franz in 1811 in blue, rose and gold, with meringue and spun sugar. Patisserie under Carême was not simply something nice to eat: it was a test of your mettle and ambition.

Carême's influence endured and spread outwards into the regions. At Madame Bovary's wedding, the three-tiered *pièce montée* (the pâtissier comes all the way from Yvetot) draws cries of admiration:

'. . . a temple with porticoes, columns and statues . . . fortifications made of angelica, almonds, raisins and orange segments . . . rocks with lakes of jam and boats made of nutshells . . . a little cupid on a chocolate swing.'

Even today this kind of patisserie extremism is alive and well in France, although it has by and large retired from international diplomacy: take the case of the 'Meilleur Ouvrier de France' competition. This competition – though it is not really a competition but a pass–fail test with no fixed quota of successful applicants (in theory they could all fail) – has existed in some form since 1924. It is the preserve of the very finest pâtissiers in the country (and yes, you do have to be French to qualify), who, after preliminary testing rounds, spend twenty-five hours under exam conditions, producing a series of unimaginably complex and beautiful cakes and confectionery.

The competition only takes place every three years and preparation for it can take half a lifetime. The percentage of the ten to sixteen candidates reaching the final who satisfy the jury is generally low: only around twenty per cent are accorded the title 'MOF' and the right to wear a tricolour collar on their chef's whites. The rules for the test are a weird fairyland of spun sugar and fiddled-with egg arcana. A question and answer section at the end of fifteen pages of instructions on the current competition includes such intriguing posers as:

Q: Can you use a brass coil to stick sugar leafwork to the masterwork?

A: *Non*.

Q: Is Isomalt tolerated in the sugar masterwork and if so, what percentage of the total mass is permissible?

A: *Oui*, Isomalt is allowed.

(The question of what percentage is not resolved, maddeningly.)

There are rules upon rules upon rules: the nougatine

must weigh 1,500 grammes; the *gâteau de voyage* (what kind of country has a particular kind of cake for travelling? One I wish to offer my lifelong fealty) must have a dominant chocolate note and weigh between 450 and 500 grammes. Finally:

'Candidates are reminded that the use of rare materials derived from flora or fauna such as ivory or tortoiseshell or certain rare woods which are subject to Washington treaty rules is permitted on condition that they are presented alongside the necessary documentation.'

On top of this, three separate teams of judges adjudicate: the first watches the candidates at work in the kitchen but neither sees nor tastes the final product, another tastes blind and a third panel assesses only the visual aspect of the finished work, which is a table of around twenty pieces of such vastness and complexity that even Carême would have had to accord a grudging nod of respect.

For an affectionate and lingering look at the MOF competition, you can do no better than *Kings of Pastry*, the US documentary film that records the 2007 event. Over an almost unbearably tense hour and a half, we watch as three candidates prepare for, then take part in, the final. They are driven men, the strain visible as they refine the composition of their entries over and over again, folding molten sugar, designing wedding cake fillings, minutely shaping and decorating. The tension ratchets up, minute by minute, as three years or more of preparation come to a head. Jacquy Pfeiffer, the candidate the film follows most closely, is an anxious, sad-eyed man from Alsace living in San Francisco:

his domed wedding dessert is planned out on a whiteboard in minute detail, with different types of cross-hatching for *genoise* and mousse. Régis Lazard, one of the other candidates, is a veteran of disaster, having dropped his major sugarwork piece during the previous competition, and he has a haunted look as he retells it.

'It's over when that happens,' he says, unfocused eyes avoiding the camera, his lips narrowed to a thin, grim line. 'There's no way back.'

After this fairly heavy foreshadowing, the inevitable does of course happen and someone – thank god, not Lazard this time, but the third chef the filmmakers followed, Philippe Rigollot – has a devastating sugar catastrophe. He places his vast sculpture of a bride and groom on the worktop just fractionally too heavily and the whole edifice shatters with a sickening, brittle crash, shards of green and brown and white sugar scattering across the work surface and clattering onto the floor. As the devastation settles, there is a momentary weighty silence in the kitchen; a collective holding of breath. Then Rigollot walks silently to the window, where he stands for a few seconds, his back to the camera, before walking out, his retreating back hunched with emotion. A bevy of tricolour-collared MOFs then sweep up with discreet, funereal solemnity.

With encouragement, you will be relieved to hear, Rigollot rallies, making 'a sort of bird' out of molten sugar in extremis and at the very end (spoiler alert) he is the only one of the three featured contestants to win the coveted title. But the most tender, moving scenes of the film are the ones where those gnarled and forbidding gods of patisserie, the MOF jury, rally around him, hands on his shoulders and waist, whispering words of encouragement as he stands, eyes filling with tears in front of the devastated remains of his work, lamenting all those years of preparation and hope. At the end, the chairman of the jury, a craggy pâtissier named Philippe Urraca who has been a severe and unsmiling presence throughout, announces the successful candidates, his voice cracking with tearful emotion.

Kings of Pastry is a tense watch. Disaster never seems more than a hair's breadth or a misplaced tweezer away. It is hard not to see imminent catastrophe everywhere. At moments, though, the concentration in the room, the silent application of the pâtissiers, is so transcendent you can forget they are basically making a heron out of nougat.

'The Samurai,' says Urraca in an interview, 'is a good parallel.' The Samurai would not misuse Isomalt.

Cake, then, with apologies to Bill Shankly who would not approve at all, is not a matter of life and death: it's much more important than that.

I derive enormous satisfaction from the French honouring of cake, because cake is just as important to me. When my mother died and everything was messy and terrible and broken, I would self-medicate with perfect pastel fondant fancies from Bettys, cheap supermarket Swiss rolls and packets of ginger buns from Thomas the Baker. After the funeral, I stood in the corner at the wake in my smart black top talking to faces from my past (even the semioticist was there!) and intercepted every plate of fruit cake that went past. I am pretty sure Louis is mainly made of cake. Here in Paris, when I buy a cake I am, briefly, entirely at home.

'*Je voudrais une part de flan*,' I say, happily confident, then I add a daring, '*pas trop cuit, s'il vous plaît*,' so that I don't get one of the burnt, leathery ones.

My exhaustive survey of the 17th arrondissement's cakes points to one clear winner: the *délice café*.

My first *délice café* comes from my sister, who brings round a randomly selected box of cakes one evening before she returns to the UK, just as an act of kindness; one of many: however sad she is, her desire to look after others seems irrepressible. It doesn't look like much – Carême would not approve, it is just a rectangular layered coffee buttercream gateau, covered in fondant icing, without any hint of Welsh hermitage – but from the first bite, I am hooked. There is thick, grainy, golden brown fondant, an almost salty coffee buttercream and moist sponge. It's not a typical Parisian cake: it has an almost ersatz quality, like a far more delicious Mr Kipling. It's a fondant fancy in a Hermès headscarf and I rapidly become obsessed.

The *délice café* comes from Contini, which is not even a bakery. It is a Jewish *parvé* deli (that is, no dairy) round the corner on the Avenue Wagram and I become a regular there. It's more of a snack bar than a bakery, selling kosher hot dogs, sandwiches and sushi, and their small selection of cakes feels like something of an afterthought. It's not an afterthought for me, though: I check every day to see if there's a *délice café* (they rarely turn up more than once or twice a week) and on the happy days I see a row of fat brown rectangles, I feel a disproportionate surge of delight. A day with a *délice* is a good day, even if I am feeling lonely and hopeless and even if I have been queuing in the Post Office for twenty minutes when the counter just decides to shut. Everything can be made OK with coffee buttercream! It becomes almost superstitious.

My aspirant Frenchness mostly fails when it comes to food. I don't like cheese (this has been a major issue in Normandy) and my fealty to Picard frozen dinners speaks volumes for my culinary incompetence. I might like watching the lunatic commitment of French TV cooking shows, the hours deboning quail and shaping quenelles, but no part of me has any interest in doing those things (or even, mainly, eating those things). But patisserie I can do. I can demonstrate as much single-minded obsession as anyone when it comes to cake and, dammit, I will.

Le Viaduc de Millau

So this is how we live in Paris. Theo goes to Am Stram Gram and Olivier goes to La Défense, Louis plays with Charline and I buy cakes. We all go to the park. Summer – the smell of warm drains in the empty city, my favourite bakeries closed, clouds of dust rising from the paths of the Parc Monceau – shades into autumn, my sister starts university and I feel more alone than ever as I watch the *rentrée* play out in the streets around the house: harried parents escorting little kids with huge backpacks to the school gates. Soon there is the first bite of cold and the leaves start to turn, then to fall, in Monceau.

Nothing has been quite as I imagined it would be. I did not really believe I would have a love affair with Daniel Auteuil, or stalk across the Place Vendôme with a perfect chignon and patent heels like Catherine Deneuve, but I am not even a micron closer to becoming Kristen Scott Thomas: and I am apparently the anti-*Amélie* to the Parisian populace, spreading unease and irritation everywhere I go. Nothing dramatic has happened to me along the banks of the Seine, except Theo deciding to stand underneath the showers at Paris-Plage (the artificial beach installed each summer along the river) until he was soaking and we had to go home early. I haven't bought a single lipstick (though I do sometimes go and walk around the beautiful, perfumed aisles of Printemps Beauté, admiring them) and I have hardly been into a clothes shop: I have only bought two Petit Bateau T-shirts since we arrived. I sit in cafés quite often, it is true, but from the moment I arrive I stress about how and when to ask for the bill (Will the waiter ever come back or will I have to seek him out? Can I just leave the money on the table?).

We hardly ever go out. I no longer know which actor the French government has decreed should be in every film, because two hours seems impossibly long, so we never go to the cinema. A big adventure for me is a trip across the river to buy a handful of *macarons* at Pierre Hermé or to gawp at the ludicrously pretty windows of Ladurée. At weekends the four of us go to the organic market at Batignolles and jostle past the wheeled shopping trolleys and gimlet-eyed pensioners to queue up for €25 chickens or we take the boys out on the RER to the swimming pool in Neuilly, the posh suburb to the west of us (it is very chic and modern, all plate glass and tropical plants). The Palais de la Découverte is a dusty nineteenth-century disappointment, one forbidding Van de Graaff generator crackling in a dark back room full of wooden benches and Bunsen burners, but the Cité des Enfants, a sort of superior science museum miles away in the east of the city where parents are younger and hipper, is a success. Sometimes we go all the way – and it is a long way – to the *menagerie* at the Jardin des Plantes, where they have a donkey with dreadlocks (it's called the '*âne de* Poitou'). You can also usually observe Kiki the giant tortoise having noisy, horrifying sex there with one of his harem of smaller tortoises. Occasionally when we take an emergency taxi back from the Jardin des Plantes, I get the full tourist spectacle of the city as we drive along the flat, grey-brown breadth of the Seine, past Notre Dame, then across the bridge and through the Place de la Concorde, the gilt on the fountain glittering. I realize in late autumn that I have barely seen the Eiffel Tower in all these months. From time to time, we round a corner and the tip of it appears, comically familiar, but I haven't been up close so I decide to take Theo.

We go down one cold foggy morning in November, walking up to Étoile to take the métro to Bir-Hakeim, Theo crammed in his pushchair in last year's yellow oilcloth coat he is growing out of, quiet, thumb in his mouth and gross comfort blanket on his lap. We are early and there isn't that much of a queue: I only have time to refuse, politely, a couple of half-hearted offers of Eiffel Tower key rings from the men who circle the Champs de Mars, then we are in the lift, whizzing up to the second floor. I have to lift Theo up to see over the barriers, to see the mist starting to dissipate over the rooftops and spires, the Jardin du Luxembourg, the Senate and the gilt obelisk at the centre of the Place de la Concorde. He's getting heavy now; he's a little boy and not a baby.

'Look over that way: that's where our house is.'

It doesn't really feel like *our* house, I realize as I say it: it's just a place we live, for now. Paris is as aloof and intimidating as it ever was: I haven't learned the special handshake yet; I'm just rolling along the pavement like tumbleweed, collecting cakes. Theo, who is probably far more at home here than I am, doesn't much care to look for the house. He is more interested in the colourful carousel of wooden horses at the bottom of the tower, and the man next to it with a tempting bundle of helium balloons, cartoon characters and dolphins and flowers, bobbing around over his head. There's nothing specially impressive about the Eiffel Tower for him, no more so than the swings in Monceau or the trains in Batignolles, but at least I feel we've crossed it off the list.

Olivier enjoys all our outings. He is as he always is: cheerful, lively and game for anything. He throws the baby happily around in the swimming pool and the baby laughs and laughs, and he pushes Theo higher and higher on the swings, or lifts him up to get a better view of the crocodiles in the Jardin des Plantes, basking immobile in their shallow water, or tries to feed the goats receipts. I hover and worry and get embarrassed about doing things properly and fitting in, but Olivier doesn't have any of those anxieties: he makes me laugh and exasperates me and I can't manage without him; I am dependent on him, far more than I ever was in London, for practical things and for moral support. At the same time, a voice in the back of my head sometimes says, 'you wouldn't even *be* here if it weren't for him' and not in a good way.

We still haven't really met anyone. I see Jill a couple of times a week to flick through old *Heat* magazines while our children watch taped *Teletubbies*, and now and then we go and see Olivier's one friend from home who lives in Paris. He and his wife are bronzed and handsome and tall and I feel like a medieval serf in their presence. No one ever tells a joke and Olivier and his friend talk about business, while I am supposed to think of things to say to his wife, but end up staring dully, like the village idiot, at her lovely hair as she talks at me. The person I like best, I think, is the man with the wolfhound down the street. He is so small and the dog is so big and he just radiates pride in Wolfie (that *is* the dog's name); his eyes light up when Theo runs across to pet him.

In the evenings, Olivier and I eat our Picard frozen dinners on the sofa and catch up with developments on the Millau Viaduct.

The Norman Foster designed Viaduc de Millau, spanning the Tarn river and part of the Paris–Montpellier motorway, is the main story on the evening news for weeks. This engineering marvel is nearing completion and it is a repository of national pride, a superlative-exhausting heap of steel and concrete. For weeks – months, it seems – before its (grand, ceremonial, forty minutes of coverage) opening, the viaduct features in some form or another on the TV news on both principal channels, the commercial TF1 and the public FR2. One night there might be a report on the company who made the girders, while the next, it will be the likely fate of the roadside cafés at either end of the suspended marvel, or details of who would be working in the tollbooths when it opens in December. No aspect of its construction, economic rationale or social impact can be left unexamined and I know everything about it, more than I have ever known about a piece of civil engineering: length (2,460 metres), height (343 metres, taller than the Eiffel Tower), number of columns (7), cost (€400m) and even how long it is guaranteed for (120 years). Olivier is a structural engineer by training and even he has reached Peak Viaduct. Still we sit and watch, because watching the 8 p.m. news seems somehow essential. If I can't belong in any other way, at least I can watch what everyone else in the building is watching and by now I feel as invested in the viaduct as if I had built the damn thing myself.

Sometimes, to break up the routine, people come to visit us. My Scottish aunties come, with Jack and Brian who were in Rome with my mum when she died. They are jolly company, dandling the baby on their laps and exclaiming at his resemblance to this or that family member, filling the flat with the comforting sound of Glaswegians at rest, long spooling anecdotes and frequent pauses for cups of tea. The aunties look a lot like my mother and sometimes, when the light is right, I get a lunatic moment of hope when one of them walks across my field of vision.

My friend Kate comes for the weekend and promptly gets stuck in the lift, leaving me to shout phonetic instructions up the shaft for her to relay to the engineers as the concierge scowls at us. We eat cake, admire paintings and laugh and I ache when she leaves, because for a little while I felt like my old self, sarcastic and silly and alive to beauty.

My stepfather comes, often, travelling with two Sainsbury's bags stuffed with stacks of back copies of the *Guardian Weekend* magazine, Yorkshire Tea and Bettys cakes, and possibly something silly that has caught his eye in Lakeland. Folded into the sofa, a serious book on his knee, he asks a lot of questions: history, geography or sociology. He wants to know who our street is named for and which way the 17th arrondissement votes, whether I have been to the Guimet Museum and where is the best place to drink coffee in our neighbourhood. We walk the streets together as he assails me with gentle yet insistent questions and sit in bars as he observes the minutiae of local life with wide-eyed amused curiosity. I find it quite annoying.

'I don't know,' I say, over and over again, crossly. I feel shown up for my own lack of curiosity and interest in my surroundings. It's all very well Joe turning up here with a multipack of Walker's crisps every couple of months and trying to pique my interest in fascinating titbits of social geography he has gleaned from *Le Monde Diplomatique*, but he doesn't have to live here. He buys a book in the end, to fill in the gaps in my knowledge: it is called 'A historical and architectural itinerary of the 17th Arrondissement' and from the outside at least, it looks like the most boring book in the world, with a dull pink and grey cover, featuring an aerial shot of Paris leached of any of its usual beauty, reduced to a blocky mass of modern towers. Turning its densely unwelcoming pages, he regales me with stuffily told historical vignettes. The substance, though, is occasionally fascinating: I'm gripped by the bits about the repression of the Paris Commune, the revolutionary scratch government that formed following France's controversial surrender to Bismarck in the Franco-Prussian war in 1870. The book relates how the Communards of the Batignolles fought like cornered tigers during the desperate final days of resistance.

'The blockades at rues Legendre, Cardinet, des Dames, La Condamine and La Fourche were defended with the energy of despair. The combatant prisoners were immediately executed in the Parc Monceau, the Square des Batignolles or in front of the town hall and buried hastily in mass graves.'

The text is accompanied by early photographs of the Communards at Porte Maillot (the northernmost point of the arrondissement), dark figures and sandbags and piles of guns. It's another, unimagined side to my neighbourhood.

My father and stepmother visit too, renting an apartment in the Marais. They're delighted with the place, which is on the Rue de Sevigné just a short stroll from the Place des Vosges, opposite a fire station where handsome broad-shouldered firemen in tight blue T-shirts can be admired polishing, tinkering and having a sneaky cigarette between call-outs. In the morning, my father goes out for coffee in a nearby bar, buying bread and fresh fruit on his way back, then they wander around the beautiful, tourist-friendly Marais, looking for a nice little restaurant for lunch or popping into a museum, then returning to the apartment for a siesta before aperitifs and dinner. They collect Theo and take him off for the afternoon, buying him punnets of strawberries in the markets and playing with him in the playground on the Place des Vosges.

I listen to their happy stories of the firemen, the beautiful raspberry tarts and the long lunches stonily: they make me feel rather hostile. I am, I realize with a shock, sort of jealous.

I want *their* Paris experience, the picture-postcard Amélie Poulain perfect one, not mine with the dogshit-strewn streets and the angry locals and the obstructive administration. I could do a great job of staying in a nice Marais apartment for a week or two – I would be brilliant at that, finding cool cafés, buying good steaks for dinner and looking at stuffed boar heads in the Musée de la Chasse. I want my old Paris back; I want to be a tourist again.

I can't really work out which bits of our constrained life are grief, which are Paris and which are simply the inevitable result of looking after two children under three. I know it feels small to me, though: there are not enough people in our lives and not enough things happening.

I feel, too, I think, the stirrings of something like home-sickness.

It's stupid that I am surprised by it: some of the things I miss are so obvious. I might find his questions exasperating but I miss the constant, careful kind of love that my step-father dispenses from his Sainsbury's Bags for Life; the way that he sits down on the floor with the children with his knees tucked under him and brings out a tiny present; I miss his Russian and German dictionaries neatly bound in brown paper with hospital corners.

I miss my expansively adoring, funny father with his aura of magical, golden confidence, the enveloping sense that everything will be all right if you just stick with him, doll. I miss my gentle, solicitous stepmother and I miss my friends, their dry – and yes, British – humour and affection. I miss Maria, our downstairs neighbour from Newman Street, still working the old-school Italian restaurants of Soho in her eighties, secreting the night's takings in her zip-up boot at the end of her shift to take to the bank. I miss lazy afternoons in the cat-hair-choked atmosphere of her flat, curtains drawn against the sun, listening to stories of sixties Soho, gangsters and nights at the Golden Nugget casino. I miss Gino and Eleanor from the café around the corner on Goodge Street, who cuddled Theo and gave me offcuts of cake.

But I miss the place as much as the people. It's almost unbearable at times. Absence brings home to me just how deeply I threw in my lot with London, how the sticky pavements of Soho and the alleyways of Fitzrovia, the soaring vault and soft light of the Great Court of the British Museum where Theo learned to walk, had become home. I miss being in the places where my mother had seen me happy, at last, where she and my father had raced, half in jest, half in deadly earnest, to my bedside in the crumbling brick and lino of University College Hospital, both desperate to see their first grandchild. I miss the dark, secretive corners of Liberty's upper floors and Marks & Spencer basement food hall on Oxford Street, where the motherly cashiers chat and smile at my babies as I buy biscuits. I miss the tiny, dirty brown mice, busy and surprising along the Central Line rails.

I miss the smells of London too, and think about them often. Sometimes when I lie in bed in the evening and sleep is elusive, I take an olfactory tour in my memory from our old London flat, choosing a route and a time of year. I might decide to think of the deep blue of a summer night and the metallic tang of the Post Office car park, the sickly coconut and cumin and incense of the Hare Krishna centre curries, lager and sweat and aftershave in Soho Square and Frith Street, then the battle of coffee grounds and Thai food down by Bar Italia. I could carry on when I needed: down through the Peking Duck and durian smells of Chinatown, to pop-corn and hamburger at Leicester Square, then a big waft of diesel as you hit Trafalgar Square and the Strand, and finally down to the faint brine of the Thames. Other times I head east in my imagination to Bloomsbury in late autumn, con-juring up the particular smell of London on a sharp frosty day, of petrol and coffee and leaf mulch, and something indefinable and smoky and exciting that reminds me of childhood. These fits of homesickness are oddly pleasurable: it's nice to know I can still feel something and on some level, this feels right. I'm in this murky hinterland of grief and it makes me an outsider; I feel unreachable. There is an obscure comfort in having the external match the internal.

On my thirtieth birthday, we do go out, for once. My sister, who has come over to visit with a lemon sponge in a tin from her father, babysits and Olivier takes me to the Michelin three-star restaurant just over the road. It is dark and intimidating, with thick carpets, shelves full of odd bibelots and a general air of granny's parlour. A group of bankers on the next table are talking incredibly loudly about office politics. Everything on the menu is so expensive I feel slightly faint.

A frosty waiter brings us an *amuse bouche*: it is a single sea urchin on a large white plate, darkly quivering, cold and gelatinous. Just as I am wondering if I can possibly hide it somewhere, Olivier puts down his spoon.

'We don't have to stay, you know,' he says.

'What? We've already ordered!'

'I mean in Paris. We don't have to stay here. It's not, you know, obligatory or anything. We could go back to London.'

I make a face. 'Yes, but . . .'

He cuts me off. 'Just think about it. You're still on maternity leave aren't you?'

'Yes, theoretically.'

'And I could easily get a job.' This is true. I have never known someone so good at getting jobs. Olivier goes to job interviews for fun, just to keep his hand in.

'But we can't just give up!' I'm horrified by this suggestion. 'We moved here, properly. You don't just give up after a few months because everything is too hard.'

The truth of this hits me – everything *is* too hard. But that's grief, surely? Anywhere would feel this shitty. And what kind of loser just leaves *Paris*? You aren't supposed to come here and be instantly filled with bliss and well-being. The whole point of a city like Paris is that you have to work at it. I am conscious I have not really been working at anything.

'We're allowed to have made a mistake, you know.'

'Hmm. I don't know.'

The waiter returns and removes my uneaten urchin with funereal solemnity. I crumble my bread abstractedly and listen to the details of Toby and Josh's ingenious swap deal on the next table.

It can't be a mistake. We are supposed to be here; this was the plan. I dismiss the idea out of hand and turn to my starter, which is some kind of scallop dish. Nearly everything on my plate is white, thin translucent discs of scallop, some kind of foamy sauce, an unidentified white length of vegetable matter (possibly salsify). It's eery, a sort of ghost dish. Olivier has *foie gras*, of course, and as he spreads some on an impossibly thin piece of toast, he waves it admonishingly in my direction.

'You should think about it. Because I can't decide this time. I pushed you into moving here; what we do next has to be your decision.'

As birthday announcements go – I'm taking you to Venice, here are a pair of Louboutins – I do not rate this one highly, but thankfully the dessert is rather lovely (it's a moussey thing with coconut and lime), and the rest of the evening passes without incident.

But now the thought is planted, I can't help but wonder. Could we possibly leave?

« 12 »

La Loi Veil

Along with my patisserie habit, I am also developing something of a pharmacy problem. There are thousands of pharmacies to choose from: it seems as if every second shop in Paris is a pharmacy, their green crosses flashing like a street corner emergency service, their windows full of seasonal urgings and warnings. I love Parisian pharmacies, and for years I have been gripped by the life cycle of their window displays, which detail all the seasonal afflictions that can befall you. In the first sunny days of April the paramilitary weaponry of anti-cellulite treatments and hayfever remedies comes out; in July there is the holiday medicine chest of Immodium, after-sun and insect repellent; September brings the 'back to school' vitamins; then winter throat pastilles and cold and flu remedies. In-between times, there are urgings to consider the benefits of magnesium, or of fish oils, of mysterious skin vitamins or treatments for the totally fictitious French affliction that is *'jambes lourdes'*, heavy legs.

'My legs!' I tease Olivier sometimes, slumping towards him Quasimodo-like. 'They are SO HEAVY.'

'It's a real thing,' he maintains, flatly. 'Heavy legs is a genuine medical condition.'

'It really isn't though, is it? It's absolute nonsense. Who do you know who has heavy legs?'

'Lots of people! Are you really telling me British people don't get heavy legs?'

'No, because they aren't real.'

I like the pharmacies because they are designed to look after you and little else in Paris is. I feel starved of kindness here, which is stupid of me; you don't move to a capital city to bathe in the milk of human kindness. If I wanted solicitous ladies who probably know at least one member of my family clucking over my babies in the street, I should have stayed in York. The acts of kindness I do find in Paris are mainly institutional. The state and the city are a munificent presence in daily life in the capital: the provision of childcare, transport and leisure are a matter of civic pride and considered a mark of civilization. It's not all functional either. I admire the activities which the city lays on in summer for residents: Paris-Plage, the artificial beach on the riverside which has spawned imitators across Europe; free cinema screenings; thoughtful, creative programmes of activities for children who aren't able to go on holiday.

But perhaps the most striking arena for this state-sponsored 'kindness' is healthcare. You will never want for a doctor in France, or for an X-ray, or a prescription. Indeed, I discover, you can envelop yourself in the delicious balm of solicitousness, that feeling that someone cares, simply by walking into a pharmacy.

I start to do this more and more often, for the children's various minor ailments or my own. Parisian pharmacists,

I discover, enjoy hearing your lengthy description of your symptoms. Perhaps it is more accurate to say that they enjoy the prospect of selling you five separate products for a modest cough, but certainly they will treat them with the utmost seriousness. They will ask you not one but four or five searching questions before pulling a bespoke selection of products off the shelves, complete with instructions and tips for use. It's extraordinarily gratifying, and soon our bathroom is full of superior multivitamins and professional-looking analgesics, antiseptic sprays and herbal supplements that promise inner tranquillity.

My habit really kicks in, however, when I hurt my knee. In October, after getting up from the floor of Theo's bedroom slightly awkwardly, my knee finally gives up after years of twinges and minor niggles, swelling grotesquely and painfully to the size of a football. My first port of call is, of course, the pharmacy up the street. There, after an initially frosty greeting, I am enveloped in a cloud of concern once I show off my hugely swollen leg. A chair is produced. The head pharmacist is summoned from the back room and a small colloquy gathers around my right leg, earnestly discussing its puffy, regrettable appearance. There is talk of ice and anti-inflammatories, of poultices and possible infection.

'Was there a fall, an accident?'

'No. Possibly a twisting movement. I heard a crunching noise.'

'Hmm. You must go to the doctor.'

'Yes, I know. I'm going on Monday. But what can I do before that? I can't walk on it. I have two small children.'

'Ah, yes. That is very trying.' Some nodding. More conferring. 'We will give you some Diclofenac. Normally, it is only available on prescription, but in the circumstances . . . And a support. We must find the right one.'

An assistant goes to the drawers and comes back with a selection of foully unattractive beige support garments, which they hold up against me, lips pursed and eyes narrowed in appraisal.

Finally, a consensus is reached on a sort of angry-looking black elastic sausage; a pile of boxed drugs are placed upon the counter and I am ready to go, slowly, with orders to keep my leg elevated, to apply ice, to eat before taking my pills, to be sure to go straight to the doctor on Monday morning. Even though my knee still hurts, I feel quite emotional: they were so nice to me! It is all I can do to resist the temptation to hide my bag of drugs, limp up the street and start again in the next pharmacy.

The sweeping magnanimity of French healthcare is often portrayed as a black hole of needy, budget-busting enormity ('*Le trou de la sécu*,' people say, 'The Hole', as if a giant financial mantrap were waiting to engulf the greedy children of the dependency culture). The vast French health budget operates with a sort of blank-faced, state-sponsored kindness. 'You matter,' it says. 'Your elbow hurts? We will send you for an MRI scan at terrifying expense. Your legs feel oddly heavy? Your doctor will send you to an approved thalassotherapy centre, where kindly young men in lab coats will make you walk in line through thigh-high baths of cold water for half an hour every morning for a week with your fellow sufferers, in the manner of racehorses with fet-lock strain.' You may have to close your eyes to some surface . . . well, disagreeableness in the process. Your doctor is likely to have strong views, for instance, on your weight; and as a non-French citizen, trying to obtain the cherished *carte Vitale* (social security registration) that opens all these magical doors is likely to leave you with psychological scars that no amount of thalassotherapy can erase. But persist. The El Dorado of a health-care system where no cost-benefit analysis applies, where no one has heard of NICE guidelines or of quality of life units, is but another eighty pages of forms and a trip to a Stalinist office in Cergy-Pontoise away.

When I do go to the doctor, my elephant knee earns me a gratifying further amount of professional solicitude and state-sponsored munificence: the doctor looks pleasingly concerned and orders me a very swift MRI scan. After she has studied the results, I get a prescription for a series of twenty-four '*rééducation*' physio sessions, each an hour long, to be cashed in at the physio of my choice (this is apparently the kind of thing Parisians actually have: a preferred physio-therapist). I find one in the phone book that seems to be relatively close, call up tentatively, and make an appoint-ment.

Christian, the physiotherapist, operates out of a sweaty basement behind the Avenue des Ternes, about ten minutes to the west of our apartment near the Arc de Triomphe. His studio is equipped with a few Swiss balls, a feeble-looking exercise bike and a couple of benches where he hooks you up to electrodes or makes you lift medicine balls. I go to the basement twice a week for remedial quadriceps strengthening and I quite enjoy it: apart from anything else, I get to talk to human beings to whom I am not related, which is a rarity. It is a cheery place. The other clients are stripped of their carapace of Parisian elegance and seem vulnerable and human in baggy T-shirts and tracksuit bottoms: it feels very normal, somehow. We do our exercises companionably to the accompaniment of middle-of-the-road pop from Europe 1 and sometimes people even chat, about the weather or the TV or local gossip. It's a weak kind of camaraderie, but I'm so grateful for it.

Christian the physio, in particular, is good fun. He tells jokes and teases his clients and asks questions: how did I end up in Paris? What is London like? As he prods and examines and chivvies me, it is impossible not to feel a little special. I find myself thinking how easy it would be to become the kind of elderly lady who always has an ailment or two on the go, a worrying cough, an indefinable weakness, to ensure I get enough of that feeling of concern, the sense that my problems merit attention. Perhaps I might develop Munchausen's syndrome? I can sort of see, now, the appeal of Munchausen's.

In the end I don't have to do anything of the sort for attention, because something else entirely unexpected happens.

Initially when I go off cake, I assume it's just a post-Christmas thing: I feel puffy and bloated too after weeks of overeating. I can't get excited about my beloved *délice café*, but I have been eating two of them a week for months, so perhaps I just need a change. It's time for the *galette des rois,* anyway, the puff pastry and frangipane Epiphany cake. Theo picks a 'Finding Nemo' themed one from the bakery round the corner, fixating on the garish crown. The *galette* is such a nice idea and I enjoy the feeling of belonging the traditions engender (the youngest hides under the table and calls out who should get each slice, then whoever gets the *fève,* in our case a tiny Nemo figurine, in their slice is the king or queen for the day), but when it comes to eating my slice I'm seized with nausea.

The queasiness continues: I can't face *flan* and I don't know what to have for breakfast: none of my usual *pains au chocolat* or Paul chocolate brioches tempt me in the slightest. I want toast and Marmite and later in the afternoons, I find myself craving cheese and onion crisps (Jill could probably help me out). Realization dawns improbably slowly, it seems so unlikely and so unfair, but one evening I am moaning about feeling sick and Olivier turns to me with a frown in the kitchen, where he is washing up, and asks:

'You couldn't be pregnant, could you?'

'No,' I say, decidedly, even though technically, I absolutely could be. We do still have sex, despite combining several of the top ten stressful life events in one convenient annual subscription package, despite the neighbours, despite everything. We aren't in a great place, but unhappy sex is not necessarily bad sex and we cling to one another, grateful for the solace of a warm body. More often than I realize, I think, we have sleepy, barely conscious, sex, a reflexive reaching out for comfort.

I haven't been taking the Pill either, partly because I am still breastfeeding and partly because it was a protracted business conceiving both boys. I can't bring myself to believe I could get pregnant accidentally. The thought of visiting a Parisian gynaecologist has put me off too – abstinence (forever if necessary) seems preferable, but then we fall into bed and have more half-dressed, half-asleep sex and the dangerous cycle continues.

I think about all this as I peel a carrot for Theo and I find I have to revise my initial assessment.

'Well, god, I *hope* I'm not.'

I need to check though, now the spectre has been raised, so on my way to see Christian the physiotherapist the next morning, I try and buy a pregnancy test. You can't buy one in Monoprix, of course; I imagine the bristling indignation of a thousand French pharmacists at the very idea: so irresponsible! Nor is there any such thing as Boots or a Duane Reade in Paris, a big impersonal drugstore where I can pluck a test off the shelf and take it to the till. This is the unwelcome flipside of all that pharmacy solicitude I so enjoy. I walk around the back streets behind the Avenue des Ternes, looking for a pharmacy which is empty, with female assistants who don't look too dragon-like, and when I do find one, I have to face a set of questions about what kind of test I want: early response? Digital? Multipack? I think wistfully of the fistfuls of cheap generic tests I used to buy in Boots when I was trying to get pregnant the first time, to total indifference from the teenage boys on the till.

'Just . . . a normal one?'

I ball up the plastic bag and stuff it into the bottom of my handbag.

My mind drifts back to the test as I lift a medicine ball between my knees and pedal desultorily on the stationary bike. I can't be pregnant. Well, I can, but I really, really don't want to be. I feel as if I have just had a baby; my body still looks as if I have too, hollowed-out and weak and sagging. It has been easier, in some ways, this second time around with Louis: nothing terrifies you like it does the first time and knowing that everything passes, eventually, makes me more relaxed. But reconciling the demands of both boys is impossible and I miss my mum, selfishly, in the trenches of babyhood. I can't cry down the phone to her or hand over an inconsolable infant to be rocked into submission or share a laugh at the impossibility of its irrational demands. Less selfishly, it makes me sad when I think of the intense pleasure she took from Theo. Nothing hurts me more immediately than the thought of her not knowing the boys and them growing up without knowing her: it feels unfair on the most basic level. This is the simplest, clearest grief I feel. I can't imagine plunging back into that again.

On my way to collect Theo from Am Stram Gram I stop off in an empty *café-tabac* I have never tried before, right by the railway bridge. I sit at the bar and order a coffee, then head down to the basement loo, which is brown-tiled and dark and smells of bleach. I pee on the stick then I put the lid back on the test and put it into my handbag and come back up to my stool at the bar. The radio is playing, some kind of debate on a doctors' strike. I drink my coffee then I square my shoulders, sigh and open my handbag.

I am totally pregnant. There is no room for ambiguity at all and I have done enough bloody tests to know: both lines are bright blue.

'Oh, *fuck*.'

I say this out loud (though not until I leave the bar), but as I say it, I feel ambivalent. I have taken so many tests in the past few years hoping for this exact result that I find it very hard to get my brain to perceive it as a wholly bad thing. Pregnant! This is supposed to be a cause for celebration, but suddenly it . . . isn't.

I stand on the railway bridge at Boulevard Pereire, looking down at the weed-choked rails, and I call my friend Kate.

'Hi, Em!' I imagine her sitting at her desk in the National Portrait Gallery. Kate had been my other salvation when Theo was tiny, drinking endless cups of tea with me in the gallery's basement café as Theo spun in circles on the floor, learning how to crawl. I wish I were there now.

'Oh god, Kate, I'm pregnant.'

'Oh!'

'Clever, eh?'

'Poor you,' she says, gently. She always knows what to say. 'That must be terribly confusing.'

I laugh, hysterically. 'What am I going to do? If I do have it, can I give it to you? You could keep it in a box under your desk.'

'That sounds lovely. I would love one of your beautiful velvety babies to play with.'

We chat on for a few minutes; I keep her talking. Her voice is such a comfort and such a wrench at the same time: when I hang up I feel further from home than ever. I collect Theo, buy a baguette, take the boys to the Parc Monceau, which is chilly in the late afternoon wintry dusk, bring them home, bath and feed them. When Olivier gets home everything is, for once, relatively calm. Things aren't impossible with the boys at the moment, I recognize that. Theo is hilarious, constantly spinning yarns, waving his favourite plush snake (Snake Snake) at people in the street, and spending fifteen minutes minutely examining a single bollard. The baby is jolly, too. He mainly sleeps through the night now and since he has learned to crawl and can pull himself up to a standing position, he hardly ever cries: the greater his mobility, the lesser his frustration. He cruises around the furniture, sticking his long fingers in everything: papers, Theo's cherished trains or the cockroach-infested kitchen cupboards. They are still exhausting, but there's a glimmer of something better around the corner.

After we've read Theo a story I corner Olivier as he's taking off his work clothes and putting his pyjamas on.

'So, yeah.' I am conscious of how very different this announcement will be to the two previous times. 'I *am* pregnant.'

He turns round to face me, features flattened with shock. '*Eh, merde.*'

'Yup.' I don't know what else to say. I feel perversely excited even though I know it's terrible news really. I follow him as he heads to the kitchen and uncorks a half-drunk bottle of wine. He waggles it in my direction, but I shake my head.

'So what now?'

'I don't know. I really don't know. See the doctor, I suppose?'

'Yes. I'll stay home from work and we'll call in the morning. Shit.'

We watch the Millau Viaduct news in uneasy silence, then later we lie side by side in bed, still silent, not touching, arms crossed like carved medieval tomb figures, as the plumbing cranks and groans around us. I don't know what to say, because I don't know what to think.

It's not difficult to get an appointment to see a GP in Paris – there are so many of them – so I manage to get in to see the stern lady round the corner who dealt with my knee by late afternoon the next day. The four of us head down there in a dishevelled procession, Theo tearing up and down the dark, silent corridor that serves as a waiting room, telling us a long story about weasels and using the door stop as a prop, Louis thrashing furiously against Olivier's chest, desperate to be free. Thankfully, there is no one else waiting and the doctor gets to us quickly, holding the door open to let us through, with an odd expression that seems to mix frank disapproval and a faint shadow of compassion. She has lovely blonde hair set in a firm wave and she is wearing a very desirable silk blouse. I vow to keep Theo far away from her.

The doctor settles down behind her desk (vast, dark wood) and raises an interrogative eyebrow.

'So . . . I am pregnant. Again. And I don't know if I can proceed with the pregnancy'.

'I see.' She takes a quick note. 'So your youngest is how old?'

'Eight months.' Theo has become fascinated with a sort of liquid egg-timer device on her desk. I take hold of his wrist as a precaution and he fights back against me cheerfully, while reaching round with the other hand to see if he can grab it that way.

The doctor grimaces ever so slightly. 'Yes, that is quite young. So you wish to consider an *IVG*?' IVG is *interruption volontaire de grossesse*. An abortion. I don't even know how pregnant I am and if it will even be possible, but we've agreed we need to start down this path as soon as we can. We can always change our minds. Or rather, make up our minds. It's not as if we know what we want anyway.

'Yes.'

'OK, well, first you need to get a dating scan to establish how far advanced the pregnancy is.' She starts writing out a prescription on a white pad. 'I'll put *grossesse non désirée*' – unwanted pregnancy – 'so they know.'

Theo breaks free from my arms and makes another grab for the timer, but the doctor is too quick for him. '*Non!*' she says smartly, shutting the timer in her desk drawer.

'The hardest thing is finding a clinic which can do the procedure within the time. You'll need to ring around. Here.' She extracts a photocopied sheet from another drawer and hands it over to me. I hand over my €30 in exchange, round up Theo, who is examining something on the floor, and the four of us exit in chaotic fashion, dithering on the threshold to check for forgotten trains and coats.

'I'm not sure she thinks we should even have *these* children,' Olivier says, pulling a face.

It's thirty years this month since the Loi Veil, which legalized abortion in France, became law. I know this because it is in the news: there have been marches and magazine articles, philosophical debates on its impact, interviews with Simone Veil, magnificent, humane, and utterly impressive.

'I would like to share with you a woman's conviction,' says Veil in clips they show on the news of the violently contested debate in the Assembly, after months of personal attacks and even death threats. She stands, chignon perfect, poker-straight, both hands placed flat on the lectern in front of her, measured, convincing and deadly serious. 'No woman resorts to an abortion lightly.' I wonder if I am about to find out.

« 13 »

Il est cinq heures, Paris s'éveille

So now I have two decisions to make, fast. Firstly, will we stay in Paris or will we go back to London? Secondly, am I going to have this baby? I have had more serene months.

There is a certain administrative momentum to the business of terminating a pregnancy in Paris. I go along with it, at least bodily, without much questioning my own motives, drifting along in the medico-administrative slipstream. First, there is the dating scan.

I go alone one morning. The Centre d'Imagerie Médicale is located in an anonymous back street behind Saint-Lazare, a fifteen-minute walk away. A *porte cochère* in a classic Haussmann block gives way to smoked-glass doors and a surprisingly stylish, low-lit waiting room filled with home decor magazines. I wait my turn, looking at seaside hotels in Brittany, Vosges linens and coir matting.

After ten minutes of instructive guidance on how to decorate my Normandy farmhouse, a friendly middle-aged man in a white coat, with a halo of grey curls, opens the waiting-room door, calls my name and beckons me to follow him, which I do, into a large, modern room full of screens and consoles. I take off my shoes and lie down on the bed, then pull up my top and push down my trousers as instructed, as the technician fiddles with the equipment. I feel more awkward than I did at the doctor's, somehow: all this fuss to deal with my contraceptive idiocy.

'Right!' he says, advancing towards me on his wheeled chair with the ultrasound wand, and dimming the lights with a remote control. Then he flicks on a large television screen I had not noticed right in front of me, angled in my eye line above the bed. A fizz of shock hits me in the solar plexus: am I going to have to watch? In England, even for my much wanted pregnancies, the technicians start off with the screen towards them, turning it around only once they have established all is well.

The familiar white fuzz and dark oval appear on screen as the technician moves the wand across my belly with practised speed. I watch, gripped and uneasy.

'Ah yes, here we are,' he says cheerily, picking up a laser pointer and aiming it towards the screen. There, quite clearly visible, quite clearly identifiable, is a foetus. His red dot picks out the outsized head and tiny limb buds. Lying in the darkness, I watch the fabulous, stubborn persistence of life. Stupid, dumb miracle.

'Your baby seems fine!' says the technician, who either has not read or does not care about the GP's note on this not being a 'desired pregnancy'. He spends a few minutes in silent scrutiny, drawing diagonal lines across the screen, measuring.

'You are approximately ten weeks pregnant,' he adds, after a short pause.

Ten weeks. I think back, calculating quickly in my head. That would take us more or less back to my thirtieth birthday and our awkward 'shall we leave' dinner at Michel Rostang, the sea urchin *amuse bouche* and the braying bankers. Some birthday present this is.

Next, eyes still fixed on the tiny form on the screen, I wonder how long I have left to get an abortion: two weeks? Four? I need to check. It feels very odd to be plotting like this while looking at the familiar shape of a baby on the screen.

'Fine,' says the technician, with an air of finality. 'We've finished. Ah! I almost forgot.'

He leans back over to his computer keyboard and flicks a switch, then wheels himself back over to my stomach, putting the wand back on my uncomfortably full bladder.

The urgent, galloping tattoo of a foetal heartbeat fills the room. *Ratata-ratata.*

'There!' he says happily, with a conjuror's flourish. We both listen, for a minute, in silence. Then he leaves, with instructions to get dressed and to go back to the waiting room while he types up his report.

Afterwards, report in a brown envelope in my hand, I walk back up the great, grey Boulevard Malesherbes, dropping mechanically into the Eric Kayser bakery. It's one of my favourites: warm and bright, with a comforting smell of yeast and butter and specialities from the east of France: *kouglof* and brioches and fat brown pretzels. The windows are still full of *galette des rois* in mid-January. I still go into bakeries: my brain doesn't remember that my stomach can't tolerate cake at the moment.

My phone rings: Olivier.

'Well?'

'I'm ten weeks. And either there was a mix-up or I had some kind of pro-life sadist, because I had to watch. And listen to the heartbeat.'

A salesgirl moves in front of me, eyebrows raised.

'Fuck. Was that . . . how are you?'

'Hmm.' I point at a pretzel, my face a pantomime of apology. The girl at the counter scowls at me – this is a major breach of the bakery social contract, but these are extreme circumstances so I scowl back unrepentantly, which seems to do the trick.

'Do you need me to come back?'

'God, no. I'm fine.' I don't really, know how I am, but there's no urgency. I walk slowly home, ripping off small pieces of my pretzel, which is perfectly salty and bland. My route takes me along the railings of the Parc Monceau and I peer in as I pass. It's bitterly cold and windy and only a few hardy, well-wrapped toddlers are staggering around the sandpit, watched from the benches by Ivorian nannies (I have learned that all the local nannies come from the Ivory Coast, for some reason. It's a closed shop) muffled against the cold.

I can't really have an abortion now, can I? Can you really hear a heartbeat and see an ultrasound and still have an abortion? I wonder if this absolves me from making a decision. But how could we possibly cope with three children? Could we stay here, even if we want to?

I just don't know. I don't know what to do about staying

or going and I certainly don't know what to do about being pregnant. So for a few days, I just shelve it: I eat crisps and look after the boys and call Kate now and then for a consolatory chat.

Olivier's position on the pregnancy seems to be the same as his position on moving: it's up to me. He is calling round clinics and looking for an opening (which is proving almost as tricky as finding a *crèche* spot) and I'm very grateful for his help – without him, I'd probably just have the baby so I don't have to talk to Parisian administrators on the telephone – but he is emphatic the decision is mine. This is very clear in his mind. I know it's meant to be considerate and thoughtful, but it feels like a monstrous imposition and I resent it. How can this all be down to me? I seethe, irrationally, and we don't really talk.

Instead, I talk to Christian the physio. I tell him, ostensibly in case it matters for Swiss ball and electrode reasons, but really because I want to confide in someone.

'I'm pregnant.'

'Congratul . . . or not?' Christian adjusts his expression on seeing mine.

'God, I don't know.' It's a relief just to say it to someone else. 'My kids are tiny. It wasn't planned. I just don't know if we can manage. I don't even know if I want it.'

'Huh. Tricky.'

He doesn't say much more than that, but he treats me normally, hooking me up to his electrodes, and it's just nice to talk to someone who doesn't care very much, but who finds me reasonably congenial company for an hour.

Finally, Olivier makes a breakthrough. I get a call as I am walking around Monoprix.

'Right, I've got one. It's in the middle of nowhere, but they can fit us in. We've got to go over there tomorrow for a pre-appointment. OK?'

'OK.' After I hang up, I test my feelings in my head. Am I disappointed he's found a clinic? I don't know. I don't feel anything definitive.

In the morning, Olivier rings in sick (again) and we trek all the way across Paris to the Institut Montsouris. It's in the 14th arrondissement, on the southern border of the *périphérique*, another part of the city I never imagined visiting. We take a long métro ride (via Châtelet, for all roads in Paris pass through Châtelet), then walk until we arrive at a plate-glass cube of great, shiny modernity.

After a lot of paper-filling farce, we are directed towards a waiting room with a sign reading 'Orthogenics', which sounds space age, but it's a normal hospital waiting room, with magazines and unhealthy-looking pot plants and anxious-looking people. I am the oldest person there by a good ten years: the room is full of teenagers. No one looks up, or speaks: it feels a little as if we are all in detention after some misdemeanour, waiting to go into the headmaster's office for a proper telling-off.

The doctor is appropriately headmaster-like: he's a severe gentleman in his sixties who barks a few questions in my direction, rolling his eyes at my stammered explanations of how the pregnancy came about. He seems genuinely angry and I don't blame him, I'm a waste of his time and resources, someone who really should know better. He gives me a brusque internal examination then snaps off his gloves.

'Yes, you're pregnant. So you are sure you wish to proceed with the termination?'

'Yes.' No. Maybe.

'Then I can confirm your appointment for two weeks from today. The procedure will be under general anaesthetic, so you need to see the anaesthetist before the procedure: you can make an appointment downstairs. I'm giving you a prescription for a drug you need to take six hours before the procedure to soften the cervix. All the information you need is on this sheet.'

He thrusts a succinct photocopy at me, and we leave, further chastened.

When I go back to see the anaesthetist, he notes my blood group, height and weight, then casts a disdainful eye at my stomach, which is struggling to withstand another assault on its already weakened musculature.

'You need to lose some weight.'

He has just weighed me and I weigh just over eight and a half stone. My jaw sags open uselessly as he fiddles with a blood pressure cuff. I am totally lost for a comeback. Again. I ride back on the métro grinding my teeth in fury.

The days pass and I still have no idea what I am going to do.

'Sometimes,' says Christian the physio, as I half-heartedly try to raise my leg as he presses down on it, 'these things just happen. Not every pregnancy works out. When my wife was pregnant with our third child, they thought there was a genetic abnormality and she would have to have an abortion.'

'What happened?'

'It was fine in the end.'

'Well, that's good.' (And totally unhelpful, I think, uncharitably.)

'What does your husband think?'

I make a face. 'We're not talking about it. I mean, he'd go along with it if I really, really wanted to have the baby but it's not what he had in mind.'

'No, I can imagine.'

'It's not really what I had in mind either.'

My mind is running along two parallel courses: one where I have a new baby six months from now and one where I don't, and they both seem equally plausible. Early pregnancy is so theoretical anyway – even seeing the scan hasn't made it that much more real. There's nothing to see and I don't feel sick any more: sometimes it feels like I must have dreamt the whole thing.

When I'm not thinking about the pregnancy, I'm thinking about whether we should stay in Paris. I have emailed my London employers just in case, to tell them I might return after my maternity leave, but I don't really want to go back. I don't know how admirable my motives are: mainly I think it would be humiliating to have to admit we've failed at Paris and I don't know how my crumbling self-image could withstand that. Kristin Scott Thomas and Jane Birkin didn't just give up, dammit. I project forward, imagine the conversations I would have to have with friends and colleagues and it just feels embarrassing. It's also sort of existential: if I'm not destined to be Parisian after fifteen years of believing that, who actually *am* I?

There are some persuasive elements on the other side of the equation, though. The boys could go back to Theo's lovely, kind, laidback nursery. I could earn proper money again. We would be closer to my family, my father and stepmother, my sister, my stepfather, all the people I miss. More even than all of those, I allow myself to imagine how *easy* everything would be: utilities companies and shops and ordering a drink. I think, guiltily, how lovely it would be to drink a proper cup of tea. I have faithfully stuck to coffee here, because the Lipton Yellow/lukewarm water/ UHT milk is worse than no tea at all and because I don't want to be a British cliché, but queasy and pregnant and repelled by caffeine, I'm left with no acceptable hot beverage options at all. I find myself imagining sponge cakes: fat, unattractive slabs of Victoria sponge and coffee and walnut, sandwiched with buttercream. I think about Marks & Spencer, frequently.

Trivial and important arguments chase around my head as the days tick by until Olivier and I can't avoid talking any more; it is two days before my appointment, and we sit, uncomfortably, on the sofa together. Olivier breaks the silence first.

'I can't decide for you.'

'Yeah, you've said that a few times already.' The pressure of the hard deadline I am facing is making me mechanically hostile at the moment; I'm seething with resentment.

'You know that I'm totally fine about us having another baby,' he says. 'I really, truly, am.'

I do believe him. He has a bit of that magic confidence my father has – the belief that he'll get to where he needs to be, even if the route turns out to be more circuitous than expected – and he's also an instinctive father. He doesn't question his own judgement or feelings. He does the best he can for our boys and he loves them: this is his job and he does it perfectly.

'But if we have the baby we won't be able to live in Paris any more and we wouldn't be able to move back to London. We can't afford it. We'll have to move out of the city to somewhere like Cergy Pontoise.'

Cergy Pontoise is one of those *zones pavillonnaires* the French build so many of. A vision of it comes into my mind with awful clarity: executive bungalows in a muddy brownfield site, a ten-minute drive to the nearest hypermarché and school drop-offs in a sensible family saloon car. It's the antithesis of my Paris dreams. If I am lonely here, imagine life in small town Cergy, six RER stops from the city. I can just picture the isolation, the awful quiet of weekday afternoons with a napping baby in a suburban estate, and it terrifies me. I know with absolute clarity that I will go mad, truly mad if I do this without sleep, without company, splitting my time and attention between three children under four.

My pleasant delusion, the happy vision of another pregnancy and another baby, fractures like crazy-paving. There isn't actually any option, or any decision to take: I can't possibly cope. If I can't imagine making the sacrifice of living out in the suburbs for this baby, how could I possibly cope with all the other compromises, large and tiny, that will come with another child? I have no support, no mother, no reserves of grit or composure and no belief that everything will be OK. I need to cling to the shreds of adult life I am painfully reassembling, not throw them all away with a baby I couldn't care for. What a stupid idea this was, how stupid I am. I feel sick at my own inadequacy, but at least I know what I have to do now.

'We don't have to have this conversation,' I say. 'It's fine, I'm doing it.'

So the next evening we watch the 8 p.m. news as usual and eat our Picard dinner as usual and at bedtime I have a shower with the special anti-bacterial soap I have been instructed to use. Then I take the first of the cervix-softening pills and it is really definitive; there is no going back now. I go to bed and fall asleep almost instantly.

The alarm goes at four and I get up and take the second pill, then I head out alone into the dark. Olivier has to stay behind with the boys, but I am happier on my own anyway.

The Boulevard de Courcelles is dim and deserted under the orange street lamps and I ride a succession of métros with the night shift workers and early morning cleaners, my mind soft and empty. Jacques Dutronc's '*Il est cinq heures, Paris s'éveille*', that hymn to the grubby city at dawn, tired and busy and ordinary amidst the beauty, trots stupidly through my head, the rumbling bass line accompanying the jolts of the métro.

I'm so relieved the decision is made, and even though I am scared, I know I can do this bit: it's simply a case of placing one foot in front of the other and surrendering myself to the absolute assurance of French healthcare. I navigate the maze of platforms and corridors at Châtelet, get to Porte d'Orléans and walk along the dark flank of the Parc Montsouris. I'm a quick walker: I have been walking this city for months now.

The hospital is shut and dark when I arrive, so I search around for a bell on the side door and raise the night porter, who lets me in. I cross the hospital, following the instructions on my photocopied sheet, and take the lift to the third floor, where a nurse shows me to my room (I have a *room*, it seems rather luxurious) and hands me a cellophane package, which contains a gown, paper slippers and a hairnet. I put them on and sit on the side of the bed, careful to keep my mind very, very empty. I look at the gaps between the ceiling tiles, the metal window frame, and watch the progression of a faint suspicion of light at the horizon, through the scrub of the park, as dawn arrives.

A motherly nurse comes in and places a cannula in the back of my hand: it's quick and painless and she smiles quite kindly when it's done. 'Not much longer now.'

When she leaves, I start counting the ceiling tiles again, with slightly greater urgency. I examine the texture of each, the veins in the material, until there is another knock on the door and a couple of porters come in, with the same nurse.

'It's time to go – lie down on the bed.'

So I lie down obediently and let myself be wheeled along a corridor in bed, even though I am perfectly well, perfectly able. There is a comfort in having absolutely everything taken out of my hands: I don't need to think any more, so I don't. We go down in a lift, along corridors, and up in another lift and finally I am wheeled through the swing doors into what is recognizably an operating theatre. The nurse and the orderlies leave and I feel cold and frightened as a masked team of four busy themselves around me.

'Right,' says the anaesthetist (thankfully it's not the one I met previously). Her face is obscured by a surgical mask and she is leaning over me in green scrubs. 'We're going to start this drip off now. It might tingle.'

I whimper, involuntarily. I'm quite scared now.

'Are you OK?' she asks, and her eyes look kind.

'No.' My chest feels tight and I'm getting black spots at the periphery of my vision. It's not doubt I feel, just stupid, basic fear.

'It's OK,' says the anaesthetist, who seems to intuit that and she holds my hand tightly with one of her surgical-gloved ones for a moment. 'It's going to be OK.' I close my eyes and surrender again.

The recovery room is a blur – someone else in there sounds distressed, but I am in a peaceful, pain-free haze. Someone takes my blood pressure a couple of times, I answer a few questions hazily and finally I am wheeled back up to my room. It's daylight now and a light drizzle has set in outside the window, obscuring my view. Olivier is there waiting, his face pinched and grey with anxiety.

'Are you OK?'

'Yup.'

I do feel OK: I feel a bit fuzzy and vague, but I have no pain and no discomfort and absolutely no regrets. Olivier has brought me a flask of tea and a croissant, it turns out unnecessarily, because a kind nurse – not the same one as before – knocks on the door and brings me breakfast on a tray: orange juice, baguette and jam. We sit on my bed, me leaning against his shoulder, and half watch *Télé Matin* (something to do with the forthcoming European referendum, I think, but my attention is fitful) until another nurse comes to take my blood pressure and remove my cannula. She sticks a plaster on the back of my hand, and tells us we're free to go.

'Thank you,' I say to the nurses huddled round the desk as we go out and I really mean it. I feel so grateful and so lucky to be the recipient of this magnificent state-sponsored care (the whole process has cost us barely anything), but also of so much basic human kindness too. Getting into our taxi, I feel oddly buoyed up: I have experienced more kindness in the Institut Montsouris than anywhere else in Paris.

I suppose this could be a turning point, the moment at which I finally start to feel at home in Paris, but it isn't. The next morning I email my head of department and confirm that I want to return to work, soon.

PART THREE

'I can hardly imagine anyone,' Lady Georgia observed,
'setting out deliberately for Brussels.'

Ronald Firbank, *Vainglory*

« 14 »

La Peau de Chagrin

It feels amazing to be back in London, far, far better than I expected it to feel. My pride has been dealt a body blow (I can see no way of glossing over the fact I couldn't hack it in Paris and that hurts), but every other part of me is filled with wild exhilaration. London! The moment we step off the Eurostar – having fought our way through the forest of French bureaucracy required to leave the country – is, for me, Dorothy entering Technicolor in Oz: everything is more vivid. We get into a taxi (a black cab! Farewell to the deserted ranks and impenetrably complicated automated telephone-ordering system of Paris taxis) and drive across the city to my dad's house, across the river, bright with reflected lights, and I feel ready to burst into song.

Our flat could not be further from our Paris apartment. It's a new build in a small block of four executive flats: light and plain, with big picture windows and laminate floors (farewell, splintery herringbone). The flat is entirely furnished with plain, unobjectionable, matching things that are not ours and it feels like a complete liberation. There is a whole, shiny, new fitted kitchen with fake granite worktops and pale-wood cupboards filled with Ikea plates and cups, not cockroaches, and a gleaming chrome and white-tiled bathroom. In order to get to our flat, which is on the fourth floor, there is a small, perfectly functioning lift that no one cares about. It is absolutely nothing I have ever aspired to, but I love it, giddily. The window to the front looks over Spitalfields market and Bishopsgate and I sit on the comfy sofa (so much better than the leather monstrosity we bought in a panic in Paris) late at night sometimes and watch the ballet of emergency vehicles, the staggering drunks and the prostitutes soliciting on the corner. I had no idea how much I missed all this, but it feels like a shot in the arm.

London isn't brighter than Paris, but it's grimy and famil-iar and satisfying. It feels as if a cloud of cartoon bluebirds is tweeting around my head as I sashay down Bishopsgate, past Benji's and Tesco Metro and Snappy Snaps. I want to embrace every cashier at Boots in tearful gratitude and shake the hand of every goth in platform boots and every waxed-moustached chap in tweed and spats (there are lots of these around Spitalfields. Sometimes I even see Gilbert and George out for a constitutional; no one bats an eyelid). I love every angry drunk and every huffy commuter pushing their way up the escalator in Liverpool Street Station. The tiny brown mice are still running along the westbound Central Line tracks, I note with delight, and the Sweet Chariot is still dispensing overpriced Spangles and cola cubes. I'm a bit nonplussed by my own happiness, but familiarity has never felt so delicious.

Admittedly, my knee doesn't feel exactly amazing. Just as we started packing up the flat, and despite all that physio, it definitively collapsed, leaving me completely immobile, stranded on a chair, crying with pain as the movers packed around me (I admit to a few dark thoughts about Christian the physio at this point). I spend the first few days in London going from doctor to hospital, getting MRIs and emergency narcotics, a process which culminates in surgery in a marble-lined private hospital in west London (thank goodness for my employer's health insurance) and the conclusion that the surgeon doesn't really know what is wrong with it, but it should be better now? Maybe? I feel fine, really, but the anti-inflammatories and the painkillers and the constant presence of pain have left me weak and shaky. I haven't been able to pick the boys up for weeks and I have had to stop breastfeeding because of all the drugs. I am also still bleeding from the abortion too, but everything is basically fine.

Things get back to some version of normal with startling speed. Theo starts back at his old nursery; it's just round the corner from the new flat and everyone is still there, the staff and the babies, Barney and Joshua and Ladybird (yes, Ladybird), all now weirdly grown up and talking in full sentences. Even the stick insects – or perhaps more likely their descendants – are still there. Louis joins Theo, starting in the 'baby room'. I hang around for a while on the first few days, marvelling at how laidback everything is, with cornflour in every crevice and kids pulling out whatever toy or book they fancy at any time of day. There are no bells and every day is different. Generally, having two small boys is much easier here: the open spaces around the market are perfect for running around and there are easy-access museums with ramps and lifts and parks where you are actually allowed on the grass.

We only get tutted at if we are obstructing the barriers at the Underground at rush hour, which I can usually avoid.

In the office, it's as if I had never left. I've had an upgrade to the coveted 'back of the room' desk (monitor angled away from passers-by for discreet, unobserved Internet browsing), but it's the same room, the same view over the internal atrium down to the canteen (staffed by the same ladies), the same timesheet system, logging my day in ten-minute increments. The people are mainly the same too (though my main office ally Laurie has moved to another firm, which is a blow) and they are lovely to me, far nicer than I have any right to expect. I get hugs and warm emails and offers of lunch.

I'm a bit embarrassed by my untimely reappearance after the card and the John Lewis vouchers and the leaving cakes (Colin the Caterpillar mini rolls and fondant fancies in the library), but I decide to brazen it out. I buy myself an expensive new Diane Von Furstenberg wrap dress and a new lipstick (the thought of a salary is making me skittish with pleasure, I have been on a delirious reunion trip around Liberty with my friend Kate, ecstatic to see both her and it) and make sure everyone knows how happy I am to be back and how ready I am to get stuck in to work again. I don't even have to pretend: it's amazing to have a function again. I walk into the office every morning purposefully, say hello to the security guards and receptionists, make my way up the back staircase to my office, change my shoes and sit down to work, grateful I still have a job.

My very favourite part of the morning, though, is my walk around the food hall at Marks & Spencer in Moorgate.

I have missed M&S more than anything, so every morning I stop off there on my way to work. I can lose ages, bathed in the cool light of the chiller cabinet, wandering from aisle to aisle marvelling at the *rightness* of it all. I like the packs of neatly chopped vegetables and the plastic boxes of clean, perfect raspberries, the fat pink prawns stripped of everything that makes them seem like a creature, lined up in overlapping curls. Going past the symmetrically stacked tubs of chocolate mini rolls and flapjacks, I smile at the cashiers – fresh, clearly, from some new customer-service training programme – when they ask me how my day is going. Brilliantly, thank you, I say. I love how I'm completely in control of these simple transactions and here, among the preoccupied City boys picking up Meal Deals in the sandwich section, I feel entirely at home.

Feeling at home, I rediscover – or perhaps discover for the first time, my memory is unreliable, flooded with London love – a taste for chat. I chat in M&S and Boots and I chat to Harvey in the deli across the market and the girls in the Shoreditch clothes shops I browse round at weekends. It feels safe to just open my mouth and say things: there is no risk I will attribute the wrong gender to a vegetable to widespread opprobrium. When we take the boys to the tiny park in Elder Street, we get talking to a nice couple, Mark and Fiona, who live down the road, and they start inviting us into their cheery, chaotic flat for tea and for drinks and barbecues. They talk unguardedly and self-deprecatingly, with a preference for a good anecdote over any semblance of dignity: Mark's drunken antics, Fiona's undignified labour, all the places their twin boys have peed. Olivier and I greet this easy sociability with open-mouthed wonder: 'This would *never* have happened in Paris,' we say to each other, thrilled. We meet up with the parents at nursery, too, by accident in the market or deliberately for picnics. I see Kate, who I have missed so terribly, and we make contact again with my half-brother, my father's son, who has a little girl and a new baby on the way. Without even trying, I have a social life.

Everything takes me back to M&S though: it's where I get wine to take to barbecues, picnic food, snacks for the boys. It is my happy place, from the neatly folded jumpers to the six-packs of knickers and the perfectly ripe peaches nestled in moulded polystyrene. I have spent the best part of a year in the world's greatest gastronomic theme park, but I would rather be here than in the loveliest Parisian market. I don't want dirt and blood and roots and angry, challenging conversations. I want the reassurance of cellophaned stir-fry packs, regimented carrot batons, perfectly cuboid chunks of mango and anodyne chit-chat at the tills. I know how to do this! I feel re-enfranchised by M&S; it is ridiculous, but true.

The really stupid thing, though, is that I don't really eat my M&S foods. I don't eat much of anything if I can help it.

'Look at you!' says one of my colleagues admiringly on my first day back as I walk into the galley kitchen. 'You look so *thin*. Is that a Parisian thing?'

It's not actually a Parisian thing; it's more of a London thing. I'm busy here, and moving has been fraught and stressful and I have things to do other than buy and eat cakes. I'm not much minded to listen to my body's demands, anyway: I feel ambivalent about it after the abortion and irritated by my crumbling knee. On top of that, the strong painkillers have eroded my appetite and left my stomach sensitive. I drink cappuccino in the morning and miso soup for lunch and pick at the boys' dinner in the evening. Work is quickly quite stressful: I get enlisted onto a big case with an impossible timetable and deadlines that follow each other in relentless succession. Lunch is for the weak, and so is apologizing in the middle of a meeting and sprinting out to collect the children before nursery closes, but I have to do that. As soon as the children are in bed, the partner in charge calls to give me instructions and I spend the evening in front of my spreadsheets and my economists' reports. The gnawing emptiness of my stomach is an odd sort of comfort, a reassuring constant.

If I'm honest, really honest, with myself, I know there's something quite unhealthy going on. I have stood in front of our bathroom mirror, stepped onto our scales and understood that I am heading down an insidious road, a road with nothing good at the end of it. It wouldn't be the first time. I had the almost-obligatory Oxford eating disorder, kick-started by a year on steroids to treat my hair loss and a censorious dermatologist who monitored my every gramme of steroid-related weight gain. I spent a year I should have spent going to parties and studying Vichy France with my head down an Oxford lavatory, my knuckles rubbed raw trying to make myself sick. I'm not doing that again: I've wasted enough time thinking about my thighs and the calories in semi-skimmed milk. Eating disorders are all about control, aren't they, and I'm totally in control now, back in a place where I can make a doctor's appointment without an hour of sweaty rehearsal.

Perhaps I'm not *completely* in control when it comes to Louis. Our usually sunny, if nocturnal, baby is going through a strange patch. He's learning to talk, which should be making him less frustrated, but instead he's suddenly angry. Most evenings he's overcome by a violent tantrum, lurching around the kitchen like a tiny drunk, screaming at me about crackers and toys. Sometimes he lies rigid on the floor and headbangs; once he even tries it in the bath, but he quickly realizes this is a terrible plan. It should be funny. There's nothing sinister going on, it's just a developmental curveball, probably something to do with the move and the exhaustion and stress of starting nursery. When Olivier's around, or when Kate comes over, it's fine, I can laugh at my tiny tyrant demanding we don't look at him and bellowing for biscuits. Even when it's just the three of us on my days off, we're fine most of the time: I take the boys to the City Farm to stroke goats and back to the lovely playground at Coram Fields, where I used to take Theo when he was tiny (I'm pretty sure it's the same grimy sheep skulking in the corner pen). We spend hours in the sandpit at the Museum of Childhood and sometimes my father and stepmother take Theo out for the afternoon. But occasionally when I'm on my own with both boys, Louis's outbursts seem to mirror some seam of violence in me. Sometimes I have to lock myself in the bathroom because I can't deal with his rages (he sits outside, banging on the door and shouting), and sometimes I need to hurt myself for the relief it brings, punching myself hard in the arm or raking my nails over my forearms until they draw blood.

Other times I stand at the window and watch the buses roll along Bishopsgate, and I imagine just running away, walking north along the old Roman road up into Shoreditch, past the Vietnamese restaurants that line Kingsland Road, through Hackney and Stoke Newington and on, onto wherever. The North. The sea. Anywhere.

It's stupid. These aren't real feelings, I remind myself; I'm just hungry. A sandwich would sort all of this out. Why won't I allow myself a sandwich? I don't know, but on some weird level I'm enjoying the feeling of deprivation. I enjoy the feel of my prominent ribs or the hard bump of my seat bones when I sit down and I like ignoring my body's demands. I get thinner and thinner, my clavicles get more prominent and my jeans get too big. I'm shrinking, like Balzac's *La Peau de Chagrin*.

It's a strange story *La Peau de Chagrin*: a fable, really. 'It deals with shrinking and starvation,' said Freud, who read it on his deathbed, but it is at least as much about the destructive force of acquisitive desire. Dissolute romantic absolutist (idiot, really; he's awful) Raphaël de Valentin has gambled his last golden louis away and decided to commit suicide (on another one of those Parisian bridges, of course) but an old man in an antique shop shows him a magic skin that can grant wishes. The problem is that with every wish granted the skin shrinks and its owner loses vitality.

From being convinced he wants to die, after wishing for and getting a dissolute, lavish party and a good income, Raphaël becomes haunted by the spectre of the skin vanishing and him with it: he wants to 'live at all costs', closing himself off from the world to avoid involuntarily wishing for anything. In the end, his desire for Pauline, his former landlady's daughter, previously disdained but now rich and beautiful, destroys him.

There's something about that narrative of bringing about your own downfall against your conscious will that makes me think of *Peau de Chagrin* now: stopping eating has that same peculiar, tumbling, inevitable momentum. I buy things, lots of things, and I watch myself shrink. It's so stupid, but I can't seem to snap out of it.

Olivier certainly thinks I'm being stupid. He thinks I'm stupid to get embroiled in this big matter at work and stupid to care about making a good job of it. He doesn't like to see me under pressure and stands over me rolling his eyes on his way to bed as I sit at the tiny desk in the corridor, phone tucked under my chin, talking to the partner as I type.

'You don't even *like* your job,' he says, incredulous, and there is some truth in this. I am no more passionate about competition law now than I was when I got pregnant twice in rapid succession and spent two years doing virtually nothing. But I like the fact of *a* job and I think he's interfering, unhelpful and naïve. Everyone I know works long hours; it's just how the City works. Also, he forced me to make a decision about moving and here we are and this is just part of it. We view the past few months very differently:

he thinks he made a gesture of love, trust and sacrifice; I feel like he abandoned me at the worst possible time and I still feel angry. I don't want to talk to him, so I don't. Sometimes whole days pass without us exchanging more than twenty words. At other times, I sleep on the sofa in mute protest, or slam out of the flat and spend the evening walking around Liverpool Street Station, grateful for the late-opening Costa and WH Smith, sitting on benches in the dark, incoherent with anger. I can see he doesn't understand what is happening, but I don't care; I avoid his bewildered eyes. We're back to that French cinematic fighting I love to watch and it's still as miserable in reality as it was ten years ago.

As work builds to a crescendo, so do our problems. One day, as I'm walking into a three-hour conference call, I get a voicemail from him: 'We have to talk in the next hour, or that's it, it's over.' I know it's desperation speaking but it feels like blackmail. The partner raises her eyebrows as I stand, paralysed with indecision and anger and fear, holding three lever-arch files. I go to the meeting. When I get home, I just explain, flatly, and he accepts it, for now. I sort of want destruction to hail down on us by this point, but nothing happens, he was just bluffing.

In July, the 7/7 bombings amplify my sense of strangeness and of dislocation. We sit in the office and watch as the terror unfolds around us, in the tunnels and streets we know intimately, people like us dying going about their ordinary London business. Leaving the office that afternoon, the city feels altered: people are afraid as they have never been before, strangers to each other, and the atmosphere for the remainder of the summer is febrile and edgy. Olivier is genuinely shaken and doesn't want to go on the tube; the nursery cancels all outings. False alarms, rumours and alerts convulse the city, and Brick Lane and Whitechapel feel tense and uneasy, even on the sunniest of weekends.

By the time work calms down (which it does in August) things are about as bad as they could be between us and they are about to get really bad in my head too. Without any immediate position papers to write or overnight numbers to crunch, I find my legs are increasingly reluctant to take me to the office. My morning wander through the M&S food hall becomes longer and longer and when I leave, I dawdle around the back streets of the city, taking in the kebab shops and the council blocks and the hidden Hawksmoor churches. Often I end up sitting in the old cemetery at Bunhill Fields between William Blake, Wesley's chapel and the Quakers. George Fox, the founding father of Quakerism, is buried here somewhere. God, I think, he would have *hated* French *Elle*. I love Bunhill Fields, the quiet weight of history, the spectre of Fox and Wesley preaching thunderously all around these streets. I love, too, the total irreverence of the contemporary city towards it, construction workers drinking cans of lager and students rolling up their trousers to soak up the sun. There is so much I love about London, so why am I in such a bloody state now we're back here?

When I finally show up in the office, I seem unable to raise myself to do more than turn my computer on, and when anyone tries to give me work I hide in the Ladies (a fine tradition, this) or lie. After a couple of hours of mutinous inactivity, I go out at lunchtime and buy clothes I neither want nor need because the adrenalin flip helps me forget my hunger. One day I go all the way to Selfridges and buy two pairs of £200 shoes I don't particularly want for no particular reason and only get back to the office at three. It's my crap, consumerist version of going off the rails.

After a couple of weeks of this – no one in the office seems to notice, thankfully – I start to feel frightened. I can't seem to make myself focus on anything, even when I want to, and waves of cold dread wash over me. A German partner is trying to get me staffed on his huge merger deal, which will mean another six months of pressure and late nights and I know I can't do it. One morning I arrive at half past ten and I can't even make myself turn the monitor on: my fingers just refuse to do it. I sit, panicking, until the trainee who shares my office leaves, then I call Olivier. Despite everything, he's still the only person I want – need – to speak to at a time like this. I can't imagine turning to anyone else.

'There's something really wrong,' I stammer. 'I can't *move*.'

We meet an hour later halfway between his office and mine on Holborn Viaduct. He puts his arms around me and I let my head rest on his chest. He smells of Guerlain Habit Rouge and our washing powder and I can feel his warm skin, utterly familiar, through his shirt. We're a still point in a dark swirling mass of lunch break office workers and I just want to stay there for a while, breathing in the comfort I have rejected for so long.

'I don't know what's wrong with me,' I say into his chest. My voice doesn't sound right. 'It's like . . . I can't breathe, I feel paralysed.' I press my forehead harder into him.

'There, there,' he says. He makes meaningless comforting sounds with his hands warm on my shoulders. 'It's OK, there, there. It's all right.'

But eventually he has to go back to work, so I go back to my office too. At Olivier's prompting I go straight down to the HR department on the third floor and I find my way to the office of the new HR lady I have only met once. I come in and sit down, uninvited. Her office smells of perfume and sandwich.

'Oh!' she says, startled, and arranges her features into a smile. 'Is there something?' her question trails off at the sight of my face, which I suspect is not pretty. I am all skinny and grey-faced and mad.

'I am having a breakdown,' I say, baldly. There is no point in sugar-coating it, after all. It isn't as if she hasn't heard it all before: people are *always* having breakdowns in City law firms; it's an occupational hazard. Legendary, probably apocryphal, stories circulate the City of people in various firms being found curled in foetal balls under their desk naked or taking heroin in the photocopier room. I attempt a smile to put her at ease. 'I need to see a doctor.'

Ten minutes later, I am sitting outside the office GP's basement surgery. It is in an unglamorous facilities corridor, near the gym, which accounts for the acrid smell of sweat-soaked carpet tile and partner testosterone. There are also showers and three windowless boxes that serve as bedrooms for lawyers unwilling or unable to go home. It's quiet down here in the mid-afternoon and I have enough time to wonder if I am overreacting, but then the doctor opens the surgery door and beckons me in. She's a nice-looking woman with short reddish hair and kind eyes.

I'm not quite sure what I say to her. I give a breathless rundown of the past eighteen months, I think: Mum, move, abortion, move, work, conflict with Olivier, Marks & Spencer. I don't know if I manage to convey the sense of perpetual dread that has crept up on me day by day over the past six months. I know I don't mention the fact I've stopped eating. I definitely don't tell her that leaving Paris means admitting defeat at the thing that has basically defined me for the past fifteen years and that I can't really deal with it. I reckon I definitely sound mad enough, though. I *feel* mad enough.

'It sounds,' says the doctor in a very measured tone, writing frantically, 'as if you have had a very difficult time.' And just like that, I get signed off work.

« 15 »

Sous Les Vents de Neptune

I have always thought a breakdown would be sort of glamorous. This feels like a rather sub-standard variety. There is no eye-gouging, no reckless fucking of strangers, no sitting on statues and shooting pistols in the air. It's a part-time, unassuming kind of thing, which I put on hold in the evenings to look after the boys.

The psychiatrist the work GP sends me to see clearly thinks he's seen plenty of my kind before. He is a beautifully dressed man with big brown eyes and a domed brown bald head and he specializes in City malaises. Hundreds of alpha personalities in T. M. Lewin shirts parade through his offices each week, with exhaustion, burn-out and other alpha afflictions.

'I expect,' he says during our first consultation, in his dark wood-panelled office in Guy's Hospital, 'you are concerned about letting your clients down. You will probably resist my suggestion that you take some time away from the office.'

I am not at all sure that I will resist that suggestion, but I nod, noncommittally.

'Is,' he probes delicately, 'the anxiety of constantly comparing your achievements with those of your peers at the root of this sense of paralysis?'

'I don't *think* so,' I venture. This encounter would actually be quite funny if it were not for the cold dread that envelops me. He's not actually too worried about my motivation anyway, because he's planning to prescribe some high-dose antidepressants and send me to therapy, he explains. They can sort me out there. I need to see a counsellor and go to group therapy three times a week at a posh private hospital just off Marylebone Road.

The hospital is a strange place in a strange part of town that seems utterly out-of-time, a throwback to another era. You almost expect to see Celia Johnson emerging from a café in the back streets by Marylebone Station, lighting a gasper and buttoning her coat. The building, too, is old-fashioned looking, a red-brick pile more like a crammer for rich, indolent schoolboys than a psychiatric hospital. Inside, there's a constant ballet of thin women with great hair in velour tracksuits and sunglasses and boys in skinny jeans and hoodies. It would have a certain louche glamour if it weren't for the fact that several sections of the building are locked and you can't get in or out without checking your name on the mandatory sign-in sheet held by the security guard at the front door. There's an edge to the atmosphere that makes me nervous before I even attend a single session: the possibility of something bad happening hangs imminent in the air.

Group therapy is interesting, in the Chinese curse sense of the word. It takes place in the basement, past the canteen and the art therapy studio, in one of three insipid, pastel rooms full of hard chairs.

I have expressed, as strongly as I know how, how very, very much I do not want to go to group therapy. I tell the blandly encouraging hospital coordinator who reviews my notes and assigns me to a group over and over again that I do not want to go.

'It's normal to be nervous,' she says, smiling at me.

'I can't do it.' If I were Béatrice Dalle, I'd be throwing a chair round about now, but I'm not; my repertoire doesn't extend much beyond apology, the British silver bullet. 'I'm really sorry, but I honestly can't.'

'It'll be fine,' she says firmly, and I realize that I am not actually in charge of this. I really do *have* to go. She ushers me down the stairs, dragging my heels.

The chairs are arranged in a circle and a handful of people are already in the room. There is a whole range of ages and types, from an elderly, aloof-looking man who must be easily in his seventies to an Asian teenage girl with a pierced lip dressed entirely in black and all points in between. Some look raw and troubled while others are perfectly dressed and made-up as if for a light lunch and a post-prandial wander round the Conran Shop. The coordinator pats me briskly on the shoulder and leaves. I hate her. Longing for her death sustains me through the next few minutes as I take a seat and more people file into the room, but it wears off and the dread returns.

Finally, a middle-aged man in a lumpy cardigan comes in and sits down. The whole circle sighs, as one.

'Hey, everyone,' he says with an anaemic smile. 'So can we all be just thinking about coming together, feeling the chair beneath our seat bones and just really being in the moment?' There is a generalized fidget of mutiny around the circle. I dare to look around me for a second and catch the elegant elderly gentleman mid-eyeroll.

'There are some new faces today, I see,' says cardigan man. 'So, for those of you who haven't met me yet, I'm Clive and I thought perhaps we could just go round the circle and just, check in? Check in on how everyone is feeling today. Does anyone want to start us off?'

He looks around encouragingly; my stomach contracts with nerves.

'I'll start, Clive,' says the elderly gentleman, spitting out the word 'Clive'. He has a lovely, cut-glass voice. 'Today is very bad, I feel very low and very hopeless.'

Clive leans towards him and nods.

'Of course,' the gentleman continues, 'it's made vastly worse by you taking this group. I believe you're a very poor therapist and I'm fairly sure everyone else agrees with me.'

There is a murmur of assent around the group. Clive nods again, unhappily.

'I'm really sorry to hear that, Jeremy. But I wonder if, perhaps, this isn't the most productive line of discussion? Maybe we could explore why you're struggling with today and how we can all help you process those feelings?'

'No,' says Jeremy, coolly indifferent. 'Right now, I need to talk about you, Clive.'

For the next fifteen minutes, various other members of the group speak in brief bursts, mainly expressing their reservations about Clive's competence, which I find very cheering. Eventually, reluctantly, the group moves on and their sad and desperate states and stories come out in tiny fragments, ineptly facilitated by Clive. There isn't time for everyone to speak and when Clive's attention alights on me, I mutter something about 'just wanting to process my feelings' and get away with it, and at last the session is over.

Over a couple of months, I go back to group therapy regularly, though I never really get used to it. A group of broken, angry people don't seem well placed to do a very good job of being careful with each other's feelings and there are spats and walk-outs and grudges and unhelpful 'feedback' between group members. Nevertheless, I learn a lot about the other people who come. There is a girl of barely twenty who has been trapped in the hospital by her anxiety disorder for months (we celebrate her walking the 200 yards to Marylebone Station one afternoon). There is a sweet, silent woman who is bullied both at home and at work, her body language a semaphore of discreet despair, and a plump, red-faced Essex lad, more a boy than a man, really, who claims to have come because of his social anxiety but who turns out to be mourning his dead baby daughter. On one awful occasion I walk in to see a work colleague sitting on the opposite side of the circle and have to run away, pursued by a well-meaning therapist trying to persuade me to stay and 'talk it out in group'.

'You can't just run away from what makes you uncomfortable, Emma.'

'Oh, I think I can.'

I avoid talking as far as possible, through the use of weaselly formulas like 'I think I just need to take some time to check in with my feelings and be in the group, today' and 'I'm not feeling very grounded right now but I think I can take strength from the group.' The therapists love this kind of thing, especially if you emphasize how helpful the group is, and I rely on this until, in a cruel failure of solidarity, someone calls me out on it one day and I have to find a new approach. There are a few people who have adopted the therapy-speak with enthusiasm and are willing to expound at length about trust and pain and what kind of person they are until someone cuts them off. In the main, though, we are all still very British about our feelings, effortfully spitting out tiny pellets of carefully expressed emotion. We're 'a bit sad' or 'feeling a little anxious today'. Mostly I look at my shoes. I still do an unconscionable amount of shopping (it's a symptom, I tell myself), so I usually have nice ones. I have some red suede dancing shoes with purple flowers on the side, which are particularly good when things are dragging.

I'm not especially interested in my own feelings and I certainly don't see group therapy helping with anything: it is something to be endured, a hoop to jump through to allow myself to stay off work for a while. I feel like that postcard I remember from my mum's office wall, something like 'I've waited a long time for this nervous breakdown and I'm going to enjoy it.' After sessions, I walk down to Liberty or Fenwick, browse through the racks and meet Kate in the café to recount the horrors of the past few hours, toying with a cake I don't eat.

'Oh, Em,' she says, eyes wide with sympathy and concern, and I feel like a fraud, because I'm not even trying to get better. I just want to get thinner and buy more dresses and continue running away from my responsibilities. In January, when my sister turns twenty-one, I turn up on the doorstep of her shared house in Nottingham with a lavish basket of fruit, a ludicrous sticking plaster for her sadness. I know university is proving unbearable for her, all those happy, undamaged kids. My stepfather's worry for her is all-consuming: it's all he wants to talk about. I haven't been in touch much, because I feel like it's my turn to be crazy for a while.

But now here I am, trying to make up for it with my feeble birthday gesture. We go for a walk around town in the January cold.

'You look very thin, Em?' she ventures cautiously at one point but I just brush it off with an excuse, all the while feeling a sick little thrill of triumph.

I don't really know what Olivier thinks, because I don't ask: I'm absorbed in my daily dramas, the ones that play out in group therapy and the ones inside my own head. He doesn't believe in antidepressants (I'm not sure he believes in depression or anxiety or any mental complaint, actually), but he has seen that they have made a difference so he has made a temporary, uneasy peace with mine. We don't seem to have a language to talk about what is happening, which becomes even more obvious when my counsellor invites him along to a session. 'You look like a concentration camp victim,' he says bluntly, when asked how he feels about me, looking straight at me, hurt masquerading as anger. I roll my eyes because it seems stupid and over the top but I think it penetrates anyway and reminds me of what I already know: that it can't go on. It's a grotesque vanity, this not-eating business, and almost aggressive in the way it pushes Olivier and the boys away. I'm too tired and weak to have much enthusiasm for trips to the park and playground. Sex is a joke: I feel nothing more than faint curiosity at the physical sensation of the new hard clash of our hip bones.

When I am not in therapy, I lie in bed in the murky afternoons, conserving my dwindling reserves of energy for collecting the children, drinking black tea and reading dark, cold murder stories. I mainly read the Scandinavians, but I immerse myself in Fred Vargas too. Vargas, an archaeologist, plague historian and crime writer who writes playful, strange stories of things that should be impossible, is one of my only Parisian cultural souvenirs. It's cold too in her newest outing for the eccentric Commissaire Adamsberg, *Sous les Vents de Neptune*: the action starts in an icy Paris with a broken boiler in the 13th arrondissement police headquarters and heads to snowy Quebec, where Adamsberg is forced to confront a buried but not forgotten story from his past and to return to the Pyrenean village where he grew up. I feel a bit like that: I have unfinished business, with France and with my mother, and I'm confused about where home is and where I am supposed to be.

At night I dream over and over again my mother is dying but I am being kept away from her; she doesn't want to see me. I scream and rage until I wake up, trembling and confused. During the day, I potter around the shops and the Internet, looking at nice things for the house and for the children. I have developed a cult-like fascination with the seasonal rituals of family life: Advent calendars and Christmas decorations and crayon marks on the wall marking the children's height. I am consumed with nostalgia for life growing up with my stepfather, coming into the kitchen after school to Radio 4 playing and some fiddly Middle Eastern dish cooking, Joe smoking a roll-up in the yard with a copy of *New Scientist*. I think more about him than my mother; the quiet way he went about making home feel like home: tins of mince pies at Christmas and hot cross buns at Easter; pizza dough rising under a tea towel every Sunday. I want my children to have the reassurance of familiarity I had and I believe, I think, that this is how you knit your family and your home together. You build it through repetition and predictability; you put in the time. I want to be as careful and slow and patient as my stepfather. I want a drawer full of wrapping paper and string and scissors and a tin full of cookie cutters and birthday cake candles. It's as if my ambitions have narrowed down to this and this alone: I want to make a nice home.

It doesn't feel like this is about my mum, although I suppose it must be, somehow. Her cakes were as thin and crisp as communion wafers and the waiters in the pizzeria round the corner knew our order by heart. She got home late and travelled across the world while my stepfather cooked and washed our clothes, a Russian novel wrapped in brown paper on the kitchen counter and Radio 4's *Analysis* on the radio. My sister and I were absolutely vital to her but so was work, and the trappings of domesticity were negotiable. It's also ludicrous. I can't offer the boys anything like this cosy Cath Kidston fantasy life in my current state, but then again, perhaps that's why it's so seductive. Nevertheless, one afternoon I set aside my Scandinavian murder and I decide to make a cake. My children have reached the age of cake: I have been to enough nursery birthday parties and oohed at the flat, wonky sponges, iced blue and decorated by toddlers.

I can't think of the last time I made a cake, a real cake. In France, of course, no one bothers to make cakes. Even Olivier's grandmother has long since given up making her famous apple tart and goes to the bakery like everyone else. I want to make a proper British one, a Proustian madeleine of a cake, so I unearth Mary Berry's *Fast Cakes* from a packing box and I set about making a lemon sponge. Lemon sponge is my family's traditional cake: everyone gets a lemon sponge for their birthday, topped with sugar flowers or jelly diamonds, depending on what we can find in the back of the cupboard. We aren't really cake bakers, not even Joe who will happily trifle with yeast, so we stick to what we know. Joe has brought me lemon sponges filled with his home-made lemon curd to Oxford and to Paris, the tin carefully wrapped up in newspaper and placed in a Bag for Life. If I'm going to make any cake, it has to be this one.

I go to Tesco for caster sugar and lemons and baking

parchment – you can't get that kind of thing in M&S – and back in the flat, I cream butter and sugar by hand because we don't have a food processor. It's hard work and I get sweaty and short of breath very quickly: I'm painfully unfit. I grate lemon rind and it's as fiddly as I remember. Gradually, I get into a rhythm, adding a little flour to my mixture because the eggs are too cold and it's starting to curdle, lining the tin. By the time I finish, evening is drawing in and I have to go and collect the boys. I put my cake in the oven and dash the few hundred yards to nursery.

When we return, the cake is ready, plump and brown and uneven, the top mined with molehill bumps. Theo is quite excited to see it – for all my domestic longings, I don't do much in the way of cooking – and clamours to try it, so I hack off a corner for him and one for Louis, then cut myself a piece. I look at it for a moment. I am weak after my efforts, and hungry. I am always hungry; hungry and cold. It's exhausting and the effort of it makes me feel detached and disengaged from everyone and everything: I'm just waiting for the moment I can go back to bed. My hip bones and my clavicles and my sternum stick out and when I sit down, my seat bones bump painfully against the chair. I am so sick and tired of self-denial, I realize. I can't even recall what I thought I was trying to achieve, but I know I can't do it any more. I am going to eat the damned cake. I put a piece in my mouth. It is slightly dry – I have overcooked the top and the crumb is coarse – but it is warm and buttery with a familiar edge of lemon acidity. My salivary glands contract painfully with the unaccustomed sugar hit. It is delicious.

I start baking regularly after this, familiar and not-so-familiar recipes. I grate carrots and chop walnuts and find buttermilk to make scones and I buy more cookbooks: Nigella's *How to Be a Domestic Goddess* and a *Good House-keeping Book of Baking*. Some evenings I bring them into the bedroom to read instead of my murders. The cupboards fill up with cream of tartar and vanilla pods, with cocoa powder and caster sugar. Baking feels therapeutic: I put on music and get out my ingredients and it is just absorbing enough. I like the steady, methodical process and the enforced precision and I take comfort from this weird notion that baking is somehow What You Do, as a parent. I see it as a way to give my children the certainty that they are loved and that what makes them happy is important. I can convey that with sponge and icing: it's my way back.

When I make my first cake, it's still winter and the afternoons are solidly, inkily dark outside our dirt-streaked fishbowl window. But gradually, the light lingers longer over Spitalfields and the sun comes out now and then and the hardier after-work drinkers start taking their pints outside. There's birdsong, from the persistent blackbirds in Elder Gardens, and Mark and Fiona, our friends from round the corner, dust off their barbecue again and lure us in for wine on weekend afternoons. Gradually, I start back at work a couple of half days a week. We've spent a full year here now, and now that I seem to be conquering whatever possessed me, it feels full of possibility. Theo and his friends chase each other around the market waving plastic lizards and Louis falls into the pond. He's not an angry baby any more: he's nearly two, wildly contrary but chatty and charming.

There is so much happening around us: Brick Lane shape-shifts every weekend, with pop-up openings and exhibitions and wild, anarchic events. Mark regales us gleefully with every shop and restaurant opening, urging us to try new sausages or doughnuts or cider, luring Olivier out on wine-tasting expeditions. I even start exercising: Fiona and I share a personal trainer, laughing helplessly as we try to stand on wobbly boards in the garden and run weakly around the market. I am finally allowed to drop group therapy, then I am referred to a grief counsellor, who is pleasant enough to chat to, in an inconclusive sort of way (I don't really feel I 'get' anywhere, but the dreams stop, so perhaps I am wrong), and finally, cautiously, the City expert psychiatrist discharges me, releasing me back into the legal community to go forth and work seventy chargeable hours a week.

'I'd like you to write me a letter,' he says. 'Setting out what you'll do if you start to get a reoccurrence of your symptoms, because they will come back, that's the nature of this kind of susceptibility. You need to write down what it will feel like, and how you are going to deal with it.'

I ignore him and never write the letter. I feel as if everything is going to be OK now. We've weathered the storm and surely we are owed a few years in which nothing awful happens? We can relax a little, enjoy our boys and enjoy our surroundings. My family is close by. My friends have been wonderful: Kate is a source of pure, uncomplicated happiness and I love every minute I spend with her, and Laurie, my law ally, is endlessly kind and funny. I appreciate them so much after a year without I can't imagine letting go again. It has been tricky, but Olivier and I have managed to survive. It is really starting to feel like we have a home here, a home that feels secure and happy, and once you have a real home, everything else, I hope, falls into place.

There is one problem with this happy, optimistic set-up. I have sort of agreed to move to Brussels.

« 16 »

Pauvre Belgique

I am utterly convinced it is a brilliant idea to move to Brussels. My theory is that it is the perfect compromise: French enough, but not too French. The whole country, after all, is a compromise. The technocrats of 1958 listed all its admirable, compromise-friendly characteristics when they argued in its favour: Brussels, a 'Committee of Experts' noted, is located on the frontier between the Latin and Germanic European cultures, has good transport links and medical infrastructure, is an important business and commercial centre and is considered neutral territory by the great powers of the European project. Perhaps not the most stirring of arguments, but very practical.

Nearly fifty years later, Olivier and I consider it neutral territory too. Before the children arrived I spent a few months there for work, taking taxis across the city with boxes of documents and sitting in the unglamorous lobbies of Commission buildings, wearing self-adhesive visitor's badges, waiting to take notes at meetings. At weekends, when Olivier visited, we explored, peering in at lives lived in high-ceilinged art nouveau mansion blocks and drinking bad coffee and *half and half* (a disgusting yet strangely moreish old lady's drink of half sweet white wine and half cheap fizz) in brown *fin de siècle* cafés next to pensioners sharing their speculoos biscuits with their dogs. It's a city that inspires domestic dreams: the houses are a riot of decorative eccentricity and quirk (botanical details and neo-classical columns, round windows, or boot scrapers in the shape of foxes' tails) and you can't help but look in and wonder what it would be like to live there. Is there a little garden out the back? What would it be like to stand in front of that round window with your morning coffee?

It's homely, but it's no one's actual home so neither of us, I reason, would be responsible for its foibles. Olivier has had more than enough of my wounded complaints about Parisian incivility, and following several long unsatisfactory nights in A&E for minor ailments and the discovery that our school options for Theo are limited to wildly expensive private rabbit hutches located in the basements of office blocks, I have been fielding complaints about the dysfunc-tional state of British public services. The last few years have been so hard, we don't need any more reasons to resent one another.

Brussels is a city of migrants too, migrants and exiles. It's a place you go when you can't stay at home. Marx wrote the Communist Manifesto there (though he didn't like it much, subsequently calling Belgium the 'paradise and the preserve of the landed classes') and in the 1850s, the newly minted country welcomed a wave of literary and political refugees from Napoléon III's repressive coup d'état: Victor Hugo, Alexandre Dumas, Charles Baudelaire and Paul Verlaine all spent time, with varying degrees of contentment, in Brussels. I like the idea of this, of course: it gives the city the kind of romantic pedigree I can get behind. Further waves of migration follow the Paris Commune, the Russian revolution, the Second World War and the declaration of independence of post-colonial Congo. Brussels residents describe themselves in dialect as '*zinneke*', mongrels, and the city has learned to welcome incomers, or at least, it welcomes the prosperous ones that work in the EU institutions or in the thousands of satellite bodies (NGOs, lobbyists, trade associations and lawyers) that orbit around them. It welcomes people like us.

The thing is, and this is perhaps inevitable with compromises, that Brussels doesn't represent anyone's dream. When you tell people you're moving to Paris, you get envy, an approving nod or a dreamy exhalation. Brussels, more often than not, gets a pause, a moment's recalibration before your interlocutor says something like: 'Oh! Is that for work?'

It's not a dramatically beautiful city. There is beauty, but it is discreet and tucked away and there are few of the kind of vistas that make your heart swell. The architects of the European project put paid to that with twenty years of hasty destruction and expedient concrete. The Grand-Place is lovely, but the streets around it are an ugly warren of kebab shops, improbable Manneken Pis trinkets (the Manneken Penis corkscrew is a favourite) and rowdy bars that periodically disgorge gangs of vomiting stags. The Sablon is undeniably beautiful too, but most of the square is used as a car park by oblivious Mercedes-driving pensioners stopping off to collect boxes of *petits fours* from the creak-

ingly formal *traiteur*, Wittamer. Most of the centre has stub-
bornly resisted gentrification and architectural treasures are
left to crumble next to Subway outlets and discount stores.
The *bruxellois* still mainly believe that the aspirational thing
is to head outwards, away from the urban unpleasantness
to the leafy suburbs: Woluwe, Uccle and Waterloo. Brussels'
equivalent of the Rue du Faubourg Saint-Honoré is the
foully congested Boulevard de Waterloo, where Tiffany and
Louis Vuitton rub shoulders with illegal waffle vans, and
huge sink holes open up in the pavements to universal
indifference. There is no Champs-Elysées and no Boulevard
Saint-Germain: there is a sort of vista along Rue Béliard in
the European Quarter from the Arche du Cinquanténaire,
Brussels' answer to the Arc de Triomphe, but the perspective
is of hundreds of office blocks of varying vintages and
limited aesthetic appeal. The Atomium has not had a chance
to become a fraction as iconic as the Eiffel Tower, since it's
so far outside the city it's practically in Antwerp. There's no
river: well, there used to be but it was buried underground in
the 1870s after one cholera epidemic too many, and instead
there's the canal, a murky industrial highway of a thing in
disreputable Molenbeek, the commune that causes respectable *bruxellois* to shiver when they mention it. Gene Kelly
and Leslie Caron would not dance along the *quais* of the
Bruxelles–Charleroi canal.

Brussels was very much not Charles Baudelaire's dream,
though he spent nearly three years in the city, exiled from
Paris by debt and scandal. Brussels disappointed and dis-
gusted Baudelaire: his lecture series was cut short and he

failed to find a Belgian publisher for his proposed new works; he found the Manneken Pis revolting and the Waterloo lion ridiculous, the Belgians bovine and provincial.

'Everything bland,' he writes in notes for a never-completed book about Belgium. '*Pauvre Belgique* . . . Everything sad, flavourless, asleep.' (Apparently this did not extend to the gingerbread from the biscuit shop Dandoy near the Grand-Place, where he was a regular customer.) 'Typical physiognomy comparable to that of the sheep or ram. Smiles impossible because of the recalcitrance of the muscles and the set of the teeth and jaws . . .'

Sebald is similarly uncomplimentary in the *Rings of Saturn*, his odd, meandering fictional account of a walking tour of Suffolk, with diversions through other lowlands in northern Europe. 'In Brussels in December 1964, I encountered more hunchbacks and lunatics than normally in a whole year,' he writes, challengingly, continuing: 'one sees in Belgium a distinctive ugliness.' The Brussels section of the book highlights 'the strikingly stunted growth of the population', detailing a series of dismal encounters under leaden grey skies with 'a deformed billiard player', a hunchbacked old woman and a 'slatternly garishly made-up sutler woman pulling a curious handcart with a goose shut in a cage'. In the manner of the earnest nineteenth-century phrenologists, both Baudelaire and Sebald try to make physiognomy revealing of character, in this case national character. For Sebald it's a physical and psychic manifestation of post-colonial guilt at Leopold II's atrocious record in Congo; for

Baudelaire it encapsulates everything wrong, mean, unseemly and peculiar about Brussels.

I have no quarrel with Belgian physiognomy and I don't think everything is bland or ugly, but it's true that I don't dream of Brussels like I dreamed of France: it's hard to be romantically inclined towards the city. Even so, I'm optimistic and positive: it looks easy to navigate and comfortable, there are schools and doctors and nice places to live with little gardens and I think we can be happy there. The job that I am applying for is much easier than my current one, too – it's a support role, so there should be no more client calls at 10 p.m. and no overnight turnarounds of research memos. It's the kind of job I have been fantasizing about since the children were born and suddenly there's a position open in my firm's Brussels office. It's the kind of opportunity that only comes around every four or five years and I feel a rare surge of certainty: I want this job and I can get it. My head, that oh-so-trustworthy organ, says it is the right thing to do.

I suppose there's some justification to ask – and people do – why I feel we need to move again. What is the rush? Couldn't we just . . . *be* for a little while, now that I'm not completely crazy and we're settled in this lovely part of London? It seems utterly contrary to uproot again, but it feels as if, for once, I actually could be in charge rather than just drifting with the current. Olivier is enthusiastic, predictably. He always favours change over stasis, always sees solutions in action.

'Do it,' he says when I bring up the idea tentatively. 'Let's go for it. At least we won't have to pay thousands of pounds a year to send our son to school underground like a mole, in a place with no outside space and NO CANTEEN' (for some, probably French, reason the 'no canteen' incenses him more than anything).

We have talked about moving to Brussels before, about how good it could be for us, so at least it's a shared vision. I really like the idea of us building something new together after these wearying years and it feels like the beginning of a sort of apology from me to Olivier, a turning back towards him and the boys after my self-indulgent solo loopiness of the last year. Perhaps I need that mythical thing, the fresh start? So I apply for the job.

I turn on the charm and call in favours and visit the Brussels office to schmooze the people I know and meet the ones I don't. I am paraded around the office – a vast nineteenth-century pile near the royal palace, it's the former Belgian Bank of the Congo of the colonial era, part of the complex of Congo-related administrations Conrad's alter-ego Marlow visited in *Heart of Darkness* – and show off my French and my experience (thankfully no one seems to remember the four months I spent as an intern in the office, hiding in the ladies lavatory to avoid all-nighter sessions working on a hideously contentious fertilizer merger). I truly believe that I can do this job and do it well and I negotiate – actually negotiate! – until eventually we reach an agreement: the job is mine. I can start in the summer.

Once the decision is made and the papers are signed, of course I start to feel anxious about leaving again. It's not so much the upheaval – for some reason that doesn't bother me – but leaving my family. Joe is always down from York, showing up with offerings from Bettys, and my sister and her boyfriend drop in and hang out, playing with the boys. It has been lovely having my father and stepmother a short tube ride away too, and it feels right, to have a sort of family life – this is how you are supposed to raise children, not in isolation. My father sometimes comes over to the flat between meetings in a black cab and takes Theo out to the Transport Museum or the zoo, and I love watching the two of them head off, seriously, in conversation. Why would I turn my back on all this?

'It's really not far,' I tell them, trying to convince myself at the same time. 'Two hours! It's no further than York.'

Before we move definitively, I work in the Brussels office a few days a month and during that time I try to find us somewhere to live. A fat, patronizing estate agent in a tweed jacket and cashmere roll-neck collects me from the office after work in his Smart car and drives me round the city for viewings. He has quite fixed ideas about what I ought to like – detached country villas in the furthest reaches of deadly silent suburbs accessible only by Chelsea tractor, mainly – and we have some thoroughly unsuccessful, if fascinating, visits. We see a perfectly preserved in amber brown and smoked-glass 1970s condo, complete with a built-in deep-fat fryer and an indoor rockery in a glass atrium ('It has so much potential,' says the estate agent. 'But who on earth *lives* here?' I marvel). We see several enormous, dull flats in quiet blocks, all magnolia paint and marble flooring, recently vacated by embassy staff from countries I could not place on a map. One afternoon we see an elegant art nouveau villa crumbling away between two office blocks, and that evening we tour a tall, thin house from a fairy tale panelled in intricately carved oak, as dark and poky as a priest hole.

I don't actually begrudge the time spent on these visits, because they are so interesting. Every house, every building in this city is so different and a confusion of eras and styles sit side by side on the same street. For a place that trails a reputation of drabness, a single look upward shatters the myth. Any possible variation of any decorative detail – balconies, windows, gabling, tiles and cornicing – has been tried by someone on some Brussels street at some time and no flight of fancy is left unexplored. We see a fully fledged fake Egyptian temple, a flock of tiled peacocks, gilded frescoes and stained glass. It seems very optimistic, this assertion of individuality: the homeowners of Brussels are confident enough to put their mark on the city. In Paris, you have to conform to the exigencies of the Haussmann standard; here you can try on a thousand different identities writ large in stained glass and paint and wrought iron and find the one that fits best.

In the end the best fit for me is really very ordinary. I fall for a plain red-brick house in a quiet street to the south of the city. I am a bit worried that the area – prosperous and quiet – is the Belgian equivalent of Fulham or worse still, the Belgian 17th arrondissement: apparently it is where all the French people live. But the smarter parts of the city, where the aspirational Eurocrats live, are regrettably too expensive with two children, and the centre has no green space. This suburb has pretty, affordable houses, good tram lines and the estate agent's seal of approval. Also, compromise is the order of the day, so here we are.

The street my house is in does not look particularly well heeled, which is something of a comfort. The house itself is half a storey shorter than its neighbours and its brickwork is stained with years of grime. It is a little dark and the tiny garden is a wasteland of mud and rubble. A great deal of money has been lavished, not always to good effect, upon the house by its rather haunted-looking Parisian owners (they are moving to Dallas, which may explain their haunted look). The white goods and door handles and sanitary ware are a festival of expensive stupidity and there is an American fridge the size of an African elephant, pointed out to me proudly by the agent. Even so, I like it instantly: it has good plain bones, the bedrooms are nicely proportioned and I fall in love with the tired but beautiful typically Belgian brown and blue floral tiles in the hall. From the main bedroom, which is light and airy and huge, you get an enchanting view over the patchwork of tiny city gardens to the rear, all lilac trees and ivy. There's nothing exceptional about the house: it's a lot like the house in York I grew up in, the house where my stepfather still lives, just taller and thinner. Maybe that's what I like about it? There's something about the intimate geography of this area, the little backyards, narrow snicket-ways and brick buildings, that reminds me of York too.

Mainly what I like about this place is that it already feels like a family home. It feels like the kind of place where you stick children's drawings on the fridge and draw pencil lines to mark their height on the kitchen wall. I can imagine us shoving our cardboard moving boxes – veterans of three moves – into the basement and not getting them out again. The estate agent's blurb describes it as a '*maison unifamiliale*', a one-family home, and I like that. I am ready for a *maison unifamilale*.

The area around the house is sleepy; you can hardly believe you're in a capital city, but there's just enough life to satisfy me. 'Where are the *shops*,' I have wailed again and again to the estate agent, who can't understand why I won't just get in my Range Rover and *drive* to the shops like everyone else, and here at least he can point to a couple: there's a bakery opposite, and a couple of doors up from the house there is an open-all-hours corner shop, a chaotic warren that smells of crumbs, cats, dust and long-discontinued sweeties, manned by a tiny frail gentleman in his eighties. Next to that is a barber's shop lined with giant painted renderings of bouffant men's hairstyles. The barber's window has a regularly changed seasonal display, from text books and pencils for *la rentrée* in September, skis and bobble hats in January, sinister bunnies at Easter. After that, the street becomes residential again, barring a strange restaurant, the side of which is covered in a giant mural of some sandal-wearing monks inexplicably waiting for a tram and carrying a duck on a tray. The 1900s shade into the 1930s then the 1950s architecturally until you get to a matronly lingerie shop, where the barber's mother sells girdles and liberty bodices in thick beige elastane, and the ice cream parlour, which is magnificent. It has retro neon signage and it is always packed: people of all ages (nervous couples on dates, elderly gentlemen on their own, groups of well-dressed Eurocrats on team-bonding expeditions) congregate on even the rainiest days for huge overblown sundaes topped with glacé cherries and whipped cream. If you go the other way down the street, there's a primary school, its windows filled with bright kids' paintings.

Olivier comes to have a look, pokes at the walls and frowns at the boiler. He's not as convinced as me – the garden is tiny, and aren't we paying over the odds for all these daft Philippe Starck doorknobs? – but I walk him around the neighbourhood, aping my companion the tweedy estate agent, pointing out the excellent transport links, the cheese shop and the hundred-yard walk to the primary school (above ground). I manage to convince him over a scoop of vanilla at the ice cream parlour (the school has a canteen, which helps) and we put in an offer.

The house purchase is as tense and long-winded and bad-tempered as these transactions usually are. The Parisian lady who is moving to Dallas has a breakdown over curtains and cries on the phone, there is a last-minute demand for us to provide a stack of cash to a dark-suited silver fox of a *notaire* in a wood-panelled office, which leads to farcical scenes running around the banks of Liverpool Street and transporting wads of cash on the train but finally we all come together in tense silence in the *notaire*'s office in the very respectable Sablon square with a pile of paperwork to sign the *compromis*, which makes the sale binding. Madame signs with the *notaire*'s Montblanc in a benzodiazepine stupor, Monsieur shakes our hands coldly and there it is, we are

Belgian homeowners. Olivier and I go a few doors down to the Vieux Saint Martin, which is possibly the nicest bar in the city, for an expensive cup of coffee on the *terrasse* to celebrate. The sun is shining and you get a delicious miniature palmier biscuit with your coffee and it feels like the start of a new adventure.

A few weeks later we move in.

« 17 »

Hunchbacks and Lunatics

On some level, I suppose I think that Belgium will be like France with training wheels, and Brussels like Paris for the psychically feeble, but it becomes very obvious to me very soon after we move in that I am wrong. Belgium is so very much not France and Brussels is nothing like I thought it would be.

The most important thing first: cake. Every corner of Brussels smells of vanilla and yeast and baking dough thanks to the waffle vans, but Belgian patisserie makes me sad. It tastes and looks like French patisserie executed by someone who doesn't actually like cake, who knows vaguely what it is supposed to be but hasn't bothered tasting anything. There is a thing optimistically called a *'flan'* you can find in some bakeries and supermarkets but it is dense and claggy, in a wet, thick pastry case with an unappetizing brown spongy top. Belgian croissants have had both their legs amputated to become a sad truncated blob called a *'couque'* which has little to recommend it, and in restaurants the safest option is to eschew patisserie entirely and go for the ever-present *Dame Blanche,* vanilla ice cream and chocolate sauce. The bakery in our street is a disaster for everything but Moroccan pancakes and none of the others in the neighbourhood are up to much: the éclairs are dry, flavours are unimaginative and anything promising is inexplicably contaminated with speculoos. Speculoos – the cloyingly sweet and insufficiently spiced national biscuit – is ubiquitous, contaminating cheesecakes and tiramisus and at its worst even game stews. Whenever I hear of a rumoured good bakery (and I keep my ear to the ground on such matters) – it turns out to be French and when I go, there is always a queue of antsy Parisian exiles, shooting daggers at whoever gets the last *baguette à l'ancienne*.

Shopping, generally, is a discombobulating experience. The corner shop in our street is a time machine to a bygone era, motes of dust hanging in the air and mysterious meats in the vintage fridge, with a smell that reminds me of my one-eyed great aunt Eve's house. Everyone in the neighbour-hood has an account, kept by the ancient shopkeeper in a giant ledger he completes in pencil, and his son (not so young, in his forties perhaps, but strangely ageless) delivers pensioners' shopping on foot in a wheeled trolley, while dispensing slightly uneasy compliments to any female under sixty in the vicinity. If you want a bag of sugar or a can of Coke, you can anticipate a lengthy wait as some doddery elderly lady does her entire weekly shop in front of you, including long discussions of the relative merits of various kinds of muscat and some painfully slow ham-slicing. While this is unfolding, you can try to stroke one of the cats who sit in the vegetable rack full of savoury crackers, but this is best avoided if you value your epidermis, or you can study the wall of small ads (mainly lost cats, presumably chased away by the ferocious vegetable rack ones).

There is nothing I recognize nearby as a proper supermarket – the local one is like shopping in a crap 1980s Asda where they hide the aluminium foil near the envelopes – and in the tiny convenience stores near work, I am constantly unnerved by the employees' desire to engage me in conversation: so I really like avocados then, she can't eat them they go right through her, what am I making for dinner, ooh, that sounds good. Weirdest of all is Colruyt. I don't know if we would have made it to Colruyt on our own, but everyone in the office is insistent I have to go there, so we do. Colruyt is a discount supermarket in a poorly lit orange hangar and it is a Belgian institution. It is famously the only supermarket chain that was not affected by the dioxin scandal of 1999 and its meat is revered in a cult-like fashion across Belgium, but as a user experience, it is challenging. The floor is bare concrete, approximately half of the surface area is devoted to beer, fresh produce is kept in an eerie refrigerated room in which it is impossible to spend more than two minutes without risking hypothermia, and the trolleys are famously resistant to being pushed. When I am struggling to try and get one down an aisle without taking out anyone's shins, a shelf stacker hails me.

'You have to look straight ahead,' he explains to me with the air of one inducting a novice into a tricky technical discipline. 'Don't look at the displays.'

'Why?'

'If you look straight ahead, the trolley will keep going, but if you look at the display, the trolley RUNS STRAIGHT INTO THEM.'

'But . . .'

'There have been studies.'

This kind of exchange is typical. The meat in Colruyt is kept behind a glass window and is not accessible to customers. Instead, you have to fill in a lengthy form detailing the kind of meat you want, and leave it in a box. Later, a tannoy announcement (in Dutch) recalls you to collect your purchases. On Saturdays, Colruyt is transformed into a giant coffee morning, with enough free samples of food and drink to keep you going well past lunchtime. The whole experience is utterly confusing.

My confusion extends – expands, even – when it comes to language. It's not so much the Dutch that bothers me, though I don't think I realized that Dutch speakers – you never say Flemish speakers, it's considered rude and inaccurate – are actually in a majority (57 per cent) in Belgium. My office mate is Dutch-speaking and I enjoy listening to her. She's ultra-blunt (this is widely considered to be a Dutch characteristic in Brussels) and explains to me how to access a late abortion and voluntary euthanasia as a sort of extended office induction, after the coffee machine and the lavatories. I'm quite tickled by the Dutch signage – I like the words I come across repeatedly like *'omlegging'* and *'endbestemming'* (diversion and terminus, thank you, the 92 tram) and I soon learn exactly how to say 'the order number 400 is ready for collection at the butcher's' (thank you, Colruyt). For an English speaker with a smattering of German it's both easy and fun to make some basic sense of Dutch.

I'm actually more perplexed by the French I hear. I don't find it ugly, but it's earthy and rhythmic and far, far away from the poetry of the lines of Proust I would recite to myself in Normandy. Yes, everyone says *septante* and *nonante* and it's peculiar and I feel self-conscious when I have to give my new mobile number, full of 70s and 90s, but there's so much more than that. Belgians use *s'il vous plaît* in the way the Dutch use *astublieft*, as a sort of 'here you are', which sounds mannered and old-fashioned to me when I first hear it. They use *savoir*, to know, when they mean *pouvoir*, can.

'*Je ne sais pas le faire avant mardi*,' the dry cleaner will tell you, shaking her head. 'I don't know how to do it before Tuesday', which makes no sense.

The word '*excessivement*' seems to me to be used, well, *excessivement*. Olivier shudders like a dowager when someone says '*il fait caillant*' for 'it's chilly', but '*la drache*' for the insistent, cold Brussels rain feels nicely onomatopoeic. Some things I love, but are just too Belgian for me – they feel wrong in my mouth. '*Non peut-être*?!' which means the opposite – absolutely – is just too colloquial and I can't manage '*Je te dis quoi*' (a sort of 'I'll let you know'), though Olivier rapidly adopts it. I could never mimic the way Belgians say *huit* either, which comes out with a sort of rounded 'o' sound hidden in it: *houit*.

Of course Brussels French is rarely the French of native speakers: most of us are just getting by as best we can in a language that isn't our own and some are barely making an effort at all. I feel much less self-conscious speaking French here than I ever did in France, because most of the people I speak to aren't any better at it than I am. It's very freeing, in a way: I can say anything to anyone, because I'll probably make as decent a job of it as most other people. But without the permanent fear of disapproval, I feel as if my French is getting worse.

In the office, we mainly speak English, but it's a peculiar kind of English. With a mix of Swedish, Dutch, French, Australians and Germans and Brits, there is no one prevailing cultural influence so we operate in a functional, but unlovely, multicultural administrative Esperanto. People 'assist to' meetings and we have *'stagiaires'* or *'referendaires'* instead of interns. My boss is fairly typical: he's Dutch-speaking Belgian, but his French is perfect and his English is exuberantly colloquial, peppered with swearing and oddities. Evening receptions involve a puzzling thing called a 'walking dinner' and the office canteen offers such delights as 'birds without heads' (it's a sort of rissole) and *'cannibale'* sandwiches (I never find out what these are as I am too frightened to try). There is a puzzling series of festivities to grapple with: 'Secretaries Day', Assumption, 'Schuman Day', even a Breughel-themed night in the office bar.

I find it hard to work out where I fit in. The young lawyers of all nationalities, here for a year or two at most, live within three or four streets of each other and go out to the same bars when they get an evening off. The partners live out in the sticks, in huge villas with gardens and wives and children and dogs, driving into the office in huge German cars. The secretaries are mostly my kind of age with children, but they stick together and live in other towns, dashing to catch their trains in the afternoon. I am not part of any group, at once too old and too young to fit in. My work, too, is self-contained, verging on dull on occasion, and I never get the usual bonding experiences: impossible deadlines, travel, absurdly demanding clients. I don't take proper lunch breaks so I can leave earlier and pick the boys up (I rush off at 5:30 to get my tram every day) and though our weekly office 'teatime' should be a good opportunity to socialize, most of the lawyers are too busy to attend, so it's usually me, the office handyman, a handful of secretaries and whichever partner has to host that week, making small talk over tiny plastic cups of tepid Lipton Yellow tea and frangipane tarts (I miss Colin the Caterpillar). Everyone is nice, lovely even, but it's hard to make proper friends.

My feeling of dislocation intensifies with the arrival of Saint Nicolas, the confusing *Mitteleuropa* proto-Christmas. Few Belgian events have the power to bewilder the migrant like Saint Nicolas. The festival has its origins in a grisly little legend in which three children are captured by an unscrupulous butcher, who chops them up and salts them in a barrel, intending to sell them as ham. The children are miraculously resurrected by Saint Nicolas, who just happens to be passing. It is a very big deal indeed in Belgium and the Netherlands, with Saint Nicolas's arrival each year by speedboat from Spain (where, according to legend, he spends the remainder of the year) televised to great national excitement.

The office pushes the boat out for Saint Nicolas, with a party for employees' children: obviously, we bring the boys. The lobby is filled with balloons, and baskets of speculoos biscuits replace the branded mints at reception, while in the library the dusty volumes of the Belgian civil code are moved aside and replaced with a lavish buffet of cream horns, frangipane cakes, M&Ms, pastel marshmallow effigies of the Virgin Mary and waffles in their many splendours.

Outside in the atrium, rows of children watch a shadow puppeteer conjure up a series of shapes in front of a rudimentary screen – the entertainment must be wordless, due to the lack of a common language among the office offspring. There's an owl, a galloping horse, then what appears to be a series of Can Can dancers. The audience, aged 2–12, is a tough crowd, restive and easily distracted by the incredible snacking opportunities mere yards away. Theo more or less refuses to watch the puppeteer when there are M&Ms to lick and discard and Louis prefers removing back issues of the *Common Market Law Review* from the library shelves, but everyone, including my children, snaps to attention when a white-gloved hand appears, tantalizingly draped over the first-floor balcony railing.

'He's here!' the whisper goes round, in many languages simultaneously.

An eerie procession descends to the main atrium, to the accompaniment of a choir of children singing the sickly 'Sinterklaas Kapoentje': dearest Santa. The saint is first. He is not fat and jolly like our Santa, but tall and imposing, with a crook, mitre, white priestly vestments topped by a red cloak and most of his face obscured by a long beard. He is accompanied by four 'Zwarte Piets' – Black Petes or 'Pères Fouettards' (whipping fathers, unnervingly) in French – his sidekicks or enforcers. The Pères Fouettards are dressed in fifteenth-century-style black and red page outfits with huge lacy collars and white gloves; most unnerving of all, they are blacked up. Some defenders of the tradition insist that Zwarte Piet is not racist: he is simply 'dirty' from the soot in the chimney and it is a 'lovely tradition', but the traditional curly black wig and earring that finish the outfit off make this interpretation difficult to sustain.

The Pères Fouettards wave and throw chocolate coins into the audience. One of them is carrying a large book: Saint Nicolas's register of the nice and the naughty. As Saint Nicolas approaches the crêpe-paper-covered dais and settles on his throne, a convulsion of excitement and something darker grips the assembled children.

'Noooo,' weeps a girl of about six in her best velvet party frock, patent-shod heels dragging on the herringbone parquet as one of the Piets beckons to her, the whites of his eyes gleaming against a full face of black make-up, one gloved hand proffering a basket full of candy. 'I don't want to go in his sack!' Traditionally, the Pères Fouettards are responsible for beating naughty children with a birch twig, before placing them in a sack or wicker basket and kicking them back to Spain. With this in mind, the atmosphere in the room is not one of joyful anticipation.

One after another, the children are summoned up onto the stage to be quizzed by Saint Nicolas, while the Fathers

Whip consult their Big Book of Children. Some smaller children are encouraged to give up their dummies, which the Fathers Whip place in a giant Nutella pot, in exchange for a gift. My sons watch, wide-eyed. They have been prepared by weeks of colouring and songs at school, but Saint Nicolas in the flesh is a whole other proposition. Finally, buoyed by chocolate and lured by the large presents the children who submit to Saint Nicolas's examination leave holding, Theo is persuaded onto the stage, where he sits for a photo, un-smiling, on the episcopal knee. Louis follows, of course: he will never allow himself to be bested by his brother and we leave clutching lavish gifts. On the way back to the car, still a little unnerved, Theo pulls at my sleeve.

'Do those men *have* to come to our house?'

There is a lot of this kind of thing in Brussels; the city is in thrall to its own folklore. In July, hundreds of people (and horses, and large papier-mâché figurines) process around the city centre in sixteenth-century costume to commemorate Charles V's ceremonial arrival in Brussels in 1549. In August a group of men called, improbably, *buumdroegers* ('tree carriers') cut down a tree – the *meyboom* – in the Forêt de Soignes and parade it through the streets of the city in tradi-tional costume, accompanied by a selection of papier-mâché giants (the men who carry these are the *poepedroegers*, which is just as bad). In November students parade through the city in lab coats with beer tankards round their necks to celebrate St Verhaegen and in March a charitable fraternity of blacked-up men in top hats and knee breeches parade around the Grand-Place collecting money. The Manneken

Pis has an association of friends and defenders and a wardrobe of some 800 traditional and not so traditional costumes from around the world in which he is dressed ceremonially (a committee decides on the introduction of new outfits, periodically, and on the rota of which ones he should wear when). On certain days, the water he pees is replaced with beer (you can check which days on the Manneken's website). In the boys' schoolyard, the children wear fancy dress as the headmaster puts a flaming torch to *bonhomme hiver*, a human effigy of winter, on a windy February day, flames licking the base of the climbing frame in an affront to received notions of health and safety.

On some level, the city still believes it is a place of guilds and merchants and princes, a prosperous city-state defined by its glorious history. ('A ghost town,' spat Baudelaire, 'a mummy of a town, it smells of death, the Middle Ages and tombs.' For Marlow in Conrad's *Heart of Darkness* it's a 'whited sepulchre.') In fact it's kept afloat by thousands of lanyarded back room politicians and lobbyists and their expense accounts in antiseptic, anonymous office blocks. I can understand, though, how that cosy sense of tradition endures, because Brussels feels nothing like a modern capital city. It reminds me most of Rouen: a prosperous provincial town. Everyone seems to go to the same places at the same times and wherever we go (the market, the cinema, the playground), we see faces we recognize. Half the street comments on the audacity of our colour choice when we paint our door cornflower blue, and when Olivier goes to the local barber, he comes back with a wealth of anecdotes on our Texan–

Parisian predecessors and conjecture on the state of their marriage. Our neighbourhood is a hotbed of PG-rated small town gossip, propagated by the barber, the shopkeeper's son and the groups of mothers who sit in the playground. Within weeks, I have an encyclopaedic knowledge of various divorces, poor school attendance records and run-ins over parking spaces.

But it's odd, too. One evening a taxi driver shows me his portfolio of miniature liturgically-themed art, which he keeps in the glove compartment of his car. Another time a fellow passenger on the 92 tram decides to engage me in conversation about whether it would be possible to milk rabbits. There's a pensioner called 'Mr Penguin' who walks the streets of Brussels dressed as, and quacking like, a penguin. One weekend we go to a gallery and a group of Icelandic performance artists, one of whom is wearing a string of sausages round his neck and another carrying a large glass pot of yoghurt, steal my handbag. A giant blue brain sculpture appears in the sky on the roof of a museum and disappears a few months later without apparent explanation, like something from a Tim Burton film or a Magritte. The city's most famous graffiti artist, Bonom, covers vast office blocks with beautiful, weird natural motifs: dinosaurs, spiders, a giant falling fox and, more controversially, a copy of Courbet's distinctly not safe for work nude *L'Origine du Monde*. At the summer Zinneke parade – a contemporary invention, intended to celebrate the city's diversity – I watch a woman on a bicycle-drawn float serve papier-mâché ice cream cones filled with paper herrings to an enthusiastic crowd. Nearer home, the man who lives next door to the corner shop sits on the street on sunny days on a bench of his own creation, which is kitted out with a rear-view mirror, a CD player on which he plays Bach fugues, a fencing foil, a sandpaper scratching post, a variety of circuit boards, magazines and pencils. Where are we? What *is* this place? Some days it seems as if everyone in the city is insane; that surreality is hard-wired in the Belgian DNA and Sebald's hunchbacks and lunatics are everywhere.

For me the lunatics, the penguins, the papier-mâché herring-filled ice cream cones, are my favourite part of Brussels: they cut through the cosily self-satisfied Mercedes-driving, tweed-wearing parts. There's a subversive heart to the city and in a place that refuses so categorically to take itself seriously how could you not be happy?

« 18 »

Les Quatre Cents Coups

When I am not at work – and I am at work far less in my new job, that was the point of it – I look after the children. We go from park to museum to musty suburban soft play area (beer is available in all these places, interestingly) and often end up in *Quick*, the optimistically named Belgian fast food chain where no one is in a hurry to do anything. More often than not, though, we stay at home, relishing the luxury of space: a garden in which to poke things with sticks, stairs to run a Slinky down and enough room to leave your crayons and Lego scattered across the floor. It is a very different existence out here in what I must accept are the suburbs; life is slowed down and stretched out to toddler pace. If the boys want to spend fifteen minutes examining a dead wasp, that is perfectly fine since we have nowhere we have to be and no one is behind us tutting. A slow meander to the corner of the street for an ice cream and back is enough to occupy most of an afternoon. I don't know how I feel about this, but the boys seem to have eased into it effortlessly. Their hierarchy of needs – juice, sandpit, digger trucks, cartoons – is met and if Theo occasionally talks wistfully of his best friend Julius back in London, they have expressed little angst at the upheaval.

I suppose these lazy, quiet afternoons are a good thing, because in the most basic way, everything has changed for both of them: they have started school now, that proper Belgian primary school down the road. Louis is only two and half, hardly more than a baby, but even he is old enough for the reception class (the *classe d'acceuil*), so every morning we trot off, the boys with their heavy school bags on their backs, to the door of the *maternelle* section, where I kiss them goodbye under the basilisk glare of the classroom assistants.

School imposes a new, bureaucratic rhythm upon our days. The doors shut at 8:25 regardless of whether someone has decided to walk backwards only on the white paving stones or has lost an essential soft toy or pebble; there is homework and gym kit to be remembered and a profusion of forms to be filled in every week, even for Louis's class, most of whose members aren't absolutely up to speed with things like walking and peeing. Even before the boys start, we are presented with a long list of *fournitures*, school equipment, which is mind-bogglingly specific. They both need a long-sleeved apron (I have never encountered such a thing in my life), a particular brand of crayons of a particular diameter, glue sticks, miniature whiteboards and the accompanying pens, various lengths of rulers and a bewildering number of file dividers. I enjoy sourcing this stuff – it is like a scavenger hunt for stationery fetishists – but it sets the tone for the school year quite precisely. Belgian school is strict: far stricter even than Am Stram Gram. Sometimes I come to pick the children up and everyone is '*puni*', heads on desks, in silence, for some minor outbreak of insubordination, and both boys are regularly punished in the schoolyard for things they don't even understand. There are frequent parents' evenings at which we discuss the evolving way the boys draw stick men and written reports on their progress. *'Rigueur'* is the headmaster's favourite word (he says it a lot at the yearly prize-giving, before we all stand and rhubarb along to the Belgian national anthem, 'La Brabançonne'). It is not one that comes to mind when I think of my own sons.

Louis starts school at the same time as all the other two-and-a-half-year-olds in our neighbourhood and he seems soothed by the regimented structures: nap times and snack times and gym time. Even so, school doesn't seem cosy or welcoming in the way I feel an infant school should and I'm spooked by the way that every drawing is identical – you must put Saint Nicolas's hat here, with this much silver foil, five balls of cotton wool for the beard, and his staff must go here. It's interesting how little store is placed on individuality and how much on conforming: it seems at odds with every-thing else I have seen in the city. With all the rules, the rote learning and *dictées*, the perfect looping, cursive script, prac-tised on repetitive daily worksheets, there's an ink-stained echo of Truffaut's sad, lovely film about a disaffected Parisian schoolboy, *Les Quatre Cents Coups*, without the navy overalls.

It's harder for Theo, who has to find his way in a class of kids who have known each other for at least two years, and he rails against it with various acts of minor mutiny. He finds the whole business of school – sitting at a desk, doing those handwriting exercises – a tremendous bore and engages with it as little as possible. We are summoned several times to the headmaster's office to discuss his lack of *rigueur* and his defi-ance and he is rapidly despatched to speech therapy and to something called a *graphomotricienne*, which is an elderly lady who makes him roll playdough balls for unclear reasons. He has to practise tongue twisters like '*en écrivant à ma maîtresse je me suis trompé d'adresse*' ('while writing to my mistress I put the wrong address') and '*Serge déguste une crêpe Suzette*' (Serge samples a Crêpe Suzette). These details tickle me, but the situation feels strange. I hate the idea of school crushing his irrepressible daftness, but there is also something about Theo not fitting in which makes me uncomfortable. The way I adapt is to try and pass seamlessly for local, to comply and conform. By standing out, Theo is blowing my cover.

But perhaps he's happy standing out? Either way, we per-severe and try to make him love, or at least, tolerate school, because its dense programme of activities (gym, theatre and beach trips, visits from farm animals, and cookery sessions) is so obviously what he needs. Both boys are fizzing with energy, exploding with exponential advances in language and understanding and physical ability.

Theo – when he isn't battling with the letter 'z' – is firing on all cylinders. He is a tale weaver, an imaginative player and a lover of all things scaly: lizards, serpents and dragons. His world has become more complex: toys are embroiled in long fanciful sagas requiring much of the contents of the kitchen and ending with them lined up in dormitory 'beds' of tea towels and kitchen roll on the hall floor. He devises a fantasy television series called 'Karate Lizards' in which we must all take on the role of a lizard super hero (Olivier is a chameleon, Theo himself is a bearded dragon, I am a skink and Louis is uncharitably given the role of 'a small lizard').

For a few weeks he suffers a full-on existential crisis, during which he mourns nightly the inevitability of death. 'I don't want to die. I don't want to be in the dark without you,' he cries, inconsolable, sitting on the stairs, clutching at me convulsively with a clammy hand. 'I want to be one of those fish from the era of the dinosaurs and never die.'

This lasts for a few days, then he moves on to something else: growing horrible insects called triops from dried eggs, constructing an arena for snail races or dinosaurs (always dinosaurs).

Louis has changed too: a head full of new stimuli seems to have calmed his temper and he is quieter now, self-contained but utterly determined. He likes things to be orderly and domestic (his favourite toys are a pretend toaster, washing machine and microwave) and he develops a very secretive side, hiding his possessions in boxes and locked drawers and forbidden corners. For a while he decides to become a parrot, and he is a parrot for several weeks, answering only to 'Rocket the parrot' and pecking his food directly from the bowl. Later, they both decide they are bats, and hang upside-down from the furniture, squeaking.

I love the ages they have reached. I get to listen to what they have done and how they feel, unpicking the multi-coloured jumble of snatched impressions and misunderstandings, and it's fascinating to have a window back into the white-hot strangeness of being small, so vivid and confusing, sometimes scary and sometimes joyous. The despatches that reach me from the front line of childhood are weird and funny: Madame is off sick because she dropped a giant ball on her foot. Joël is my enemy. I have lost my dead moth. The boys remind me of the children in the scene in *Les Quatre Cents Coups* where Antoine and René sit in the back row of the puppet show in the Jardin du Luxembourg. Truffaut films the illuminated faces of the much younger children around them, rapt, their expressions a magic lantern show of joy, fear, concentration. Life is so extraordinary and absorbing when you are that age and I get to share it. The only thing is, they tell me everything in French.

This is my fault. After three moves and three countries, I am so keen to smooth their path to assimilation; I would do anything to help them fit in. Communication seems both basic and essential to me so as soon as we arrive, we switch to French. We speak only French to them and make them watch French cartoons, and over the summer their grandparents come and take them away for an intensive French-speaking holiday in Normandy. Of course, the boys understand French: Olivier and I speak it all the time. But until now their spoken vocabulary has been limited to a handful of nouns: *maman, papa, doudou, pipi,* which slot into English sentence structures.

For the first couple of months after we move, their language is a chaotic jumble of English and French, English interspersed with French school jargon for which they know no equivalent: *sieste, journal de classe, collation.* But quickly, astonishingly quickly, it takes on a more coherently French shape. It's a shape I am simultaneously learning, thanks to the rigours of primary school grammar: subject, direct and indirect objects, qualifying adjectives, *complement indirect du groupe sujet*. This insistence on the naming of the parts is a long way from the 'naming words' and 'doing words' we learned at my primary school; it's as if you need a far clearer instruction manual for French than English. But it works: when they share a bath, or squabble over Lego together, they start, spontaneously, to fight in French, the language of the playground. *'C'est à moi . . .' 'Je vais dire . . .'* From time to time, I even get called *madame*, which I suppose is better than calling your teacher *maman*.

In the afternoons and at weekends, the TV resonates with sanity-eroding Anglo-Saxon kids' shows mangled into French. Theo favours *Les Totally Spies* (a gang of high-pitched crime-fighting bimbos) and Louis *Dora L'Exploratrice*. Both of them will happily watch *Les Héros d'Higglyville* (talking matryoshka dolls having soporific community-minded 'adventures') or *Bob l'Éponge* who lives in an *ananas dans la mer* and whose pants don't get a mention in the French version. I hate all of it. The voices are astonishingly awful to my ears: high-pitched and idiotic; why, with all the reserves of beauty and poetry spoken French can command do all French voice-over artists sound so grating? Can they not find work in any other domain due to their vocal handicap? The home-grown Francophone Belgian fare is no better, which seems a shame given the proud tradition of cartoons in our adoptive land: there is a stupid hippopotamus and dog double act who are cruelly unfunny and Titeuf, a grotesquely unpleasant-looking cartoon child, a bit like Bart Simpson but without the wit. The Barbapapas – those benign, shape-shifting colourful ovoids – are Truffaut in contrast, but no one at school watches the Barbapapas, who are universally rated '*trop nul*' (lame).

Because now my children have peers whose opinions are important to them and we live in the slipstream of playground crazes, bright, hard-edged things with their own TV tie-ins and Anglo-Saxon sounding names: Pogs and Bakugans and Beyblades. A lot of English words are bandied around, but they are so distorted you can't even tell they are English any more. Dark Wolf becomes 'Dar Kweulf'. Battle, 'Batteule'. I don't think the children recognize their mother's tongue in them; they occupy another part of their brains. I play along – I like a practical way to further the assimilation process – and we trail to the local toyshop to stock up on whichever piece of Japanese-inspired plastic is the essential must-have item of the month.

The greatest, the most enduring of all these enthusiasms, is Pokemon, the world-dominating Japanese cute creature battle universe. My house is full of Pokemons: our lives are filled with powers (*pouvoirs*) and life points (*points vie*). Back in London I used to work for a client who produced Pokemon products, so I know more about Pikachu and Ash and Jigglypuff than any thirtysomething should, but now I have to relearn everything and the names are all different. It's Rondoudou, not Jigglypuff, Salamèche not Charizard; I sometimes wonder who on earth sat down and found appropriate French names for several thousand fictional creatures.

What a job. We watch the TV series endlessly, singing along with the theme tune: '*Un jour je serai le meilleur dresseur,*' the boys bellow. '*Je me battrai sans répit.*' It sounds far more poetic in French (I still believe almost everything does). For a while it feels as if we live in a brightly coloured Franco-Japanese bubble of cartoon violence.

Far better are the picture books. I buy armfuls of them, because in my mind, the way to love anything is through books, of course. If you avoid the dull 'here are some things and their names' books, which French publishing seems inexplicably to favour (*Les Insectes, Les Plantes*), they are beautifully illustrated and terribly dark. Louis falls for an intricately drawn book in which a snail grows a shell so gigantic and decorative it can no longer move and starves to death. We acquire another book with accompanying rock opera CD called *Moitié de Coq* (Half a Cock), in which a cockerel on a quest shoves a wolf, a fox and a river up its arsehole. This is exactly what it says: 'arsehole' (*trou du cul*), which seems startlingly rude in a book aimed at six- or seven-year-olds: '*rentre dans mon trou du cul*' (go up my arsehole), the cockerel instructs everyone. Perhaps most surreally terrifying of all is *Monstres Chéris*, a sort of picture book family tree for a group of monsters. The father monster is called Papadamour, which makes him sound like a Haitian dictator, and he terrorizes the family with an axe (he cuts off mother monster's toe when they first meet). There is also Tante Andrée la Fumée, who is just a curling ball of smoke. She gets dismembered too.

My very favourite picture book, however, is *Les Larmes*

de Crocodile, Crocodile Tears, by André François. This 1956 classic is long and thin like a crocodile and it explains how to go and catch a crocodile by going to Egypt with a long wooden box ('UNE LONGUE CAISSE A CROCODILE'), acquiring a fez and a dromedary and sitting on the banks of the Nile pretending not to watch as all the crocodiles try the LONGUE CAISSE A CROCODILE. The little bird that cleans the crocodile's teeth comes back in the boat and sits in a glass in the bathroom next to the other toothbrushes ('*Les crocodiles ont de drôles de brosses à dents*', crocodiles have strange toothbrushes). It's vivid and elegant and funny: it's everything I fell for in French culture.

In all this ebb and flow of cultural enthusiasm, I take the lead: Olivier doesn't really get involved. He seems sort of semi-detached at the moment; present but not entirely there. Some combination of the stress of another move, job uncertainty (he's been left in a sort of semi-freelance position which is perilous) and impending global financial meltdown is keeping him preoccupied. He worries about money and security, constantly, and he seems to have little time for the boys. When he comes home in the evenings, I often hear him sigh at the mess, before he says hello. The detritus of life with two small boys seems to be wearing him down and I think he feels like I just facilitate the creation of more chaos, that I'm not capable of behaving like a responsible adult. His role, more and more, with the boys is telling them to tidy things away, and to behave. It's sad and strange, because he's always been so playful, so full of joy at the basic nuts and bolts of being a dad. We still see flashes of it, but more often than not it gets submerged in fatigue and irritation.

The end result of my intensive cultural hothousing is inevitable: we become, to all intents and purposes, a French-speaking household. Soon, when I speak English to the boys, they reply in French, offhand, naturally. You can almost see the geography of their speech rearranging itself week by week until they are both perfectly fluent. French is their default and their mother's tongue is no longer their mother tongue. Soon English words are relegated to a sort of garnish, the odd noun or expression dotted here and there. Eventually, there is nothing really left but swearing.

'*Je sais*,' says Theo sorrowfully, confessing to a lost coat, '*que tu vas dire* "fucking hell", *Maman* . . .'

Their French is beautiful, with that instinctive grasp of genders and tenses that no English person will ever attain. Soon they can even use the past historic properly: I have never said anything that ends with *ûmes* or *inrent* without a frisson of terror. I speak to them in English and they reply in French, then I speak to them in English and they tell me they don't understand in French, so I find myself giving in, speaking French to avoid the pantomime of confusion. I should persist, but I don't. It feels a bit fake initially – *I* feel a bit fake – but gradually, it just becomes normal. Sometimes all three of them absent-mindedly correct me when I stumble over particular blind spots, confusing the gender of lighthouses or dishwashers, and I feel a weird mixture of shame and pride.

At this point, surely, we have got as far as we need to go:

the boys are assimilated, their magnificently flexible child brains have adapted. I should try and redress the balance with English, but for some reason, I don't, I still speak French with them. It's that stupid vanity: I still love the way French sounds and I feel a wholly unjustified pride at their linguistic prowess, as if it is somehow a positive reflection on my parenting. The truth of the matter is that I actually *want* French children: having them gives me some additional stamp of francophone legitimacy. I don't want the kind of French Children Who Do Not Throw Food that Pamela Druckerman has been selling the world in recent years, obviously: mine would never be paragons in Bonpoint knickerbockers. The images of French childhood I cherish are the urchins in Cartier-Bresson photographs. These grubby, wisecracking, stone-throwing savages represent some kind of ideal of French irreverence for me, even if they are as pure a fantasy as Druckerman's.

Initially, my glow of pride is only punctured by occasional sadness at the cultural highlights of my own childhood, which are summarily cast aside or never get an airing. *The House at Pooh Corner* languishes unread and the *Tale of Samuel Whiskers*, even my most beloved pictures of Tom Kitten burritoed in pastry, arouse nothing but stony-faced puzzlement. No one understands when I sing the song we sang throughout my own childhood: 'Everyone makes a fuss / Of birthday girls who are not us' (from Russell Hoban's *Bread and Jam for Frances*). In a fit of nostalgia I order a dog-eared copy of *Miss Jaster's Garden*, in which a short-sighted elderly lady mistakenly plants a hedgehog with brightly coloured annuals, which the boys disdain. Nothing has much success, but I let it go, I don't insist. I accept that after their laborious handwriting homework and their bafflingly annotated maths, they want to watch the shows that everyone is talking about in the playground and watch them in French. How can I deprive them of that means of belonging, when belonging has been so capital to me?

The reality of my dream come true starts, very gradually, to make me obscurely uneasy, as if I am not quite at home in my own family life. That unease is compounded when we go back to England for holidays: the boys struggle to communicate with my father, which is sad after all those trips he and Theo took to the Transport Museum, and with my sister who has put in all those hours playing with and caring for both of them. They feel the frustration themselves when we meet up with their cousins, my half-brother's kids, and they can no longer play the way they used to.

But this is what I wanted, wasn't it? To be immersed in Frenchness, and we are. I am so immersed myself that quite often Belgians ask me if I am French, when they can't quite place my accent, which gives me an adolescent thrill. And it's not as if the children are lost to me, of course they aren't. They are still mine and I know every curve and angle of them. They are funny and wilful and imaginative, wearing socks on their hands, or communicating only in squeaks for a day. They still run to me with their scraped knees or their existential angst or just for the animal comfort of a sleepy head resting on my chest. Even so, I can't help but feel there's a semi-permeable membrane between us, the imminence of incomprehension. I don't play with language so much, I find, now. My jokes fall flat so I stop telling them and whenever they fail to understand me, I get a chilling sense of a distance growing between us, as if we are becoming strangers to each other on some basic level. The boys' language is a tangle of TV and school and playground slang, things that have no recognizable English translation, and I struggle to keep up. There is something lost when you can no longer play with words and every time I have to explain something with the deadening qualifier *'c'est un jeu de mots'*, it's a play on words, I feel bereft. I think it is the first time I really feel what is lost living as an expat.

Of course, there is more to this estrangement than language. When the boys lose a tooth they believe a mouse collects it (how, I ask, can a normal mouse collect all those teeth? At least a fairy has magic on her side). At Easter, chocolate is not delivered by a bunny, but by *'les cloches'*, the bells, bringing eggs back from Rome. This bothers me.

'But how do the bells carry the chocolate?' I ask Olivier.

'They fly upside-down, filled with chocolate,' he replies, flatly, as if this is entirely obvious.

'But why are the bells in Rome in the first place?' I persist, unconvinced.

'To see . . .' His certainty seems to sag a little at this point. 'The Pope? Anyway, how does the rabbit carry chocolate with those tiny paws?'

'It has a basket!' I protest, stung.

My children do not know a single Christmas carol ('that

is *not* a carol!' I snap automatically when they sing 'We Wish You a Merry Christmas', just as my mother used to chastise the half-arsed teen carol singers on our doorstep in York), and instead of a nativity play, there is a yearly school *'fête'* where they lipsynch to popular songs of the francophone 1980s or, one memorable year, sing the beer-themed Belgian novelty song *'Chef, une petite bière on a soif'*. They go on school trips to the Magritte museum and the Côte d'Or chocolate factory, and at the age of five they are despatched to Ostend for four days of bracing seaside pursuits including careering around in *cuistax*, the murderously dangerous, ankle-attacking go-karts that are the Proustian madeleine of a Belgian childhood.

I cannot win them over with British food, either. When I send them to school with jelly cubes as a treat, they come home mortified, because their friends say they are 'Martian food'.

I try to make toad in the hole (*'crapaud dans un trou!'* I say, encouragingly, as if this would make it more appealing) to universal displeasure.

'It's *toad*? We're eating toad?' Theo's face is a rictus of disgust.

'No, it's just *called* toad. It's sausage. In a sort of . . . pancake?'

'So . . . the sausage is the toad?' Olivier takes a delicate fork to my golden batter.

'Yes.'

'And that makes this . . . *pâte* . . . the hole?'

'No, of course not. The toad is in the hole IN the *pâte*.'

'But . . .'

Louis is clearer: *'J'aime pas.'*

One day, I go to school to collect the boys and Theo runs across the schoolyard cheerily to meet me, handing over his vast school bag.

'We had horse today!' he says brightly (in French, of course). 'I LOVE horse.' His face takes on a dreamy cast. 'It's so tender. Mmmmmm *cheval*.' He continues in this vein on the superior qualities of horsemeat for some minutes.

It is plain to me by this stage that I am raising aliens.

It's hard to admit to myself, but in this strange land, with my strange children and my unhappy boyfriend, I am a little homesick. I'm still repelled by the odd kind of expat life I see lived out around me, with imported cereals and English book clubs, and I am not unhappy with where we have landed. I love the city in all its exasperating strangeness, the loopy public transport encounters and the unhurried chat of the supermarket cashiers, the oddity that lurks under the mantle of bourgeois comforts. But I miss so much about England. Occasionally I list the things I miss to myself.

I miss Marks & Spencer, of course. I miss buying *Heat* and *Grazia* magazines on a Tuesday lunchtime and reading them in the weird, empty café on London Wall that gives you free chocolates. I miss Kate and I miss Brick Lane early on a Sunday morning before it gets busy. Dairy Milk – actually all the iterations of British chocolate: Caramels and Crunchies and Rolos. Bettys tearoom of course and everything in it, including the cake samples under the plastic cloche, the melancholy evening pianist and the copies of

Yorkshire Life neatly hung from wooden rods. Coram Fields playground with its two gloomy sheep. Barnitts, the pride of York and best hardware store in the world. Proper-flavoured crisps (Belgian crisps come in paprika and Bolognese flavours, both of which are appalling). The Lakeland catalogue with its primary-coloured assurance that your life will be instantly revolutionized by lettuce scissors or nestable Lock & Lock containers. Mist over the Ouse in York and the smell of After Eights from the Rowntrees factory.

I know things are bad when absence starts to make my heart grow fond of things I don't even like: Battenburg cake, Fig Rolls and Ribena, Scampi Fries and *Antiques Roadshow*. On one bleak Saturday when I am pining for the *Guardian Weekend* magazine, I make Olivier take me to the awful 'English Shop' out near the airport, a thoroughly eccentric enclave of the kind of little England expat life I profess to despise. It looks and smells like a Cotswold Spar, half-timbered and lino-floored, and I walk its aisles in a trance, picking up bacon and Creme Eggs.

Most of all, though, I realize I miss my language, after all these years trying to escape it. In French, even my vocabulary still feels sparse and unimaginative. I can 'pass', but I'm frustrated by my own limitations and lack of wit and imagination and I don't seem to get better, however much TV I watch. Having hit this ceiling, rather than being spurred to improve, I find I want the ease of my own language. At work, I hear English and speak English, but it's not the same, it's a convenient simulacrum of English invented by non-native speakers and the more I am immersed in it, the less I notice its oddities and imports and artifices. I want to speak real English, I want to feel agile and clever again, to tell jokes and spin yarns. Without any of this, my sense of self feels fragile: what am I, exactly? I'm still not French but I'm losing my Englishness too.

But, really, I need to shut up about what I want. I brought us here, it was my choice and my decision and I have got what I wanted. Olivier has more than enough on his plate, trying to make a living, squirrelling money away, and dealing with the boring minutiae of being a homeowner I can't be bothered to engage with. This is my problem, and mine only.

So I deal with my homesickness on my own, and in a couple of ways. Firstly, I start to make British cakes. I locate the box where I have stored the baking kit I acquired back in London and start churning out scones and fairy cakes for school events and children's parties. I am not very good, but the standard at school is gratifyingly low (the cake table is usually limited to a couple of half-hearted chocolate fondants and a selection of bought loaf cakes), so I rapidly get a reputation as a master pâtissière, with my Spiderman cupcakes and edible glitter. Soon, I get more ambitious and order a selection of complex cake-decorating equipment and books. I start producing fondant-covered dragons, Pokemon cakes and Halloween biscuits, and it feels lovely: it is gently creative but also very structured and absorbing and it makes me feel obscurely in touch with my homeland. I don't come from cake-baking stock, but it taps into a reassuring sort of folk memory of coffee mornings and Brownie bake sales. The baking does not endear me to Olivier at all: the kitchen is regularly covered in clouds of icing sugar and I stay up late, fiddling with my designs when I should be doing other things. I like the late nights when the house is quiet and I can roll out fondant and place sweets in restorative peace, but it is true, it means we spend even less time together.

Secondly, I start a blog.

« 19 »

Nouvelle Star

Having a blog is amazing, almost immediately, which makes me wonder why on earth I didn't do it sooner. During all those weird, awful years, why wasn't I writing this stuff down?

I don't know what pushes me finally, but one afternoon in the office, I just open up a basic blogging platform, pick a title (Belgian Waffle) and a template. I like reading blogs. I have become addicted to the way the format offers a voyeur's window into quite ordinary lives, click after click, reading hungrily through stories of relationship struggles, mental health issues and parenting all woven up in the mundane minutiae of daily life. Recently, I have started to think I can tell my own, so when I get home, after the boys are in bed, I start writing. I'm bored and homesick and lonely, but it's more than that: there's a head of steam of frustration building up inside me that has no outlet. I have so much to *say* and I want someone, anyone, to laugh at my jokes and I want to write about this absurd, under-appreciated city.

My very first post is about needing to go to the dentist and after that, I write in rapid succession about the music they play on the Brussels métro, French reality TV, the fact that Greggs, the low-rent British bakery, has opened an outlet in Brussels and an incident in the schoolyard where I am informed about an outbreak of penis-waving among the children. I have plenty of good anecdotes saved up from the previous few years, stories of madness and grief and getting poked with walking sticks by Parisians, and I write them down, mixed up with sillier, frothier things: tales of tram encounters, domestic squalor, the maddening frustrations of life with small children. There is a lot of nostalgia for Yorkshire and some contemplation of shoes and novelty chocolate.

It turns out I love writing. It is such a pleasure, so much so that it seems bizarre to me that I haven't ever tried it before. I haven't written anything since university apart from long emails to Kate and my law friend Laurie, in which I try to extract the last dregs of comedy from office life. Sometimes, in the throes of the worst or most ridiculous times in my life, I have imagined awful incidents reframed as fiction, but it has always seemed like a distant dream or an idea for retirement. Being a writer is just a fantasy, impossibly difficult and inaccessible, something you daydream about. How do people *do* that? My stepmother has one friend who is a journalist and sometimes I imagine . . . what? Pressing something I have written into her hands? It's ridiculous; I've only met her twice.

But of course, the Internet has changed everything, cracking open a closed shop: online writing is exploding. The blogs I read are almost exclusively by people who have no professional writing experience and they are fresh and unguarded and funny. That unmediated, unedited immediacy is compelling for a reader but also for a writer: I feel caught up in that excitement and I write all the time, in notebooks and in my head, late at night and on my lunch break. I am full of words, English words, things I have never said out loud or half remember from childhood, snippets of poems, phrases from P. G. Wodehouse, and jokes. I feel sort of myself again; perhaps more myself than I have ever been.

Writing for pleasure is one part of the blog; writing for an audience is even better. Because the Internet, it turns out, is my new French *Elle*: it is where everyone who likes the same stuff as me hangs out and, better than French *Elle*, they want to talk back. People comment and react and email and I am gradually drawn into a vivid community of funny, eccentric introverts who have strong feelings about cake and P. G. Wodehouse, patent leather shoes and capybaras. A significant number of them even know about Bettys and Barnitts hardware store (the York diaspora is surprisingly over-represented on the Internet). From my francophone bubble, those shared frames of reference feel precious. There are people out there in the ether who have read the same books and listened to the same music as me. Sometimes I make an offhand reference to some obscure indie group of my teenage years or quote a favourite book and am astonished at the number of people who recognize and respond.

The things I write about, whether it's missing London or the weirdness of grief, or a self-coruscating confession of some act of stupidity, always seem to generate an answering echo from someone – a virtual 'me too'. I quickly become the perfect example of online disinhibition, that new phenomenon: I say things on the blog I can't imagine ever saying to anyone face to face and I am rewarded for it by that answering echo, so I do it again and again. The blog comment box creates a safe space and in it, people confess to hopeless crushes and doomed love affairs, financial incompetence, petty acts of unkindness and secret ones of revenge. It's giddying to discover them: there are people out there who are just as confused and tentative, chaotic and scared, as I am. Corporate law did not throw up very many of those, but here they are: clever, funny and awkward, hanging out on the Internet, hiding red bills and unable to make a phone call without half a day's preparation. Loopy stories emerge: there's a woman who keeps relics of her unrequited love for her best friend (including a used chip fork) under her bed and another woman who sabotages her horrible husband's collection of fountain pens in secret.

A lot of the people who comment seem to be isolated by circumstance or geography and, like me, this is where they make connections: this corner of the Internet is populated by people living away from their homelands or otherwise lost in some way. For me and for some of them, the blog becomes a warm, dysfunctional, hug of belonging. The hard core of regular commenters are completely real to me: I worry about Red Shoes' medical problems and Kath's grumpy husband and I get a clear sense, too, that they worry about me. People send me things: chocolate pigs from Bettys, books and cards and weird home-made crafts.

Better even than the comments and the parcels is the

discovery that you can actually make friends – real, proper friends – online. My first is Helen – online moniker 'Violet Trefusis' – who writes me a long email quoting extensively from Bertie Wooster's speech to Roderick Spode in *The Code of the Woosters* and adding some thoughts about the hypothetical political leanings of various brands of luxury shoe ('tomato patent leather is screamingly fascist'). We strike up a correspondence that soon becomes a real friendship of drunken dinners and rueful breakfasts, punctuated with poetry, anecdotes from the world of luxury magazines where she works, and confidences. She is elegant and wistful, kind and funny, and her life is unimaginably glamorous viewed from suburban Brussels: I feel a bit star-struck knowing her.

Soon after that both Helen and I meet Tom, a London art student who calls me his adoptive mother ('Waffle mère', which makes me sound like a Lake District B&B) and starts to send me silly Photoshop images and absurd crafts ('I have just made a Mexican Day of the Dead gingerbread house with a roof of shattered Dorito shards,' he emails me one day). Next a man called Benjamin sends me a short film of an owl riding a skateboard and a follow-up selection of acerbically funny complaints about Belgian life (sample: 'I have just seen a shoeless man on the métro at Louise carrying his own poo in a plastic bag'). He is a stylish New Yorker perplexed by exile in Brussels, a lawyer and a lover of absurdity and animals, and we exchange gleeful daily emails on Belgian life and meet for drinks. There are many more: Lydia and Lindsay, Frances, Kathy, Maija and Simon, people who go from a tiny thumbnail picture of a dog or a cake to becoming real flesh and blood friends. At blog meet-ups in London pubs and shy coffee dates in Brussels parks I forge more friendships than I ever have, more than at Oxford, where I was always disappearing to Normandy, and more than in London, where I put paid to a social life by getting pregnant at twenty-six.

As my world expands with all these clever, funny people I realize just how starved of fun I have been. I laugh more in that first year of blogging than I have for a decade, easily, and at the silliest things. Everything is just *so* silly: I run a virtual Village Fête on the blog over the summer and people carve me horrifying vegetable animals and bake ugly cakes. I instigate weekly Confessionals, where everyone admits to their daft transgressions. The 'me too', the answering echo of the Internet, becomes immensely, probably excessively, important.

Most important of all, though, is Madevi, my new best friend.

I first encounter Madevi via her cartoon dinosaur alter ego on Twitter and via the blog, where she issues me with a challenge to take two inflatable plastic dinosaurs into my office and pretend to have a meeting with them. I wimp out on the challenge, but soon after that, she emails me. 'I am the Mother of Dinosaurs,' the email starts (she is the co-creator of a cartoon series featuring two dinosaurs in corporate middle management), which is promising, and then goes on to describe a horrifying tax situation in which she is embroiled. Madevi is a few years younger than me; she works as an animator and describes herself as 'a Frenchie exiled in Scotland for the past ten years'. I reply, she writes back and soon we are emailing and chatting online multiple times a day.

I have never encountered anyone who loves so many of the things I love, or who shares my sense of humour so closely. We soon establish that we agree about almost everything except jelly (she loathes it) and *galettes des rois* (I hate them). In the first few weeks of knowing her we talk about breadmaking videos, Fred Vargas, special cellulite pants, why ham is considered a vegetable in France, whether Bonne Maman or La Laitière make the best crème caramels, our respective credit card debts and weird crushes, her job folding scarves at Hermès, childhood comfort blankets and the best places for éclairs in Paris. We talk endlessly, greedily, without awkwardness or ever getting bored. We discuss writing, and gossip about people on the Internet, and every day – every single day – we discuss what is for lunch. Everything makes us laugh: jugglers, awful French rap, Internet acquaintances. She starts writing an advice column for my blog, taking on the persona of an easily angered, plain-speaking capybara, Dr Capybara, who has no time for middle-class whining, which becomes enormously popular.

It is quickly inconceivable for us to spend a day without talking. What I especially love about Madevi is that when we talk, I can just say or write whatever comes into my head in French or English. Our chats are a delicious, lazy mix of both languages, in which I can write something to her like: 'Louis has just told me a chicken called Fleurette came to school on an educational visit today. All he would tell me was that its tongue is "*pointue*" and its *crête* is "*très chaude*".'

. . . and she understands. We finish each other's sentences, riff off each other's jokes and know exactly what absurdities will make the other laugh. When one of us is being self-indulgently gloomy, the other one croons Brassens' '*Le Petit Cheval Blanc*', the saddest song in the world about the death of a brave, hard-working horse who never gets to see the sun, at them.

It's a completely new experience, playing with both languages in this way, and when I talk to her, something feels reconciled, as if I can be completely myself.

Of course, I should be able to have that feeling with Olivier. After all our years in London, his English is excellent and we could be this playful, this free in the way we speak to each other, but we aren't. We're stuck in our habits, our French-speaking habits (it was his Frenchness I fell for initially, after all, so I hang on to it now), and frankly, we're hardly talking at all, because that seems safest.

One of the things I find myself confessing to often on the blog is problems with Olivier: arguments, disapproval from him and small acts of defiance from me. An undertone runs through the first eighteen months of the blog's life of a relationship in deepening crisis, even though I try to play it for laughs.

Olivier did not seem bothered when I started the blog and was happy to help me out with various bits of silliness, but as the months have gone by, he has become less and less comfortable with the hours I spend blogging and the weekends I spend trying to carve out time to hide away with my laptop. He doesn't understand the confessional impulse at all and while he doesn't actively disapprove, the way my world is expanding and my hunger for new connections jar with his own current instinct, which is to circle the wagons, to keep the family close and safe. It is 2008 and the world is spinning into catastrophic financial meltdown: Lehman Brothers collapses and the sub-prime catastrophe plays out week after week on the news, an unnerving snowball of economic doom, gathering speed. I feel expansive and excited about life, busy making myself a beard out of Post-It notes because I hope it will make some people on the Internet laugh, but Olivier is anxious. As the British government scrabbles to bail out the banking sector, I am blogging my failed attempt to make a papier-mâché dinosaur or carving a large courgette into a crocodile. Olivier is glued to the news and wondering whether to put our money into a safe deposit box. We are further apart now than at any point in our relationship, I think. It is apparently not conducive to conjugal harmony to come home worried that the world financial system is imploding and to find your partner adding fondant teeth to a cake in the shape of the Belgian politician Guy Verhofstadt.

I am looking outwards, I tell myself, while he looks in. But in looking outwards, I also look away: from him, from the family, from our life. Every incident and exchange becomes material and I frame and reframe things in my head to make them as pithy and entertaining as possible. I mine chore-filled family weekends and exasperating evenings with the boys, who are funny and maddening and wonderful, for comedy. It makes them easier to tolerate, but it also keeps me somehow separate: I am presenting family life as a spectator sport, not fully taking part, and Olivier knows it. When he tries, eventually, to suggest I curb my online time, I get sullen and mutinous: how dare he try and spoil my fun?

To avoid conflict, the time we spend together becomes necessarily very bland. We deal with the practical necessities of parenting (we do not even necessarily agree on these) and when we are alone together, we sit on the sofa and watch French reality TV, shows full of sound and fury and manu-factured outrage. The mainstream French channels have recently woken up to the potential of imported formats and our screen is full of ersatz *Supernannies* and *Weakest Links*.

We watch *Koh-Lanta* (French *Survivor*), in which twenty French people (sometimes there is a token Belgian who is rapidly ejected) are dropped on a desert island and have to try and survive on their wits and a dwindling quantity of rice by dint of endless arguing, aided by the scout-master-style encouragement of presenter Denis Brogniart, in sensible Rohan slacks. Grown men are reduced to tears as a saucisson is dangled tantalizingly before them, then snatched away if they can't balance on a log for long enough. We watch *Un Dîner Presque Parfait*, the French *Come Dine With Me*, in which, boringly, everyone behaves impeccably. There are no scenes of shameful drunkenness and no fights. No one says things like 'I can't eat lamb because it's cute' or 'I don't eat vegetables' or 'what's a mille . . . foy?' and no snakes defecate on the dining table. In *Un Dîner Presque Parfait*, even feckless early twenties ravers will comment seriously on whether the table decorations were appropriate and have an opinion on the use of deep-fried leeks in the starter. The 'entertainment' is extraordinarily straight-laced too, parlour games, the re-enactment of local traditions and *le rock 'n' roll* dancing.

Sometimes, when things are good between us, we amuse each other imagining French versions of other television shows.

'French *Don't Tell the Bride* – literally just an hour of menu planning.'

'French *One Born Every Minute* – very boring because a patronizing obstetrician just comes in and orders everyone to have an enema and an epidural.'

'Then afterwards the midwives lecture you on making sure you have sex with your husband very quickly.'

'Someone asks about a water birth and everyone laughs uproariously and tells her it's unhygienic.'

'French *Apprentice* – no food-based tasks because it would be carnage, with everyone fighting for their own regional interpretation of the sausage.'

My favourite evening distraction is *Nouvelle Star*, a French *X Factor* with an eccentric judging panel composed of the tiny, apoplectic rock journalist Philippe Manoeuvre, 1980s still-beautiful teen star Lio, gimlet-eyed and rude veteran funk performer Sinclair and my favourite, the pianist André Manoukian. I have something of a crush on Manoukian, who looks like the tedious pop philosopher Bernard-Henri Lévy's sexier, plumper brother and has a penchant for quoting Roland Barthes at bewildered teenagers.

André is my ideal kind of Frenchman, with his excellent hair and great erudition: he represents what France does best (talking in immensely abstract terms while being sexy). Olivier isn't really like this.

Olivier is very clever; he's cleverer than I am. He has done an MBA in a foreign language and fought his way into demanding, highly paid jobs on his wits alone, but we never talk about literature or art and he can read the same issue of the *Economist* in the evening for three months, because he falls asleep after thirty seconds. He'll try anything – opera, performance poetry, probably even Morris dancing – once, but most of the time, he doesn't share my interests. Now I have the Internet, and I have Madevi, I feel this absence acutely: how can I share my life with someone who has never read *Scoop* or *Cold Comfort Farm* or *Under Milk Wood*?

My vision of the life of a couple is skewed, I think, by spending too much time reading Simone de Beauvoir's memoirs. For Simone de Beauvoir and Jean-Paul Sartre, culture is a joint enterprise: every other sentence starts '*nous lisions*' (we read). 'We read Virginia Woolf,' she says, or 'We read all the young Russian authors'; then she and Sartre discuss their reading, spurring each other on to new discoveries, and it all sounds idyllic. This, absurdly romantic a notion as it is, is what I want. It's the model I know from childhood too: my stepfather would trap us at the dinner table and read seventy-five lines of some Louis MacNeice something we have said has reminded him of, or some particularly revelatory passage from Mary Midgley. We glazed over and my mother turned up *The Archers*, but sharing words, poems, thoughts, is how I conceive of a relationship and of a family and I can't see how we can achieve that. Failing that, *Nouvelle Star* night is our moment of détente. I put aside my laptop and we watch together, becoming deeply invested in the fate of Cedric, Amandine and Ycare.

Apart from *Nouvelle Star*, the fun, vivid parts of my life and the sense of connection I crave are increasingly online. There I can be frank and raw and funny, but in real life I am detached and impatient. All my energies are turned towards the blog and the people I have met through it; that space has become more important than almost anything. Going on the flattering feedback I get, Internet me is far more likeable than real me: I am brave, or hilarious, the comments say and while I don't really believe them, it's gratifying. Nothing I do in my real life generates this kind of response: my non-Internet friends are few and far between, my family are preoccupied with their own lives, beset by poor health, work and ongoing sadnesses, and I feel quite strongly, at the moment, that Olivier doesn't even like me. It's no surprise, perhaps, that I become ever more dependent on this virtual validation.

It is not just my family that suffers either: my limited (at the best of times) commitment to the law dwindles as writing begins to seem like a real possible alternative career. Journalists and editors contact me and I start getting commissions to write for magazines. An agent gets in touch to ask if I have ever considered writing a novel. Helen introduces me to her contacts.

Caught up in the excitement of everything, I go a bit off

the rails. I don't have to be a lawyer all my life! I have found something I am genuinely good at and it feels amazing. On top of that, I have a new, exciting, delightful group of friends who are showing me how much bigger and better my life can be. I interpret these events as an expression of manifold destiny: I am supposed to be doing this. My French period is over and now it is time for me to reaffirm my Englishness and forge a new life.

With this sense of destiny comes a growing conviction: Olivier and I need to split up. The distance between us has become too great and I don't have the will to try and bridge it. It seems suddenly very simple and I am quite, quite determined that it is the right, indeed the only, thing to do.

« 20 »

Madame Bovary

Splitting up is nothing like it looks in films. I thought we (I) would just decide and then it would be done, but it doesn't work like that at all, it turns out.

First we get a dog, in the manner of people having a child to save their marriage. I have wanted a dog for such a long time and now I have reduced my hours at work (I am only working two days now, to concentrate on writing; Olivier has been utterly supportive of this even though it means I am barely earning anything as a result), I can finally do it and Olivier is keen, so we do, on impulse, in the cold dark days of early January. I collect the puppy from a farmhouse in a gloomy hamlet somewhere north of Amiens: it's a whippet, that classic signifier of Yorkshire, but a French whippet, which seems appropriate. The children are thrilled of course and for a couple of weeks we live in a cloud of oxytocin puppy-bonding bliss.

In the longer term the dog, Oscar, does not repair our rift; if anything, he makes things worse. While undeniably sweet, he is also an incontinent, shoe-chewing, demented mess, which is not exactly what Olivier wants more of in his home. Between the puppy and writing, I devote no time whatsoever to keeping the house from descending into squalor, then when Olivier arrives and casts a jaded eye around the dirty coffee cups, chewed tennis balls and shredded paper, I am defensive and snappy. When he suggests I could spend less time blogging, I feel a steely resolve not to do anything of the kind. I'm not trying to provoke him, but the blog feels as vital as oxygen and I just can't imagine not doing it. Instead I stay up after he goes to bed, writing and chatting with Madevi until my eyes can't focus, then sneaking into the bedroom in the dark. I hate where we are – what kind of relationship is this, where I'm playing the mutinous teenager and he's the parent? – but I make no attempt to try and improve things. In my head, I've already checked out.

We have a proper fight in February, during which we explicitly discuss splitting up (though 'discuss' is the wrong word, it's a mess of fear and anger and not very many words, both of us circling a black hole), then immediately thereafter, we have to go on a long-arranged skiing holiday with Olivier's parents, the six of us in a tiny Alpine apartment, where it gets dark at four. The chaos and upset mean that we forget to bring any clothes. 'We look,' I write on the blog, 'like the survivors of a natural disaster from which fleece was mysteriously spared.' In the face of this potentially hideous situation, Olivier and I acquit ourselves pretty admirably. It's obvious we can't talk in any serious way, so we are kind to each other and just get on with things. We have breakfast with Yves and Jacqueline, we dress the boys in their many layers, retrieve forgotten gloves and poles and carry their skis to the Spartan-inspired École de Ski Française classes (where pick-up time brings an extra frisson, as you are never sure whether they will just leave your child on a mountain to die because his skis are insufficiently parallel), then we go off and ski ourselves.

Skiing is one of those French things I cannot embrace. The whole business is alien to me: I find the idea of exercise for fun repellent and I have always thought France was fairly enlightened about this, but skiing seems to be the exception, because here is all of Paris, exported to the Alps in brightly coloured performance fabrics, exercising. I don't understand how the stylish French can associate themselves with an activity that requires such awful outfits. Beyond that, my balance is atrocious and the terrible, selfish, non-queue for the ski lifts where everyone jostles and elbows their way to the front causes me almost physical British person pain. I do not like most of the supposed consolations of skiing, all those queasy cheese-based blow-outs, *tartiflette*, *fondue* and *raclette*, and there is a limit to how much mulled wine I can drink because I need to keep my wits about me to avoid the murderously careless teenagers on snowboards. I just can't fake Frenchness here: I ski like a startled crab, stiff with terror as Olivier and his father swish insouciantly past (his mother wisely sticks to bracing Alpine walks and taking in the sun in a deckchair, trousers rolled up to her knees). Even back in the apartment the combat continues: the constant friction of man-made fibres creates a crackling halo of static electricity and I get repeated shocks from the metal door handles. I hate skiing. Olivier, of course, is brilliant at it:

quite often he'll ski backwards down a hill to encourage me as I lurch erratically towards him, whimpering.

But in this hostile environment and at this most awful time, Olivier and I look after each other. We roll our eyes and make jokes, we sneak off for bad, expensive white wine in bars manned by surly Alpine alcoholics and we take the boys swimming in the horrifyingly cold outdoor pool. When I get tired on the mountains, Olivier waits for me and when I get paralysed with fright in narrow *couloirs*, between rock faces and vertiginous cliffs, with leathery Parisians whooshing past me on every side, he coaxes and encourages me, helps me down, then installs me in a café with a hot chocolate. Sometimes, when the sun is shining, making the snow sparkle, and we find a quiet slope, I can almost imagine enjoying it. In the evenings, Olivier's mother cooks and then there is the usual box of cakes: coffee éclair for Yves, chocolate for Olivier, *flan* for me. There is no wifi, of course, so, chased away by ancient dubbed action films and wooden home-grown drama series on the TV, I read, while he dozes beside me. It is peaceful and humane and I feel hopeful for us.

But once we get home, the tension ramps up again as we revert to our current, unsustainable norm. I return to the Internet (while we were away my blog was selected as one of *The Times*'s Top 100, bringing me more attention than ever and a pressure to produce good new material) and Olivier gets frustrated. We also do unhelpful things like go and look at other houses, as if a bigger garden might fix all our problems.

At this point, I also become infatuated with a married man.

The married man is from the Internet, of course he is, and perhaps more important still, he is English. He emails me via the blog and I email back and we strike up a conversation that becomes, over a couple of months, more and more flirtatious and intimate. When we finally meet, it is in the almost parodically English setting of Claridge's bar.

I note the similarities between us, delightedly, both generic and specific. We are more or less the same age; he has two small children, has lost a parent and is married to someone who isn't English. But it's also about the fact that we both grew up watching *Saturday Swap Shop*, drinking Ribena and eating Bourbons. We're drawn to music by pasty undernourished northerners with guitars, read the *Guardian* and like football. By the time we meet, I have already been seduced by the self-evident rightness of it, the simplicity of interacting with someone like this and the neat way our cultural baggage fantails. This, I tell myself, as we trade barbed witticisms, is the kind of person I am supposed to be with. Someone who *gets* me. This is how British people find a mate, with teasing and booze and no discussion of our feelings.

Obviously it would be much more French just to have an affair with the married man and stay together. The national predilection for adultery, from Madame Bovary to Jacques Chirac (who is famously nicknamed 'Monsieur 3 minutes, shower included'), is one of the most enduring of French clichés. But, oh, anything but that. For all its beauty (and it is *so* beautiful, especially about rural Normandy: the lacy effect of the dew on cabbages; the silvery bark of the willows reflected in the still, deep water of the river), Madame Bovary is so sad. It's desperate really: Emma is a horrible creation. She's in love with the idea of love and after the initial thrill, disillusionment comes swiftly: nothing ever comes close to her reading ('it was all love, lovers, sweet-hearts, persecuted ladies fainting in lonely pavilions'). I know I could be an Emma, sulky and bored and destructive in my provincial comfort. I can't bear to be an Emma, despite my name.

Even so, there seems to be a current of French thinking in which affairs are presented as the enlightened solution to long-term relationships (which are desirable, essential even, but impossible to sustain). I have read Lucy Wadham's fascinating and clear-sighted *Secret Life of France*, in which after-dinner orgies and civilized *cinq à sept* arrangements are the norm for at least a section of the metropolitan bour-geoisie. Adultery is the *cartésienne* way. At one point in our discussions, Olivier even says to me:

'Take a year. Stay with us, but do whatever you have to, I won't ask anything of you, just wait and see.'

But I just can't see how this would work. I can't imagine gallivanting around Europe like an Amish teenager on rumspringa then coming home to my family. I might be disgustingly self-indulgent, but this is beyond me: I'm not brave and I'm not candid and I don't have the emotional maturity to make that work. By this point in my life I am pretty clear that I can't reason my way out of guilt and shame thanks to the light of pure positivism. I need to break away,

I can't see any other solution. 'Everything is black and white with you,' Olivier tells me often and I suppose that's true.

So I say it again more explicitly:

'I can't do this any more,' I say. Or I think I say. Something like that. I don't know, but I think my facial expression is a bit clearer this time, because it feels more definitive somehow, and from the set of his jaw, I can tell Olivier feels it too. He disappears for half an hour and when he comes back, he tells me we are going on a day trip, so we get in the car and drive to Bruges.

'We've never been to Bruges!' he tells me, firmly. 'If we're splitting up, we need to have been to Bruges.'

This is pretty stupid, but I quite like this impulsive Olivier and at least something is happening at last. It's raining and Bruges is grey and greasy, the belfry obscured by cloud and the squares and narrow streets clogged with tour groups in waterproof ponchos. We arrive so early that nothing is open and drink bad coffee from paper cups staring at the same shop windows we have in Brussels. We have to bring the dog and he whines because it's cold and we can't go into any restaurants or churches because of him, so we sit in a bus shelter, then we sit on the main square at a tourist bar while it drizzles and then we drive home again. I don't know what he says and I don't know what I say: our discussions are bleeding into one another and it's exhausting. I'm sick of myself, sick of hearing my lame justifications.

We still don't split up. 'Give it the summer and see how you feel in September,' he says, and that seems reasonable, so a few months later, we go on holiday again. We go back to

Normandy, where it all started, just the four of us. Olivier chooses the place and it is perfect. I have never stayed anywhere quite this beautiful and I can't imagine how much it must have cost him, but he's in a 'what the hell' mood about life and throwing everything he can at trying to save our relationship. This is his Hail Mary holiday. It's a large, airy white house with huge windows, actually *on* the beach, a vast expanse of soft and deserted white sand just up the road from Deauville. We can open the door in the morning and the boys run out to play, collecting hermit crabs and racing them, or splashing in the shallow waves. The sun shines almost constantly, which is unheard of for Normandy, and the sunsets are ravishing, a shimmering pink haze on the water as we drink dry cider and watch strings of horses walking silhouetted at the shoreline. It isn't all portentous and poignant: we have a laugh too. We find a book in the house about how to petrify fruit and vegetables using the power of your mind and spend a fun afternoon trying to petrify a lemon. We teach the boys to play chess and all four of us play long inept tournaments with our early evening aperitifs. Late at night when they are asleep, we watch films in bed, his head on my shoulder, then we turn off the TV and open the window to listen to the waves. It's so strange: everything is wonderful but it's awful too. All the anger and artifice has fallen away and I'm implacably calm; I just know what I want. I spend a lot of the time sitting on the immaculate cream sofa, writing, while Olivier plays with the boys outside. Most of the time he is bouncy and fun, throwing them into the sea as they laugh and squeal and pushing them around on their inflatable alligator. But sometimes he gets sad.

'It's such a shame you can't be happy with me,' he says, as we sit out in the late afternoon sun. He gestures around at the boys who are building a den for a dead crab from seaweed and stones, the beach, the exquisite house. 'With us.'

And he's right; it is an awful shame and at that moment I really, really wish I could. This lovely man would do anything to keep us together and our boys are wonderful and we have had such a laugh and such strange moments of tenderness over the past few months. But I am so, so sure. I can't explain it to him satisfactorily, which makes it worse, so I just repeat myself: I can't be with him any more; this can't be all my life. I am thirty-five years old and even though I have had two children and buried my mother, I feel as if I haven't really lived. Depending on Olivier – and he is so perfectly dependable – has made me weak and cowardly and lazy. I need to go out and make some mistakes without his loving, stifling, safety net.

We have a final French holiday to celebrate, after a fashion, Olivier's birthday, on a grey September weekend at a B&B in a crumbling chateau on the northern coast near Le Touquet. It's a strange place, remote and draughty, run by two gruff brothers out of their scruffy kitchen. There's a herd of Shetland ponies, baby rabbits and guinea pigs to pet and a donkey you can take out for walks, which we do, the boys taking it in turns to sit on its back. On the Sunday morning while I am out with the boys petting the guinea pigs, Olivier finds some notes I have scribbled, full of thoughts of escape and of the married man. When we get back he starts to pull away properly, angrily, going out for hours at a time, then one morning he comes into the bedroom and looks at me for a moment, then he just says, simply, 'You don't want to be here. You should go.'

So I do.

PART FOUR

C'est Paris en chemin
Et toi qui m'attends là
Et tout qui recommence
Et c'est Paris je reviens.

And it's Paris on the way
And you waiting for me there
And it all starts again
And it's Paris I'm coming back.

Jacques Brel,
'Les Prénoms de Paris'

« 21 »

La Cristallisation de Stendhal

And just like that, the slow, affectionate, exasperated un-tangling that seemed as though it would never end is over. Things accelerate vertiginously: we are really splitting up and I have to find somewhere to live. That is what we agree, late at night, huddled in the back garden after the children are in bed: we will share custody equally, a week each, and I will move out.

I start to look for a place to live, armed only with a wildly optimistic back-of-an-envelope calculation of my income and my own prejudices, and settle on a house that is almost the carbon copy of our current one, a ten-minute walk away: another sleepy street, another hairdresser a few doors up. It hasn't had the Texan–Parisian luxury treatment and every-thing in it is cheap, greige and utilitarian, but it's big and solid and it feels convincingly like a family home. I don't consider very seriously whether I can afford it: I'm so caught up in the momentum of the blog and writing that I truly believe money won't be an issue, because I'm going to write a bestseller, or become a broadsheet columnist or something. I'm optimistic about everything, including the separation: I look to my parents' example, remember the pair of them taking me to Paris long after they separated, how much they still made each other laugh (it's a mark of success for a divorce, I find myself thinking much later, if your children don't realize the huge efforts involved in that appearance of ease). I know we can do this. I just ignore how grey and unhappy Olivier is as I extricate myself from our family home, because it doesn't fit with my rosy and enlightened vision.

Milestones follow one another in rapid succession over the following weeks: I sign a lease; we split our savings; we tell the children. It becomes very real at this point: Theo cries instantly then Louis cries because his brother is crying and we hold them tight and I mouth all those platitudes about still loving them and liking each other, we're just living in separate houses now, and even though it's all true, it really is, I feel hollow and dishonest. I look across at Olivier. He looks ill and deflated, as if someone has gutted him like a fish. But what can I do? I can't give him the only thing he wants, which would be the news that I have changed my mind. I haven't. So we push on, reassure and console, blow noses, and then we sit on the sofa and watch cartoons. After a week or so, as the boys' immediate attention turns back to school and Pokemon and who has taken whose biscuit, the shock fades; gradually it becomes another hard thing among all the hard things Olivier and I have done together. I organize a removal firm and box up my books and clothes and trinkets and one day in November, when Olivier isn't around, I move out. The stupid dog comes with me (this is something of a silver lining for Olivier).

Initially, there are parts of separating that are quite exhilarating. I am so sure that it is the right thing to do that there's a kind of excitement to it for me, as if this is a difficult but necessary stage towards becoming the person I am supposed to be. The process has a fierce forward momentum and there are so many things I have to do that I have very little time to brood. Many of the things I have to do are the kind of tasks I have always left to Olivier. I deal with my new landlady, who is horrible; a desiccated, gimlet-eyed, tweed-clad matron with a rigid helmet of grey hair and a strong line in wordless disapproval (I fall victim to a classic bait and switch: one day I am signing the paperwork with her fat, jovial husband, then before the ink is even dry, the temperature drops ten degrees and Tweed Nosferatu is released from her underground lair. I never see or hear from him again). I have to buy furniture then put it together and make the television work. I deal with the boiler, procure a washing machine and fridge and source an energy provider, grown-up tasks for which I feel wholly unqualified, lost in a tangle of SCART cables, Allen keys and rawl plugs. I do a lot of driving too, which I hate and have spent my adult life thus far avoiding. A month after I move out it is Christmas, and I have to persuade a car hire company to rent me a car without a driving licence (I have, of course, lost mine), then drive it, plus children and dog, to York and back in treacherous, icy conditions. I manage, but it takes a week afterwards for the pain of my tensed shoulders and wrists to fade.

Nevertheless, it feels sort of salutary, all this admin: this is what adult life is like, I tell myself, without the security blanket of an ultra-competent, ultra-grown-up partner and I can do it, sort of: I can pick up the phone or go to the bank when there is no one else to do it for me. Whenever anything is difficult or frightening, I tell myself that this is what I wanted, and it is about time I shaped up.

But as much as our separation is about the serious business of being an independent grown-up for the first time, it is also about sheer escapism. The possibilities of solo living make me giddy: I go to nightclubs with my friend Tom, drinking too much gin and watching a procession of Belgian drag queens, calves clad in thick American Tan hosiery, stomp up and down a tiny bar. I start a baking business of sorts with Madevi, selling home-made biscuits stamped with rude words at craft fairs. It's a vast amount of work and we barely break even, but it's so much fun working with her: we laugh and laugh and make other people laugh too. I buy myself self-indulgent home furnishings I cannot afford: silk quilts and children's beds that look like castles and a large plastic dog that glows in the dark. I have never made these kinds of choices alone before – the only places I have ever lived alone were during those few weeks before I met Olivier in Normandy and my college room in Oxford – and I'm determined to enjoy them, hang the expense. I say yes to everything: concerts, drunken evenings with acquaintances, terrible German performance art, an air guitar contest in a bar in Flanders and an urban safari round Charleroi's abandoned factories and slag heaps in the back of a dilapidated transit van.

It's fun, a lot of this stuff, but it has one serious consequence. I become more distracted than ever at work, preoccupied with writing and my messy personal life, drifting in late and compulsively checking my messages under the desk. It should come as no surprise – though I am still shocked – when I find out I am next in line for redundancy. Olivier is very cool and kind about it when I call up and blurt it out: dramas of this kind never seem to faze him. He takes me out for a meal and reminds me how much I want to do other things with my life. I know that's true but I feel sick at having put myself in such a precarious situation. After a couple of weeks of panic, though, I find it sort of bracing, having no income – bracing like the North Sea in January. I can't just float around making biscuits and trying to write a novel, so I knuckle down to finding as much work as I can, scrabbling to do editing and translation and unglamorous writing jobs. The big break I was so certain was just round the corner remains elusive. I'm not sure I think I can make it as a blogger now: I'm finding my former levels of candour harder and harder to sustain. It's as if I have only just realized that other people are involved and my writing does have consequences.

In other ways, though, the redundancy shock makes me reckless; indifferent to consequences. I get drunk often, with abandon, taking unwise late-night trams and even less wise late-night walks through the city, then get home and fall asleep with my shoes on. I feel untethered, although I suppose that was sort of the point.

What does tether me is the boys. When they are with me, our days have a rhythm I find intensely reassuring: we walk to the tram in the mornings and I ride the two stops to school with them, then walk back with the dog and work all day. In the afternoons, I pick them up and hand over some small change for the vending machine and we walk back home, an awkward shuffle of school bags and Kinder Egg wrappers and the dog winding itself between our legs, Louis hanging off my arm and Theo telling me about Mexican wrestling or the monster he has been drawing. After they do their homework, there are cartoons then dinner, a story and then bed, and once they are tucked up I tidy up and do the washing, pairing socks and folding T-shirts, straightening the basic building blocks of family life. These basic and necessary things feel vital to me: the routines I felt were burying me alive a year ago are what keep me afloat now.

But in the weeks when the boys are with Olivier I have none of that routine or certainty and now not even a job to give my days structure. I go out as much as I can because the house is too quiet and too empty; it isn't home without their trails of discarded toys and clothes, without the elaborate *tableaux vivants* of soft toys on the sofa. Whenever I can, I leave the country altogether, raiding my already depleted savings in order to run away to London and Paris.

I run away so often in this period that the Eurostar terminals become a second, third and fourth home. I know which of the border control officers is ponderously, pedantically slow and the corner behind a pillar where you can always find an empty space. On the train, I have a preferred carriage and seat and I weave efficiently, powered by muscle memory, through the Disneyland crowds in London and the stag parties in Brussels, the packed ticket hall at Gare du Nord. My passport becomes dog-eared from constant handling and the gilding rubs off the front. I like the way that, on the train and in the terminals, I can choose to be whomever I want that day: friendly, aloof, French or British. It's what my friend Helen calls 'identity tourism'. Who *are* you when you are no longer half of a couple? This is what I have been so anxious to find out.

Most of the time, my assumed identity of choice is Londoner. I have pined so hard for London over the past few years and it still feels more like home than anywhere else. I have no idea now why I thought we should leave. When I visit, I want to gobble the whole city up, even the worst bits: maimed pigeons and discarded copies of *Metro*, slow moving crocodiles of language students shuffling down Oxford Street and the Northern Line. I stuff my bag with magazines and packets of chocolate digestives, spend hours in Liberty and John Lewis just wandering the aisles, drink pints and pints of tea (with real milk, not UHT), sit in Bloomsbury squares and linger in the streets inhaling bus fumes. London is where most of my friends, old and new, are: I sleep on Helen's sofa, hang out with Tom, visit Kate, and organize drinks with Internet acquaintances. These are the good bits; the happy bits. The bad bits are when I try and see the married man.

This episode is already ridiculous. There is nothing really going on between us, but he represents some kind of ideal for me: the easy, teasing familiarity of Englishness; a shared cultural shorthand. I know it's daft, but I can't help myself:

I'm infatuated, not with him but with the *idea* of him, the path not travelled. He has come to represent something more than he actually is.

My idiocy reminds me of Stendhal, a man who knew something about behaving like a fool in the grip of a powerful cocktail of emotions and his theory of *cristallisation*. Visiting Salzburg's salt mines in 1818 (nineteenth-century tourism certainly knew how to have fun), he was struck by the glittering crystalline formations on every surface and the way in which the most unexceptional twig was transformed by this improbable chemical reaction into a gem-encrusted marvel. Human sentiment, Stendhal realized, could effect something similar and in his 1853 treatise on love, *De L'Amour*, he describes *cristallisation* as the process by which, when you fall for someone, you idealize them and reshape them in your own mind in the way that suits you best, so that everything they are and everything they do, even their defects, take on a treacherous fairy sparkle bearing little relation to reality. This, I think, is what has happened to me. My skewed perception 'crystallizes' this ordinary chap and he sparkles even brighter for his unavailability (*'une frequentation discontinue de l'être aimé'*, infrequent contact with the loved one, is one of Stendhal's conditions for this alchemy to operate). Something similar is happening, I realize, with London itself, longed for and far away. The maimed pigeons glitter like birds of paradise; rude Tesco Metro cashiers become sparkling wits.

Of course, you can't be dazzled by a heap of salt crystals indefinitely and I'm not; it fades. Beyond a shared fondness for grubby indie boy bands of the nineties and a sort of dissatisfaction at the way we have led our lives up to this point, the married man and I don't really have any kind of connection and soon I stop hoping; stop trying, stop crystallizing.

Before I get to this point, however, I find out that I was wrong about the most fundamental part of what attracted me to him: communication. Because it turns out that even in English, where I master every bloody nuance and subtlety, I don't know how to express my feelings. If anything, I'm worse, and on the rare occasions we actually meet, I become increasingly clipped and silent, spitting out the occasional tiny haiku of a sentence, heavy with unexpressed feeling. Mostly my mind gallops and churns just as fruitlessly as it did with Olivier. It seems I am just a terrible communicator in *any* language: I am the problem, not French. How can this be? When did I start to believe spoken words are as powerful and impossible to control as bullets?

Forced to contemplate my own failings yet again, the puffed up daring that has carried me through this early part of my grown-up single life deflates. All my feelings about the separation, my mother, the last five years, the mess I have made of things and the trail of hurt I have left behind coalesce and swirl around, threatening to engulf me. Finally – and I suppose it's long overdue – I feel truly sad.

That sadness makes me stupid. I lose things – wallets, tickets, shoes – and even when I haven't lost anything, I think I have, checking my bag over and over again for passport and keys. I fall over frequently, as if unhappiness has gone to my inner ear. On one London trip, I take a train out to see Kate and her new baby (I mainly cry when I get there, in her lovely, warm, pretty kitchen, which feels so much like a home compared to my grubby, cold Brussels house, as she feeds me home-made cakes) and on the way back I fail to mind the gap and fall from the carriage, misjudging the distance from train to platform. I scrape my leg right open and walk around the city bleeding and confused, tears trickling unchecked and making my make-up run. Another time, I break the heel off one of my fancy shoes and end up with both knees bloody and gravel-filled, like a kid in the playground; I even drive a borrowed car into a wall in a fit of particularly awful distraction. When I tell Olivier my misfortunes (which I am often tempted to do, although I know that really I shouldn't), he makes some mild expression of concern, which I find momentarily hurtful, but my problems are my own now, this is exactly how it is supposed to be.

In this state of mind, London itself feels spoilt to me too; the shine wears off its streets and parks and shops. I have messed the city up for myself and now it is associated with this awful mixture of regret, bad behaviour and longing, my trips there freighted with hope and disappointment. I find it almost physically hurts to go back to some parts: Spitalfields makes me cry, just because it's still there, living its life, and I wish I were too, wish we had never left. Out west, my father and stepmother are lovely, just lovely, when I arrive at their house late at night in a whirlwind of smudged make-up, drunk and chaotic, and they never make me feel anything but welcome, but I feel keenly how much of a worry I must be in my current ridiculous state. 'I'm such a mess,' I cry to them over lunch on one trip, head bowed, fringe dangling in my spaghetti, disarmed into candour by tiredness and alcohol. 'I'm a *disaster*.' Madevi and I coin the term 'facepasta' to describe this self-loathing low and we use it again and again: my life seems to lurch from one facepasta event to another.

Brussels, meanwhile, is as messy and cluttered with chores and responsibilities as my kitchen table: my heart sinks when the train comes through the unlovely architectural mess of the suburbs and into the low-ceilinged concrete chaos of Midi Station. I feel constantly nagged by an endless cycle of unfinished admin and perplexing household maintenance: the overgrown garden I need to tackle because the neighbours are unhappy, the mysterious smells and the non-functioning dishwasher, the lost pieces of paper that must be provided to some obstructive Belgian bureaucracy or another. The landlady comes round uninvited, purses her lips and makes warning noises about my deposit. I feel embattled; judged and found wanting.

The house doesn't matter so much, but the boys do and I worry about them constantly. Are they coping? How badly have they been affected? Can I do this alone? On weekends with them, the expanse of empty time to fill frightens me. It's not that they are terribly demanding – they would happily stay at home and watch TV in their pyjamas, all they really need is me, sane and stable and comforting – but I doubt my own ability to give them that basic comfort and with good reason: my track record thus far has been pretty shitty. I don't feel as if I am enough on my own and Olivier is such a solidly good father, certain of his own abilities. I miss that. I miss him. I don't let myself think it very often; I try not to think it, but there it is.

I shouldn't be thinking of it, because here I am, *une femme seule* after all these years. I could do anything! I tell myself, and then all I actually do is sit in my dirty house, hunched over my laptop in pyjamas for eight hours at a stretch without speaking to anyone, eating Bonne Maman Crème Caramels for breakfast, lunch and dinner.

Thank goodness, then, for Paris.

« 22 »

Je voudrais que quelqu'un
m'attende quelque part

The first time I go back to Paris I am on a mission: I am finally going to meet Madevi.

It is a strange thing, meeting your best friend for the first time. I get the train from Brussels and make my way to the Tuileries, where I sit on some dusty steps nervously waiting for her, clutching a poster of mythological creatures we have been laughing over online and a bar of Côte d'Or chocolate (the caramelized almond variety, with a touch of salt – she has been very specific). We are like naïve Internet daters who have become soulmates over a series of increasingly fevered emails without ever actually meeting, and there seems to me to be a very real danger that we might not get on, a pair of prickly introverts forced, blinking, into the daylight. I might come over well virtually when I can pick and choose my words, but in person I know all too well how stilted and uncomfortable I can be: shyness can come across as coldness. What if I have nothing to say to her? What if she doesn't like me?

It is strange, too, coming back to Paris. I am not sure, before I get off the train at the Gare du Nord, how it will feel to be back as a tourist, but it's nice, actually. The sun is shining and the familiar forecourt of the station with its angry ballet of taxis, drunks and fast food joints is a jolt of adrenalin after stolidly predictable Brussels. I like how the city makes me stand up straighter and move faster, and the crackle of my synapses remembering short cuts and métro lines I haven't taken in years is strangely satisfying. I make my way down to Châtelet and along the Rue du Faubourg Saint-Honoré, past cheerful groups of tourists taking photos of the window displays at Colette, then I walk through the beautiful Place Vendôme, where my mother once got the giggles taking pictures of a rowdy demonstration of striking lawyers ('you should be a lawyer here, Em, it looks much more fun').

Madevi appears from the Rue de Rivoli and even from a distance it seems as if she just fits in. I don't know why I think that, exactly: the set of her jaw perhaps, the pace of her walk or the take-no-shit aura she gives off. Momentarily, this makes me more nervous still, but she catches sight of me and laughs at my gormless expression and my silly bag of presents. We hug, she brushes dust off the back of my coat ('Have you already been rubbing yourself up against the park ponies, you pervert? We were supposed to do that together!') and I know it's going to be OK. We eat tempura in a basement bar on the Rue Sainte-Anne, Paris's Little Tokyo (I nearly drop a prawn in a woman's handbag), then we walk through the Passage des Victories covered nineteenth-century arcade: I have never been in all my years visiting Paris and it's so beautiful. Finally, we hop across to the Left Bank to buy the definitive cappuccino éclair we have been discussing for weeks and slump in a café to eat it. My first impression is right: even though she hasn't lived here for years, Madevi passes as emphatically, perfectly Parisian. There is no excessive politeness or apology with her, just a brisk efficiency that commands respect. I feel gauche and clueless trailing in her wake, but my confidence is bolstered by osmosis to the point that when an elderly lady tuts and brushes at the back of my still-dusty coat, I laugh.

Madevi and I come to Paris a few times together and when we are not there, we egg each other on to greater heights of longing for the city, a latter-day Masha and Irina languishing on Google Chat. I see it through new eyes with her: greedier, happier, sillier ones. We drag our wheeled cases through the drug dealers and pavement hissers of Barbès and eat Vietnamese food, full of fresh mint and coriander, straight from the containers. Madevi takes me to an un-marked outlet shop out in Mouton Duvernet where they sell cheap Maje dresses and to Du Pain et des Idées, her favourite bakery, with its baby-blue and gilt exterior, the scent of butter and yeast carrying all the way down the street. We buy still-warm croissants and neat, salty goats cheese parcels and eat them on a bench next to the Canal Saint-Martin, then python-stuffed with carbohydrate, we try on dresses we can't possibly afford under the censorious eye of etiolated salesgirls in empty boutiques. We go to La Grande Épicerie and to Lafayette Gourmet to buy Christine Ferber jam (Madevi has instructed me that these are the only jams worth eating) then eat large steaks and drink Bordeaux in the food hall brasserie like proper grown-ups. Madevi drags me, intimidated, into Hermès to relive her scarf-folding student job glories and to Printemps Beauté to test lipsticks. One sunny afternoon, we sit in the Jardin des Plantes under the low branches of a flowering cherry tree Madevi remembers from her undergrad days, then take pictures of the '*manège du dodo*', a weird carousel where you can ride on extinct creatures of every imaginable variety: the horned tortoise, the sivatherium (a sort of giraffe-deer) or the Tasmanian wolf. Best of all, we go to Stohrer.

This is a pilgrimage of sorts: we have been talking about Stohrer for months, each of us in front of our laptops in cities a long way from Paris.

'What cake would you like most in the world?' Madevi asks me idly one day. All our conversations come back to cake eventually.

'Hmm. Coffee and walnut. Or a good *flan*.'

'Boring. You always say a bloody *flan*. I want a Stohrer éclair.'

'What's Stohrer?'

'You don't know Stohrer?'

'No. Should I?'

'You've never been to Stohrer! God, I dream of Stohrer. Look it up, go on. Mmm, the "*religieuse à l'ancienne*", it's like a miniature *pièce montée*. The éclairs are pretty good too, small and bitter. Look.'

She sends me a link to a picture of the *religieuse* on the Stohrer website, which is an old-fashioned thing in curly, fussy script. The *religieuse* is a pyramid of stacked alternating coffee and chocolate éclairs, topped with a miniature *croquembouche* of caramelized choux buns. It is ridiculous, nonsensical. How would you even cut into it? I want it, badly.

'That's . . . I'm speechless. That's a real thing?'

'I can't believe you've never been. Can you find a picture of the *macaron pistache framboise*? Oh god, I want one now. Juicy fat raspberries. We'll go together.'

So we do.

The Rue Montorgueil, in the 2nd arrondissement near Les Halles, is a verging-on-the-Disney perfect Paris street I don't remember ever walking down: cobbled, pedestrian, lined with counters of perfectly stacked fruit and vegetables, rotating roast chickens and glossy fresh fish, elderly ladies overdressed for the weather in camel hair coats and mufflers pulling wheeled trolleys, and dark cafés. At one end, the Escargot Montorgueil restaurant announces its mission with an outsized gilt snail balanced on the wrought-iron door frame, antennae glinting in the sun and a busy herd of smaller snails crawling along beneath it. At number 51, under a yellow awning, is *La Maison Stohrer, Pâtissier, maison fondé en 1730*, the oldest patisserie in France. It is tiny, with a blown-glass chandelier, pastoral murals and mirrored walls crazy-paved with age. We don't buy a *baba au rhum*, even though that is what you are supposed to get because Nicolas Stohrer invented it, or a *puits d'amour*, the eighteenth-century deep-filled custard tart that is the house speciality. Instead, we both get a *macaron pistache framboise* and take them to the café next door. We eat in reverent silence, pistachio cream, crisp shell and fat raspberries. How could I have never discovered this place? I am starting to realize how warped my mental vision of Paris is. Like my France, it's patchy and partial: there's the tight web of streets in the 17th I know too well, then the rest of the city is an adolescent's fantasy, a collage of films and Cartier-Bresson postcards. With Madevi, it starts to take on real shape.

Madevi comes with me too, when my friend Trish throws a New Year's party.

Trish is another Internet friend – we bond over a picture of Noirmoutier butter with salt crystals – but she is also someone I know of from my French *Elle* reading days. A cookery writer, a long-time expat Parisian, glamorous and beautiful, she has until now been utterly distant from my life, a gorgeous image on a page. Now, thanks to the magic of the Internet, we've traded confidences and expat horror stories and now she has invited us for New Year. Madevi and I look anxiously at false eyelashes and new lipsticks in Printemps and agonize about what present we could possibly bring, but we need not have bothered, because Trish makes us instantly at ease and the party is wonderful: generous and funny and uproarious. I had always assumed adulthood would be full of this kind of event, but until now, it never has been.

From the outside Trish's Haussmann block on the Left Bank is as chilly and disapproving as ours was, but inside there is champagne and dancing, the unsanctioned throwing of ice cubes from the balcony, The Bee Gees and haggis. At one point there is even a small fire, when a box of meringues gets too close to a candle. The neighbours come up to complain and are effortlessly incorporated into the festivities. In the early hours, Trish, Madevi and I sit amidst the candlelit carnage of the evening eating *crème de marrons* straight from the tube and speculate, laughing, about the year ahead, which just at that moment seems big and bright. ('Icing sugar will be big this year,' says Trish dreamily. 'Stoats,' says Madevi, with conviction. 'This will be the year of the stoat.')

At dawn, when Madevi and I finally collapse into the tiny beds in Trish's daughter's bedroom, you can see the Eiffel Tower from the window, quiet now after its midnight paroxysm of pyrotechnics. In the morning I wake to find Madevi has already left and after a quick coffee and whispered thanks I walk back across silent Paris in my creased party dress, head still spinning. The gilt dome of Les Invalides is sparkling in the wintry sun and there are treacherous, glittering patches of frost on the ground. My phone has died so I have to guess my way back across the city using maps in métro stations and half-remembered routes. Before we head off to our trains, Madevi and I share a box of tiny, beautiful treats from the Japanese pâtissier Sadaharu Aoki, little green tea, dark chocolate and citrus morsels, and as I sit on my train home, I think to myself that this is how Paris is supposed to be: a beautiful adventure.

For a while after this, it is as if I have passed some kind of initiation ritual and Paris plays nice for me. I don't exactly feel as if I belong, but I at least have the right stamp in my visa; my name is on the guest list. I finally let go of my wounded perception of the city only as a chilly, disapproving sepulchre and Paris becomes the City of Light again: joyful. Every time I get off the train at the Gare du Nord I forget my money worries, my domestic and emotional inadequacies and my fears for the children for a few hours of pure escapism. Leaving the station is the start of a little escapade and even the dirtiest métro carriages seem redolent, not just with urine but with possibility, every warm body an invitation. I hold eye contact a little too long, stand a little too close; I wear my nicest clothes, my highest heels and my brightest lipsticks. On one occasion I walk down the Rue de Sèvres and it feels as if every eye is upon me: I think for a moment I have tapped into some hitherto unimagined reserve of sexual magnetism but then I realize my skirt is tucked into my knickers. Nevertheless, Paris is a holiday from myself at a time when I need it urgently; when it's hard to see myself as good or lovable, or even just OK.

I go to dinner at Trish's often. These dinners are a source of wonder to me: if you had asked my teenage self to describe the perfect Parisian party, they are exactly what I would have conjured up: sharp wit, beauty, humour and deliciousness. The food, unsurprisingly, is memorable: we have new season asparagus, strawberry soup with lemongrass and mint, chicory Caesar salad, smoked butter, twenty types of goats cheese and elaborate Pierre Hermé desserts. But the company is just as good. Trish has a magical ability to take odd mixes of people and just make them *work*, somehow. I meet all sorts of people: photographers and theatre directors, loose cannon expats, fast food empire heirs and proper French establishment types. There is often an element of uncertainty: a wildcard guest Trish doesn't know and has invited on impulse, or someone who might or might not turn up. Every evening is an adventure and before the night kicks off, Trish and I sit down and talk about who is coming and what might happen. One evening we babysit a handsome pâtissier's sausage dog while he goes clubbing and another night, a photographer friend of Trish's sweeps me off in a taxi to meet a transsexual barmaid he needs to talk to at Les Bains Douches, the famous Marais nightclub. There are intrigues and disagreements, flirtations, gossip and laughter, so much laughter.

One evening I arrive to find a defiant sign on the wall in the entrance hall of the building – 'Tonight we are having a dinner party (5th floor left) and we will make a NOISE. We may even LAUGH and WALK AROUND' – and this fuck you to Parisian *froideur* delights me so much I laugh out loud: Trish has endured plenty of Parisian neighbour hostility but she's gloriously, exuberantly unbowed.

In high summer, I come back to Paris with Benjamin and his new boyfriend, Ian. The two of them are headily, demonstratively in love and while it could be strange or lonely, here in the hot, sexy, narrow streets of the Marais (we travel with another single friend who can't cope with the suffocating romance of it all and goes AWOL for the weekend, causing great confusion), it isn't: it feels festive and charged with possibility. It's so hot, the backs of my knees are slicked with sweat when I sit down and I stick to the basket-work of café terrace chairs where we drink too much cheap rosé. As Ian dozes back at the hotel, Benjamin and I walk slowly, languorously round the shops, cleaving to the odd patches of shade and chatting about love and cardigans. In the evening, a man I met at one of Trish's parties comes to take me out on his scooter and we weave through the Saturday night crowds who have spilled out of bars and into the streets, then zoom along the Seine, faster and faster, the warm air on my face, the city lights reflected on the water, the sky deep blue. It's magical and, just for a few minutes, I feel like one of my teen cinema idols.

Back in Paris for another party in the autumn, I bring the dog. The train is delayed and circuitous and we end up chugging in on a tiny suburban shuttle, but he's perfectly behaved, sitting sphinx-like under my seat, and when we finally arrive in the Gare du Nord he bounces out with me into the early evening, where a soft yellow sun is warming the sandstone. It's unseasonably warm for the time of year and I am wearing a silk dress and bare legs again, enjoying the stolen autumn warmth of the sun on my back. Oscar trots beside me as I head west along the Rue de Maubeuge, enjoying the simple pleasure of knowing where I am going, past corner shops and opticians and small gravelled squares where the leaves on the horse chestnut trees are just on the turn and onto the Rue des Martyrs. Rue des Martyrs is one of those cartoonishly perfect Paris streets, like the opening sequence of a romantic comedy: the rakish dark-eyed chap with the beautifully knotted scarf salutes the wizened Algerian greengrocer perfectly piling his clementines, Cartier-Bresson schoolchildren gawp in exaggerated wonder at huge meringues or *baguettes à l'ancienne* perfectly dusted with flour in the baker's. There is a shop that sells nothing but beautifully coloured choux buns, plump and pretty. The dog and I sashay through the middle of it all, like Gene Kelly and Leslie Caron in *An American in Paris*, all lightness and romance, and people *smile*. I have never seen anything like it. Is this all it would take to fit in here? A whippet and a nice dress? If only I had given birth to puppies instead of children, perhaps everything would have been different, I think, a little sourly.

The next morning I head home and stop off at a café on the Rue du Bac, sitting outside with a cup of coffee, Oscar at my feet. It occurs to me suddenly that this is it: this is my teenage dream, give or take a few details. Here I am, alone in Paris with a dog, sitting outside a café and drinking coffee, writing for a living. I acknowledge the moment, but it doesn't feel quite how I expected it to.

That fantasy of myself as solitary, self-contained and independent, stalking through the streets of Paris, is so powerful it has endured undimmed since my teenage years, but it doesn't hold up to real scrutiny. Even Simone de Beauvoir, whom I idolize for her resolve and her rigour and her willingness to do brave things alone, was avidly hungry for connection (by her own account, life only starts to make sense with Sartre). All those actresses that fuelled my Paris visions aren't truly solitary either: that would make for a terribly dull film. They are all waiting for someone, thinking of someone, trying to forget someone. I have wanted the confidence to be alone, but it just shows up what is missing and I have learned by now that the wrong warm body is no comfort at all, not really.

With all the time I spend in trains and on platforms, my feeling of dislocation intensifies. There's often a moment when I get off the train and scan the crowds at arrivals and feel a tiny pang that no one is waiting for me. *'Je voudrais que quelqu'un m'attende quelque part'* ('I wish someone were waiting for me somewhere') keeps running through my head – it's the title of a book I see over and over again in station newsagents and bookshops. I buy it on one trip: it's a book of short stories by Anna Gavalda, a slight, wistful mix of longing, dreams and disappointments. The story the phrase comes from doesn't really resonate when I finally read it (it's a melancholy account of a young man permanently upstaged by his older brother, though he gets the girl in the end) but that phrase stays with me. It's a ridiculous feeling (the story says that too: *'c'est con'*) because no one has *ever* waited for me like that, not since my mum met me off my flight back from Casablanca, but it represents something, some kind of absence. If no one is waiting for me, does it really matter where I go, or what I do?

« 23 »

Sous Le Pont Mirabeau

After my year of making up with Paris, I don't go as often. I can't keep trying to run away from myself, much as I might like the idea, and I certainly don't want to run away from my two lovely boys, waiting back in Brussels. The city's sparkle hasn't faded, but I feel as if I have to let go and accept that it's not mine; I am just an occasional visitor. My Paris experiences are the tiniest strand – a Wikipedia stub (*une ébauche*, a sketch, the French version calls it, which I like) – in my life. '*Méfiez-vous de Paris*' sang Juliette Greco and I *am* wary now, it's so beguiling, but it's not for me, or at least it's not for now.

More practically, all this travelling is ruinous and I need to settle and live in one place. I have made some progress with Brussels. Sometimes now when my train approaches Midi Station and I spot the strange white elephant of an art deco church that marks the highest point of the city, Altitude 100, I feel a little spark of belonging. Climbing into a dangerously decrepit taxi that smells of pine air freshener and cigarettes and getting into a lengthy discussion with the driver (who is *never* the person on the photo permit that hangs on the back of his seat) about the best route to my house, over the soundtrack of Nostalgie radio playing France Gall or Alain Souchon, I feel at home, sometimes.

The city has taken shape in my head and I know how it fits together. I am more in tune now with my sleepy, surreal suburb's weird rhythms too: how, for ten days in spring some blossom or other makes every side street and every back garden smell of honey, and how, a few weeks after the honey, we get the lilac, an explosion of scent that vanishes as suddenly as it comes. I mark the arrival of summer with the arrival of the eccentric neighbour's decorated bench, with the queues of people lining up at the ice cream shop to – inexplicably – then sit in their cars with their ice creams. After that comes the interminable school pageant, in which the boys have to dress up as Indian chiefs or the Duke of Wellington, and prize-giving, sweltering in the gymnasium. In late July Brussels just empties, the Eurocrats vanish home and the Belgians go on holiday, and it feels as if there is no one but me and a few stray cats left in the city.

On the odd occasions I do go to Paris I don't see Trish so often, because she has moved out to the pretty market town of Saint-Germain-en-Laye out to the west, at the other end of the rail line Theo and I used to watch from the Batignolles park. I do still visit sometimes: she has a beautiful apartment overlooking the park and the chateau and it's quieter now, just us and her kids. The moment for wild festivities has passed, at least for now. In the dead of winter, we go out for oysters in a snowstorm, sliding around the snowy streets, Trish in a furry trapper's hat, me in leaking impractical suede boots, laughing at the wild weather. I admire Trish so much – she has done what I never could and made Paris her own – but even with all her chutzpah, beauty and brilliance, it still doesn't look easy, fitting in here. No wonder I fell on my arse. *Trop belle pour toi*, says Paris, like that Depardieu film with all the Schubert I watched so many years ago at Quaker school. *Trop belle pour toi*, even in your best dress, even with a dog.

I head back into the city early the next morning to get my train to Brussels. Saint-Germain is looking beautiful, muffled under a carpet of snow, but I'm worried about getting home. Even so, as I sit on the nearly empty early-morning RER in a puddle of melting ice, I decide, on a whim, to stop off for cake. Every trip I have made over this past year has involved cake. I just have to buy at least one of my favourites to have something, a waxed-paper-wrapped parcel or a pretty box, to cheer me up on the way home. It's a way, too, of remembering my other Paris year, somehow; my tiny gesture of belonging. I have a shortlist of favourites: there's Pierre Hermé's famous *Ispahan*, a raspberry *macaron* with rose and lychee cream and fresh raspberries, a flavour combination so sensuously satisfying it has spawned a generation of imitators. Ladurée's *Saint-Honoré rose-framboise*, another favourite, is arguably one of those imitators, but this ludicrous, blousy pink Barbara Cartland over-indulgence of a cake with flounces of Chantilly and rose petals always cheers me. Madevi has won me over to the Stohrer éclair too, neat and bitter, almost restrained. And I'm always in the market for a good *flan*, so I keep my eyes open: Pâtisserie des Rêves does a splendid one with puff pastry and intense vanilla crème.

Today, though, I want a *Bamboo* from Sadaharu Aoki. The *Bamboo* is a riff on the traditional *Opéra*, using dark chocolate and matcha tea, alternating impossibly thin layers of genoise sponge, joconde biscuit, chocolate, and green tea-infused cream and it is topped with a beautiful dusting of matcha and icing sugar, shading green and white like a bamboo stalk. I think it might be the prettiest cake I have ever seen. I want one for my journey home, which promises to be arduous, and the easiest place to find one is Lafayette Gourmet. I get off the RER at Auber and take the short walk round the back of the Opéra to the Boulevard Haussmann and Galeries Lafayette.

Lafayette Gourmet is on the first floor. It's not the most extravagantly beautiful of food halls – La Grande Epicerie is prettier – but it's wickedly well stocked, with smart men in black chef's jackets carving Serrano ham, *macarons* from Jean Paul Hévin and, my destination, the Sadaharu Aoki counter, with its jewel-box-perfect display of patisserie: matcha and black sesame éclairs, thin, crisp, salted caramel tarts and acid bright rectangular ganaches, perfect as an unused child's paintbox. I pick up my *Bamboo* and a bar of Aoki's crispy caramel chocolate then, with a little time to spare, I wander on through the store, straying into the jams, the dried pasta, the 'British' section (Tiptree marmalade, oatcakes, misfiled Lucky Charms and marshmallow fluff; I would be offended for British gastronomy, but I gave up that fight years ago). I don't seem to be insulated by the protective layer of euphoria I usually have when I come to Paris and as I walk, memories of walking these same aisles during our Paris year start to drift to the surface.

I remember coming down to Lafayette Gourmet a few times, in search of treats on special occasions. I recall looking for a nice dinner for Olivier's birthday, regretfully dismissing truffles as too expensive and wondering about hand-carved pata negra ham, wandering the aisles and leaving, frustrated at my lack of resources and imagination, with a single chocolate chip cookie. I had been back around my own birthday in search of treats from home and stared blankly at boxes of Twinings teabags and shortbread, trying to buy a comfort I couldn't find anywhere else. Finally, at Christmas, Theo and I went to look at the window displays. The windows of the *grands magasins* are a seasonal tradition in Paris, miniature tableaux of wonder and colour, featuring hydraulic magic and glittering lights. The streets are packed and the stores provide little wooden steps and walk-along platforms to allow children to see the displays, but Theo and I only managed a couple of windows before the five-deep crush and the shoving chased us away.

Looking back, I feel, suddenly, incredibly sad. I have this glib account of our year in Paris I trot out when asked – the comic clashes with awful neighbours and the on-street aggression – but I have never really thought about what unhappiness, overlaid and muffled and hidden under the ordinary hard business of looking after tiny children, ran through it. I remember, now, Olivier, throwing all his energy into trying to buoy us up, again and again. My sister, hiding behind her curtain of hair, wishing for the earth to swallow her up. My stepfather, coming to visit and trying to weave connections and make sense of his shattered life. I remember how lost and out of place I felt in these aisles and walking through them today opens up a Pandora's box of long-suppressed sadness, so I hide behind the expensive canned tuna and cry.

Once I start crying, I don't seem to be able to stop. It's not discreet, silent weeping either, I'm gasping for breath and snotty in the tinned fish aisle and oblivious Japanese tourists keep reaching across me for sardines, so I stumble out, half blind with tears, into the street behind the shop, all delivery vans and cheap noodle bars and sales assistants muffled in down coats on cigarette breaks. I like the ugly back end of the *grands magasins*, the behind the scenes bit; *l'envers du décor*, they say in French. Sometimes too much beauty and too much opulence are oppressive and today the shabby Rue Saint-Lazare is a great comfort.

I drop into a loud Vietnamese café with Formica tables and a strip-lit display cabinet of trays of bright orange sweet and sour pork, brown, sparsely garnished noodles and rows of those plump, tightly clingfilmed rice paper rolls. There are hundreds of them, all over Paris. I order myself a bowl of noodles, dry my tears on a scratchy paper napkin and find myself thinking of Olivier. This is nothing new. I think about him often, sometimes irritated, sometimes guiltily, usually unconsciously. He's always in my mind somewhere. When I lie in bed I get a muscle memory of how he would reach across in his sleep and take my hand or let his fall into the hollow of my hip. Now, though, I remember him in

Paris. I imagine, for the first time, what it must have been to live with me, angry and sad and silent. I remember how tired he looked in the evenings and his eternal bounce and optimism nonetheless. I was often furious with that optimism and his insistence that everything would be all right. How the hell could he know that? I appropriated all that sadness for myself, rolled myself up in it and paraded it around, but in fact it was shared, painfully, lovingly shared. I thought Olivier couldn't comprehend my loss, but I realize belatedly that he had lost the life we shared. He had also lost my mother, who adored him, and in every meaningful sense he had lost me. His love, despite all this, seems like a miracle I just ignored. Now I see it; I feel it.

I walk back up to Saint-Lazare to catch a métro to the Gare du Nord and the streets feel charged with memories in a way they have not on previous trips. This is the place I took my very first train to Normandy on my own as a nineteen-year-old. Here is the road up to the Batignolles bridge and that bloody intimidating organic market where I was always too nervous to ask for anything (and where I once cried in the queue for a chicken and told an old lady I missed my mum – she was quite nice about it, actually, and told me she still missed hers). But here too are the streets where Olivier bought me cakes and made me laugh and held my hand.

When I get back to the Gare du Nord, my train is delayed, of course. A cold wind is insinuating itself around the concourse, which is packed with angry commuters and patrolled by machine-gun-toting CRS riot police, and as I wait for more information, I get that panicky feeling again, as if I have lost something. This time, though, I don't need to check through my bag for my passport and my keys: I know exactly what I have lost. I just don't know how, or if, I will ever get him back.

I do not run back to Brussels and tell Olivier I still love him in dramatic, cinematic fashion: actually, I don't even consider it might be an option. You can't get it back: '*Ni temps passé / Ni les amours reviennent*,' says Apollinaire in 'Sous Le Pont Mirabeau'; time and loves don't come back, however much you might wish they would. Initially, the realization that I have walked away from something extraordinary feels like another painful dose of self-knowledge. Intimations of my own inadequacy come thick and fast this year: 'just another shitty personal growth moment,' someone says on the blog apropos some other act of stupidity and that is exactly how it feels: like a long series of shitty personal growth moments, necessary but painful. I don't really think there is any way back from the place I have landed myself.

What I *do* do, eventually, after weeks of ruminating, is go round for coffee one morning after I drop the boys at school and shoot my mouth off, vaguely. It's almost as if I don't really know how to say what I need to say, but I know I need to say something, so I just open my mouth and hope for the best. 'The only real problem with us,' I say to him, 'was timing. We met each other far too early.' I am all worked up and confused and over-caffeinated and this is unusually frank for me. Even so, I'm not scared: I can say most things to Olivier and we never stopped talking when we split. We still *like* each other, liking each other was never really the problem. 'We're actually really compatible,' I say, warming to my theme, 'but I just hadn't *lived* at all, so I couldn't know.' It's hardly the great romantic speech, but for me, it's huge.

Olivier smiles: he looks almost amused. He seems healthy, a long way from the grey wraith of a couple of years ago. He spends his free time climbing, playing squash and roller-blading. He has started volunteering for a suicide helpline and he's made what seem to be a really lovely group of friends who won't let him take himself too seriously. He is about to go off to visit an old university friend in Canada. It's interesting, I think, how his world has expanded without me. He's lost some of his previous closed-off intensity and from the outside, at least, he seems *bien dans sa peau*, at ease with himself. But what do I know?

'You reckon?'

'I think so.' I don't say I'm sorry, but I'm thinking it, hard. How did I not see you, I think. I drink my coffee, which is excellent (Olivier has invested in an eye-wateringly expensive coffee machine, which is whirring and spitting in the corner of the kitchen) and get ready to leave. It's strange how somewhere I know every brick isn't mine any more and it's strange to be back here, just the two of us. I could find my way around this house in the dark – I have done enough times – put my hand straight to every light switch and avoid every creaky board. I feel the same about Olivier, in some ways; not at all in others. What's going on in his head right now? He nods as if I have proposed an interesting thesis.

'We should spend more time together,' he says. 'It would be good. Let's get a drink sometime soon.'

'Sure, when you get back from Canada?'

And I think no more about it, because what exactly is going to happen? Nothing. He's just being pleasant.

But when he does get back from Canada, he comes to pick the boys up, tanned and happy and full of tales of riding quad bikes on frozen lakes. Then he comes round again. The four of us watch a film squashed up on the sofa in my house one Sunday afternoon and it feels good, but so confusing. The next time, he comes round when the boys aren't even with me and we have a drink. After that, he takes me to a concert on the back of his motorbike. Days pass, weeks pass. Then one evening after we have been out for a couple of drinks in the bar round the corner and we are chatting about nothing very much, he kisses me, just like that in the kitchen and I kiss him back and I think 'Oh!' and 'Really?' and it feels as if after all my missteps and stupidities, my idiotic vanities, I have cheated time somehow, because my love is back.

Then I don't think any more: the noise in my head stops, for a wonderful moment, and everything is still and quiet.

« 24 »

État des Lieux

The French language has a word for what is happening to us – *retrouvailles* – the explosion of emotions generated by a reunion. It's one of those words that ends up in lists of the notoriously untranslatable, as if it were a feeling that only French people have, or feel the need to label. Our *retrouvailles* are both wonderful and terrifying. It should be my happy ending, but I go a bit off the rails. Again.

We don't go public straight away. For a few months we sneak around and take things slowly: we date, I suppose. Olivier comes to see me in the evenings when the babysitter has the boys or vice versa and we go out on his motorbike to bars and restaurants in areas neither of us know. In the school holidays when the boys go to stay with his parents for a few days, we spend a weekend in a hotel in a vineyard near Bordeaux. We sit out in deckchairs in the weak early spring sun and cautiously expose our pale limbs in the still chilly pool. In the afternoon we lie in bed in those thick hotel robes that make your limbs impossibly heavy and try and make sense of everything. I rest my head on his chest. It feels strange, the dissonance of new and familiar all at once.

I feel incredibly, improbably lucky – I love him, he loves me, this is an amazing outcome – but it feels almost too easy. There has been no hardship and no drama, which is unnerving. Can it really have happened? Our reconciliation has a surreal, nonsensical quality, as if we are doing something a bit ridiculous, and sneaking off for weekends and evenings just adds to that. I wonder if we can make it work and more specifically, I wonder if I can be trusted not to mess it up again. Having got everything so wrong and having been so certain I was right, I have no faith in my own judgement any more: most days I barely trust myself to cross a road.

Olivier thinks it's easy. He still has that lovely certainty that reminds me of my father: just stick with me, doll, and everything will be OK.

'Do you love me?'

'Yes. Yes! Of course, but . . .'

'Then the rest is just logistics.'

There's a bit more than just logistics to worry about: first we have to explain to the children. It's an unnerving carbon copy of telling them we were splitting up: the same room, the same febrile atmosphere. They are not touchingly delighted.

'We've got something to tell you,' says Olivier, carefully. '*Maman* is going to move back in, we're getting back together.'

Instantly Theo's face crumples in anger and distress and he starts to wail, inconsolably, overcome with some impossible to digest cocktail of emotion.

'Too much change!' he cries. 'Too much change!'

He's only nine; his brother is seven. Olivier and I have been so careful to try and make things OK for them, so scrupulous in keeping our relationship good-humoured and harmonious, but so much has happened in the past few years: three countries, four moves, a separation and a reconciliation would be far too much for one twice his age. I try to hug him but he's tense and tight and his face is hot. Louis watches, as wide-eyed, silent and wary as a bush baby, as Olivier puts his arm around his shoulders and gives him a reassuring shake.

'It's OK, Loulou.'

'I'm happy,' he says thoughtfully, but he looks uncertain. I reach across and give his knee a squeeze, my arm still around Theo.

'It'll be OK, Theo. Honestly, it's OK.' There doesn't seem to be much more we can say – the only thing that will make these words true for him is time. I want everything to be smooth and happy and uncomplicated for them now, but life isn't like that. Will it be OK? In the meantime, we go for an ice cream.

Even the logistics are horrible, as I try to move out and back in, dismantling the life I have been putting together, piece by piece. First I have to give notice to the gorgon land-lady, who has grown in my mind into such a towering figure of menace I half expect her stiffly waved helmet of hair to turn into a nest of snakes. She blames me for the flood in the house next door (as if somehow I have engineered the burst pipes through solid brick) and her way of dropping in and looking round the house in disgust, as if someone has defecated on her beige linoleum, has unnerved me to the point of genuine terror. Preparing for the *état des lieux* (the exit inspection) is one of the most stressful experiences I have ever had, during which I use up more cleaning products than in the rest of my adult life and at one farcical point end up hiding, lying flat on the floor, when I spot the land-lady's Volvo parking up outside. I focus all my terror for the future on the frankly irrelevant question of whether I will get my deposit back – god knows, I have thrown more money away on less important things in the past few years – and even when we reach an agreement, I live in fear of a call or a registered letter saying I am being sued for some forgotten misdeed or unfiled piece of paperwork.

Once that is done, we give away my fridge and store my TV in the attic, roll up the mattress and try to decide between two sets of toasters, kettles and microwaves. The wasted expense – all my savings gone – makes me feel sick and the confusion is exhausting. At one point the dog has an actual nervous breakdown at all the toing and froing between houses and sits down in the street, refusing to move in either direction. 'Too much change,' his eyes say: he doesn't know where he lives any more and I don't either. I have to carry him back to the house, where he whines when we go upstairs and pees on the fridge. It takes me forever to work up the nerve to tell my father and stepmother Olivier and I are back together, which is stupid, it turns out, because they are delighted. My dad pours a lot of wine and calls Olivier up to tell him how happy he is, then he calls up several other family members too.

My stepfather and sister are easier, somehow, probably because they've been in contact with Olivier throughout. He has been part of the family for so long that even if we had never got back together, he would always have been part of their lives. My sister is studying and working in Paris now, helping in shelters for the homeless and working with autistic kids. She has bottomless reserves of kindness and compassion I can only wonder at: her most recent flat share fell apart when she brought home a homeless kid she found sleeping in a park. I feel happy to see her settled and a bit discomfited at how much better she manages Paris than I ever did: she has a Navigo pass and a flat in Montreuil and a gang of mates, and she knows how to use those intimidating Vélib bikes. Her relationship to it is very different from mine: she hasn't read all those novels or watched all those films and her Paris is real, it's a world of children in distress and illegal immigrants and she is doing what she can to make it better.

It takes me ages, too, to tell people outside the family we are back together because I just sound so stupid to my own ears. Logically, I know that we have both changed during our separation and that things *are* different, but I'm ashamed of the trail of damage I created along the way. When I finally screw up my courage, if my friends are bemused, they don't show it. Helen reassures me over a lunch where I cry uncontrollably for reasons I can't quite fathom. Trish says it's 'wonderful and romantic and full of hope'. Kate is gentle and reassuring and Benjamin, who is in the process of moving to Scotland, trades terrors and gets me drunk. 'For what it's worth, I'm happy for you,' says Madevi, then we go back to watching a video of a manatee eating carrots.

To make matters even less relaxing, the minute I move back into the house, so do the builders. Olivier has big plans, ones that involve planning permission, load-bearing walls, a loft conversion and a ground-floor extension. For months as I try to deal with shutting down my old-new life, my new-old life is filled with drilling, dust and the thwack of mallet on masonry. The walls are daubed with paint samples and catalogues full of sinks and bannisters clutter every surface. At weekends, there is always something we need to go and examine in a far-flung builder's merchants. We have to eat squashed around a fold-up picnic table with a nest of spiders in the centre and for six months there is just a giant hole in the exterior wall in the house, blocked up with hardboard and duct tape. I would not have chosen this, not now. It's chaos, dusty, noisy chaos, and there is no refuge anywhere, no space of our own to crawl into. Instead, I take the dog for long walks around the neighbourhood and question my sanity. I'm so happy about the basic fact of having Olivier back, but everything else is weird and frightening. When he comes out walking with me, I question his sanity too.

'This isn't all some elaborate trick, is it? When all this is over, you aren't going to turn round and say "actually *I* need some space now" are you?'

'Pffff.'

I don't really believe it, but I have to sound out my fears, because I am scared all the time. The evenings, when Olivier and the boys are around, are tranquil and reassuring and life makes absolute sense when the four of us are together, but in the daytime when I am on my own, I go a bit odd. The situation seems far more than I deserve, too good to be true, and waves of dread consume me. How could I get it so catastrophically wrong and still luck out like this, back with the man I love? Everything seems terrifyingly fragile: when I ride on the back of Olivier's motorbike I imagine the crunch of impact, shattered glass and limbs, and when anyone goes out, I fast forward to the knock on the door from grave-faced Belgian police constables.

So I hide out in the attic, turn down good offers of work and obsessively review my awful behaviour over the past couple of years. My finger hovers over the button to delete the blog: the archives feel like an embarrassing catalogue of things I'd rather forget and I don't know how to be unguarded on there any more, the stakes are just too high. I want to be strong and unrepentant and happy but quite frankly, *je regrette* everything, every misstep, flawed conviction and casual cruelty. So mostly I stay at home, sitting in the attic, wearing the same awful pair of unflattering, slightly shiny black trousers, which I dub the 'occupational therapist' trousers, every day for weeks. Now I'm the one circling the wagons: I just want to huddle with my family. I don't know what my place in the world is, really, except with them.

Three things get me out of my funk. The first is that the boys start speaking English again. I decide that I just can't have children who don't speak my language and can't speak to half their family, and I can't bear another dubbed *Bob l'Éponge*, so I insist they only watch English TV. The BBC steps in where I have failed, making the most of the licence fee I am not paying and on a diet of *Horrible Histories*, *Blue Peter* and *Hacker and Dodge* (a pair of lary Mancunian dog hand puppets), within months they are fluent again, not just fluent but making jokes, singing along to Furniture Warehouse adverts and speaking to me in English even when I forget and talk to them in French. I don't understand how it happens so fast and I certainly did not expect it to be this easy: the incredible plasticity of children's brains astonishes me. Louis develops a fondness for homophones – he likes 'knows' and 'nose' and 'we'll' and 'wheel' and drives everyone demented with his laborious punning. Theo discovers LOL-cats and starts texting me gnomic, idiosyncratically spelled messages: 'tniy', 'awsemom', 'I aftoo clean my theets'. Soon, the four of us can sit down and watch *Father Ted* together. Perhaps I shouldn't be so delighted to hear them chorus 'arse, feck, girls' but it's exactly what I thought I might never get and it makes me truly happy.

The second thing is that I start working on a big translation project with a Congolese-Belgian rapper and poet, Baloji. I'm not sure I've ever done anything harder in my professional life: Baloji is so demanding (my first drafts are never good enough and often my second and third drafts aren't quite there either), and the way he uses language is so intricate and clever it makes my head ache as I stumble over his double meanings and plays on words, but when I get it right and he's happy, the satisfaction is enormous. A lot of his work is about identity and exile: Baloji left the DRC to live with his father's extended family in Liège when he was three and didn't return or see his mother for twenty-five years. Having never felt he really belonged in Belgium, on returning to Congo, he realized just how European he had become: a veil of incomprehension separated him from his mother and his birth culture. When you don't go home – even if that decision is imposed upon you and entirely passive – your relationship to home is irrevocably altered. What is especially interesting to me, though, is how he chooses to view this 'in-between' identity: it's a wrench and a loss and perpetual puzzle, but it's also a positive identity of its own and a creative force. You can do more than just try and reconcile the different parts of your identity: you can build something unique from them. At its best, Belgium itself, that uneasy mix of French and Flemish, transient incomers and strong diaspora communities, feels like the consecration of that idea. More often it feels like a mess, but the idea is powerful and optimistic.

Finally, I just give myself a talking to. 'What is *wrong* with you,' I hiss to myself as I drag the reluctant, still freaked-out dog round the empty summer streets, which are strewn with discarded ice cream wafers and warmed to a state of perfect torpor. Would Béatrice Dalle be flipping out with self-flagellation and doubt? Would Catherine Deneuve? Lots of wonderful things have happened in the last few years, not just shame and misery. Would I want my life without Madevi or Helen or Ben? And isn't it, actually, a great thing I am no longer the world's worst competition lawyer? More important still, I don't see how Olivier and I could have survived without some kind of shake-up, violent and hurtful as the one I engineered has been. We are different now, freed from the roles we spent so long stuck in. We're gentler with each other's foibles, we definitely laugh more and, sometimes, I even manage to talk about my feelings (not often, but I try).

Perhaps, I think, walking yet again past the strange neighbour with the bench, who is currently busy applying a waterproofing spray to the inside of his umbrella, I did not appreciate how long and circuitous and strange losing my mother would be; the effect it has had. Grief, I think, as I walk the dog, has not been like a bear hunt for me. You *can* go over it, under it, around it, meander around the edges, it takes forever, but you get to the same end point, eventually. I have made a mountain of mistakes and caused all manner of hurt, but here we are: if Olivier can forgive me, surely I should forgive myself. All this sackcloth and ashes is doing no one any good and there is simply no time for more sadness. Sometimes there is no time left at all, I know that all too well. So I think of my mother and her favourite unrepentant alley cat Mehitabel and turn my attention to locating my *toujours gai*.

Gradually, too, as the building work takes shape, my perspective starts to shift. I begin to see the transformation of the house, dusty and chaotic and nightmarish as it is, an act of love and of hope. Olivier is pouring all his optimism and generosity into making this place new and perfect for the four of us and it works, what he is creating is wonderful. He has made me an office – a place to write that is all mine – and we have a new, bright room big enough for a proper table downstairs so we can sit and eat. It's still home, but it's new and brighter and it's his way of saying that things are different and better; that *we* are both different.

But I wonder, actually, if it is even necessary. Because the place that is ours, the bolthole, the burrow where I feel safe, doesn't have to be physical. My safe place is the space between our bodies when I reach out and grasp Olivier's hand in bed. It's the space that is created as my long-limbed boys perch on my knee for comfort and the space around the four of us as we sit on a grimy picnic rug in the rubble-strewn backyard to eat sandwiches, chased from the house by more drilling, the dog hovering greedily over our shoulders. We have our space.

« 25 »

Ce Plat Pays

Our wedding is tiny and ordinary. Nourished by novels, egged on by films, the Emma Bovary part of me still expects everything to be big and bright and dramatic – grief, love, myself, life – but this is indubitably small. We don't have a bucolic Normandy blowout, unfolding over multiple days and meals, with cousins in their Sunday best, drunken incidents, fights and children sleeping under tables. It's not a secret, black-clad, witnesses-only piece of urban chic and we don't elope. Rather, we get married on a wet, blustery day in February in the swirly-carpeted town hall function room, presided over by Belgian bureaucrats and watched by our parents and our children, almost twenty years exactly after we first met.

Before the wedding, our families converge gradually at our house. We haven't given them much warning, because the whole thing was an impulse, a moment of joint tipsy daftness over a strange meal a few months ago, when Olivier gesticulated at me with a forkful of pigeon upon which some unspeakable culinary crime had been perpetrated and said, 'Let's get *married*!' largely as a joke and I said 'Yes!' and meant it.

Olivier's parents arrive the night before and sleep in our spare room. They wake early and potter around the kitchen, warming coffee and spreading butter in the good wedding suits that have seen so much use at all those Normandy nuptial marathons: cousins, second cousins, nieces, nephews and godchildren. This is not that kind of wedding but at least, for once, we are inviting them to a party and not the other way around. Later, after several peremptory text messages, my father barrels in, a whirlwind of bonhomie and ebullience. 'Hello, darling!' he bellows and sets off on a round of shaking hands, ruffling hair and teasing the dog. My stepmother follows, warm and funny and carefully considerate of everyone, camera at the ready. As I make more coffee I field texts from my sister who is on her way, possibly, perhaps late, and needs a pair of tights. My father and Yves fuss over Theo's tie. He has gelled his hair to a rigid peak and, we eventually notice, has his pet rat in the breast pocket of his jacket. Louis is quieter, hanging off my arm in a borrowed tie. He's not keen on fuss or dressing up, although he's happy to see his various grandparents. The boys don't mind us getting married, but it's certainly not 'epic', Theo's epithet of the moment.

Olivier has a new suit and I am wearing a violet silk 1950s dress, bought in a rush. I think I must have yet again taken leave of my senses when I chose the dress, since it looks a bit like something a stout Brussels matron might wear to the opera, but Madevi has lent me her tulle dancing petticoat to wear underneath, and at Helen's insistence I have bought myself a shiny pair of navy Ferragamo pumps I can't really afford, both new and blue. I put on the pearls my mum gave me for my eighteenth birthday, because if you can't wear pearls to get married, then when? I've been wearing them to bed for the past few weeks, because that was what Mum told me you should do to keep their lustre; another one of her unexpected pieces of wisdom.

We cram into our car and Olivier's parents fit the stragglers into theirs and we head down to the town hall – a rather plain, square building, scene of many of my battles with the Belgian administrative authorities – in the driving rain. My stepfather meets us there on foot, padding up quietly to meet us with his good suit under his cagoule, smoking a last-minute roll-up; a brown-paper-covered Turgenev in his pocket. My sister appears in her usual whirl of chaos and forgotten essentials. She looks beautiful in a blue mini-dress and less haunted than she has done for years, laughing and chatting. Paris seems to suit her, far more than it ever suited me. We have a flurry of kisses and hellos and photos, then a civic official in an impressive gilt chain beckons us up to the *salle des fêtes*, where another official in a tricolour sash is ready to do the honours.

I never wanted to get married. The first year we met, Olivier asked me to marry him, but I obfuscated and changed the subject and wouldn't commit, because, well, I don't know. It didn't fit with the image of my life I held so preciously in my head, free and solitary and sitting outside Le Flore with my Scottie dog.

I have, however, considered marriage in the past for two reasons. The first is Olivier's name. His surname is impec-

cably, utterly, *Tricolore*-textbook-perfect, cliché French. You
can't get any Frencher. Mine is impossible to say Frenchly
('*Madame* [hesitation] *Baïe-dan-ton? Bé-dine-tan?*') and I
have spelled it wearily over the phone so many times I am
heartily sick of it. With Olivier's surname, my credentials
would be irreproachable: for administrative purposes at
least, I could be completely French.

The second reason is Eric Sax. Eric Sax is the eerily
smooth and mahogany-tanned deputy mayor. He in charge
of all sorts of local festivities and I often see him in the local
free rag, shaking the hand of centenarians, opening fêtes
and presiding over weddings. Sometimes I even see him in
person, driving around in his Eric Sax branded Smart car,
his blond highlighted hair perfectly set in steely waves. I
want to meet Eric Sax very badly indeed.

On the day, however, it turns out that Eric Sax is not
presiding. I don't suppose it's worth him doing his luxuri-
antly highlighted hair for such a tiny, B-list gathering, so we
have a large, bossy lady who is almost certainly a primary
school teacher in real life given the way she orders us around.

It feels strange, the ten of us in this huge room with its
neo-classical friezes and oversized oil paintings of Belgian
pastoral scenes, and the briskly unsentimental ceremony
doesn't make it any less strange. It's short, almost comically
so, and the only thing we have to do is say '*oui*' once, which
we do, as indicated. We have rings, but there is apparently no
protocol for when and how we exchange them and no vows,
so we just fumble it after the '*oui*', then kiss awkwardly, self-
conscious in front of this bossy stranger. I am beginning to

think it is one of those life events from which I am going to feel a bit detached, it has that remote, slightly unreal quality, when the registrar beckons us to sign the register and the familiar soft swing piano intro, with its ripple of applause as Nina Simone's live version of 'Just in Time', starts up. We don't agree on much music, but we agree on Nina.

'*Just in time*,' she sings as we take up the municipal fountain pen and sign the enormous blank page one after the other.

'*You found me just in time.*'

And I realize it's true and I can't believe my luck. I have been spinning off my axis for ten years and most of my certainties have proved as brittle and insubstantial as a sugarwork heron, but even so, despite it all, here we are. What were the chances? My legs go a bit wobbly, so I hold on tight to Olivier's arm and blink back tears as we sign.

It turns out that in Belgium, you can't take your husband's surname and actually, I realize, this is ideal: I am completely happy like this. I don't want to marry Olivier for some green card or rubber stamp of Frenchness. But I am not French, not now, not ever and that is OK. I am a Beddington and some essential, perpetually apologizing, scone-loving part of me will always be British. If I want to get married to Olivier, it is because he is home, home like the lilac tree in our backyard, home like Bettys tearoom or the last verse of 'Dear Lord and Father of Mankind', home where my head is finally quiet and my heart is full.

Theo, who is in charge of our camera, takes a picture, and then all of us line up together for the man in the giant ceremonial chain to take another one of us for the local magazine (where we will appear regrettably without Eric Sax) and then as we all start to wonder what happens next – is that it? Can we really be married already? – the town hall stereo starts to play Jacques Brel's 'Bruxelles'.

'Bruxelles' was our other musical choice, though not because it has any sentimental value for us: we just like the idea of a nod to our home (host?) city. I have more and more time for Brel these days. I came to him late, compared with Gainsbourg, and he always seemed a bit square, with his giant mouthful of teeth and his verging-on-mawkish theatrical love songs. Gainsbourg has that effortless French *désinvolture* (though I think now some of it is shyness), whereas Brel seems sincere and sincerity is never cool. But I have watched a lot of old Brel performances on YouTube in my anxious attic over the past few years, the young Brel, all angles, sweaty and electric, and realized how wrong I was. Because Brel is caustic and clever and angry and his lyrics are beautiful, from paeans of regret and tenderness to razor-sharp social satire.

The boys have sung '*Ce Plat Pays*' at school – you can't get through a Belgian primary education without singing a couple of Brel songs – and it is proper poetry, lyrical and funny and clear-sighted all at once:

> *Avec un ciel si bas qu'un canal s'est perdu*
> *Avec un ciel si bas qu'il fait l'humilité*
> *Avec un ciel si gris qu'un canal s'est pendu*
> *Avec un ciel si gris qu'il faut lui pardoner.*

With a sky so low that a canal got lost
With a sky so low, it begs humility
With a sky so grey, a canal hung itself
With a sky so grey, it must be forgiven.

I wonder if my children think this flat land is theirs. I suspect they won't know themselves for years, if ever. Where do any of us fit? I think of Madevi's peripatetic life and Trish who has devoted so much of her life to France but is drawn inexorably back to Ireland, of Benjamin exiled in Scotland for love, and of Baloji making something wonderful in the uneasy interstices of two cultures. Isn't that just life, a quicksand of compromise and accommodation where nothing is completely stable? My boys will be at home wherever they choose, eventually, and it probably won't be anywhere I would have predicted. I'm happy here, for now, in our strange, sleepy suburb. A Picard has opened up down our street and there's a rumour Marks & Spencer is coming back to Brussels next year. Forever? Who knows?

'Bruxelles' is so irresistibly jolly that as we leave, the three civic officials sway gently in time to it. We take another couple of pictures on the steps, but the wind is really up, whipping our hair into our faces, so we give up quickly and head home for tea, where everyone sits round the kitchen table conversing in an awkward, but good-humoured, confusion in French and English. Later on, we have lunch in an eccentric guesthouse nearby (the proprietor keeps trying to interest us in his novel design for self-warming dog leads) and then there is a cake, of course there is, there must be cake.

It's not the wedding cake I would have imagined for myself. If I had considered it, I would have thought we'd have a towering *pièce montée*, like the pâtissier from Yvetot made for Emma Bovary, a *croquembouche* or perhaps one of Stohrer's alternating chocolate and coffee éclair *religieuses à l'ancienne*, the ones Madevi introduced me to. But time was short and nothing ever works out how I imagine it, so instead, I've asked a girl I know to make a cake for us: a lemon sponge. It's a very good lemon sponge, light and not too sweet and filled with home-made lemon curd, but it's far from an aesthetic triumph. It's a bit flat and wonky, topped with a cursory sprinkle of hundreds and thousands (we are too drunk by the time we cut it to even remember to put the little 'just married' sign on the top). Nevertheless, it's a surprising success: everyone likes it. Even my father who never eats cake approves.

Later, Yves gets out a ceremonial bottle of his grandfather's Calvados, one of the last ones in their dwindling reserve, and we all drink too much of it. My stepfather and sister are lurking in the muddy garden, deep in conversation, smoking roll-ups, Olivier's mother is explaining something very loudly to my stepmother, the boys have slumped in a corner to play video games and my father, who has toasted and laughed and generally been the life and soul of the party, has fallen asleep with practised efficiency at the table. I catch Olivier's eye over the stained tablecloth and the spilled wine, our lopsided family and the remnants of our lopsided cake, and I smile and he smiles back. Then we go home.

Acknowledgements

This book took shape slowly and many people helped it along the way. I owe the hugest thanks to Patrick Walsh for hand-holding, cheerleading and general loveliness, and to George Morley for her endless patience, wit and reassurance as well as editorial brilliance. Thank you to Carrie Plitt for her invaluable assistance and kindness, and to Laura Carr, Nicole Foster, Nicola Evans and all at Pan Macmillan for making a real book out of some repetitive muttering about éclairs.

Thanks for shrewd professional advice, well-timed shoves and touching generosity to Laura Cumming, Trish Deseine (and Karl), Sarah Franklin, Tamara Gausi, Harriet Green, India Knight, Charlotte Mendelson, Eireann Lorsung, Jojo Moyes, Marina O'Loughlin, Alice Wignall and Sasha Wilkins.

Thanks to my magnificent friends for the solace of shared complaint, animal videos and gin, past, present and future: my precious first readers Helen Brocklebank and Fernanda Moore, Nathalie Bouhana, Benjamin Brust, Laurie Horwood, Tom Houser, Kate Jaram and Maija Krastina.

Thanks to all from the blog, a true fellowship of hilarity and shared crapness. Thanks particularly to Frau Antje, BB, Carolinefo, the Cephalopod correspondent, Patience Crabstick, Cruella, the Fat Controller, Jane, Kath, Lee, Lydia, Margot Leadbetter, Nimble, Non-Working Monkey, redfox,

Acknowledgements

Soleils, Xtreme English and Z, and apologies to all omitted in haste and stupidity. Thanks to all the anons, lurkers and emailers and special thanks to Wanstead Birder for the subtitle.

Thanks for dinosaurs, facepasta, my sanity and everything else to Madevi Dailly.

All love and thanks to my family for patience, support, babysitting, gnomic texts, lemon sponge and taxi money: Joe, Julia, Dad, Caroline, Yves, Jacqueline, and to Les and Rob, my almost-family.

Thank you to my sons, Theo and Louis, for making me laugh, usually at my own expense.

And for everything, always, Olivier.